The Pubs of Leominster, Kington and north-west Herefordshire

The Pubs of Leominster, Kington and north-west Herefordshire

by

Ron Shoesmith & Roger Barrett

Logaston Press

LOGASTON PRESS
Little Logaston Woonton Almeley
Herefordshire HR3 6QH

First published by Logaston Press 2000
Copyright © Ron Shoesmith & Roger Barrett 2000

ISBN 1 873827 07 5

Set in Times by Logaston Press
and printed in Great Britain by
MFP Design and Print, Manchester

This book is dedicated to the memory of Anne Sandford who was the Curator of Hereford City Museums and Art Gallery for many years. Before her tragic death she took a keen and active interest in this project and provided much help with the first volume— *The Pubs of Hereford City*. Several of the photographs used in this book were first used in Anne's various publications.

Dick Vowles, when Mayor of Hereford, issued a 'Poetic Licence' to the author of *The Last Great Pub Crawl* to 'render description of the pubs, alehouses and hostelries of our historic city, and to further write humourously so long as it be without malicious intent about this city and its good people'.
This book follows in that tradition throughout north-west Herefordshire.

Contents

Sources of Illustrations

Hereford County Library:
    pp. 21, 23, 36, 204, 205, 207 (upper), 208 (upper) 259
    (lower), 278, 280
Hereford Record Office:
    pp. 16, 17, 19, 20, 31, 57 (upper), 60, 61, 62, 63 (lower), 67,
    96, 103, 116, 118, 126 (upper), 166, 167 (lower),
    168 (upper), 180, 192
Hereford Times:
    p. 52
Derek Foxton:
    pp. 34, 105, 181, 288, 290
Ken Hoverd:
    p. 174
Chris Powis:
    pp. 144, 145, 169
Frank Bennett:
    pp. 2, 30, 40, 44, 59, 88, 121 (lower), 122, 123, 157,
    213 (upper), 250
David Gorvett Village Archive
    pp. 49. 50, 51, 53 (upper), 54, 55 (upper)
Heather Hurley
    pp. 32, 33
Simon Whitney
    p. 72
Lion, Ferney Common
    p. 78 (lower)
Queen's Head, Kington
    p. 93
Old Fogey, Kington
    p. 106
Geoffrey Hodges Estate
    p. 277
Anne Sandford Estate
    pp. 38, 141 (upper), 151, 260, 303 (upper)

Acknowledgments

The interest in *The Pubs of Hereford City* encouraged Logaston Press to consider the potential of rural Herefordshire. It soon became obvious that this was an undertaking of considerable complexity. Information had to be garnered from a variety of sources, photographs had to be borrowed and copied, others taken, directories consulted, and in some cases original documents, now stored in the Record Office in Hereford, had to be deciphered.

This volume is therefore the second in a growing series on the inns and taverns of Herefordshire. It is hoped that the third volume, dealing with Bromyard and Ledbury, and the fourth volume, covering Ross and southern Herefordshire, will both be completed before the end of 2001.

The preparation of this volume would not have been possible without the cooperation of many people who have spent much time and effort in producing information and photographs.

Some of the material used was provided by the late Anne Sandford, then of the City Museum; Derek Foxton provided several of the older photographs; the old photographs of Eardisley are from the David Gorvett Village Archive lodged in the County Record Office; Heather Hurley produced a copy of the detailed sale notice for the Kite's Nest; Ken Hoverd copied some of the older photographs; Ben Shoesmith produced the maps—without their help the task would have been much more arduous. The staff of the Hereford Record Office and Hereford City Library provided much information and allowed us to copy material; the *Hereford Times* provided two photographs—our most grateful thanks to them all.

Following various requests for assistance through the columns of the *Hereford Times,* and the Hereford Family History Society, many people phoned or wrote with information about various inns, both open and closed and special mention should be made of Eddie Hatton, who produced much information and introduced me to Skarrett's Diary, which contains an immense amount of background information on Kington; Chris Powis, now of the Wellington at Wellington, who was born at the Red Lion at Upper Hill and provided original family documents; Frank Bennett who loaned items of postal history associated with Herefordshire inns; Eric Turton, who provided booklets and lists of pubs in Leominster; Jon Cooke, who sent me notes on the many pubs he sampled whilst working at Wigmore Castle; Clare Westbury from Calgary in Canada, who stimulated the search for details of Orleton where her ancestors once lived; the kind people who live at what was the Seven Stars at Monkland and provided an old photograph; John Eisel, who provided notes from his searches in the *Hereford Journal,* and to the many others who, by an odd phrase or comment, helped this book on its way—our thanks to them all for their encouragement and their permission to use the material.

When it became obvious that this book could well not be finished within my self-imposed deadline, Roger Barrett was press-ganged to assist, and apart from providing much direct help and encouragement, took over the production of the chapters on Leominster. Andy Johnson of Logaston Press, as always, has been a constant help and encouragement. My daughter, Katy, provided endless cups of coffee as the book neared completion. My thanks to all for their kindnesses and understanding.

The sources of many of the illustrations used in this book are listed below. Others are from the author's private collection and a few are from unidentified sources.

Ron Shoesmith
October 2000

Introduction

The roadside inn, the large town centre hotel, the old-established tavern and the street corner public house are all particularly British institutions that have grown through the ages both as a matter of need and as a result of a complex series of Acts of Parliament. For many centuries they have provided the opportunity for people of all classes to meet, to drink, to eat, and, particularly, to talk. They have provided accommodation, sometimes good and sometimes poor, for the traveller and his steed, be it a horse or latterly a car. They have provided entertainment—from bear baiting and cock fighting to billiards and bowls. They have provided food, from the simple ploughman's to full *à la carte* menus. They comprise many of our most historic buildings, for the wholesale rebuilding of licensed premises came only with difficulty and after much pressure.

No attempt has been made in this book to include all the information available about the inns and taverns of north-west Herefordshire. Such a work would be of almost encyclopaedic length, for the information available in the official records, in newspapers and by word of mouth, is immense. The main danger in writing this book has always been that it would end up as long lists of names; not just of licensed premises, both open and long-closed, but of all the men and women who were the licensees. Every effort has been made to avoid this pitfall, but in the presentation there has had to be a degree of organisation of the information to ensure that the record is reasonably complete.

The easiest method of presentation would have been to produce an alphabetical list, but this would have had little attraction and would inevitably have been boring to the reader. An alternative approach has been chosen which, it is hoped, will provide more general interest and be more readable. The first chapter consists of a basic history—an attempt to show how the British inn came about, what it served and how, as a result of varying legislation, it has changed through the ages. The second chapter deals with the most important products of our inns—cider, ale and beer—where it was made and how it was produced.

The following chapters each cover a distinct area of the county. Chapters three, four and five follow the main roads from Hereford leading westwards and north-westwards towards the Welsh Border. Chapters six and seven concentrate on the public houses in Kington, the most north-westerly town in the county. The next two chapters also follow roads from Hereford City's boundary, but northwards. The second of these leads naturally to Leominster, a main cross-roads and the home of many inns that necessitate three chapters to cover the whole town. Chapters thirteen and fourteen respectively follow the courses of the Arrow and the Lugg upstream from Leominster, and finally chapter fifteen deals with the areas to the north and north-east of Leominster.

The *Pubs of Hereford City*, first published in 1994, generated, despite my best endeavours, much more information on the city's inns and a second edition followed. We suspect this book may also prompt many memories—please feel free to share these with us and perhaps this title will also need updating in due course.

Ron Shoesmith
Roger Barrett
October 2000

CHAPTER ONE

Alehouses, Taverns and Inns

It was during the 350 year period when Britain was within the boundaries of the Roman Empire that roads were first laid out on a formal basis in this country. In the first instance they were built for military purposes—to enable Roman troops to travel quickly and safely from one part of the country to another. During the early Roman occupation of this area the main road, built by the army to join the legionary fortresses of Chester and Caerleon, probably crossed the river Wye at one of the Hereford fords. After a while their engineers constructed a bridge near *Magnis*, the Roman settlement at Kenchester, and the line of the road was diverted to this, the first Hereford by-pass! To the north it follows the present A4110 through Canon Pyon and Knapton. At Stretford Bridge the modern road takes a more easterly course for a few miles, to pick up the Roman road again at Mortimer's Cross. After Aymestrey the alignment is again lost, for the Roman road went through the middle of Weobley Marsh on its direct route to Leintwardine, the *Bravonium* of the *Antonine Itinerary*.

Magnis was only a small town, but it would have provided refreshment and accommodation for travellers on this Welsh border road. In addition, immediately to the west of this early road was the Roman military area that covered the whole of Wales. With its broad main street and large public buildings *Magnis* would, without any doubt, have had guest houses providing overnight accommodation and places where soldiers, returning from a stint of duty in Wales, could drink and enjoy themselves. Alcoholic refreshments would doubtless have been available to those who required them—the Romans imported wine from other parts of the Empire and made every effort to grow vines in the southern part of England. They

1

The City is denoted by red and the respective Hundreds of the County by different Colours, which distinctions are peculiar to the superior Edition.

Map of Herefordshire from an 1805 Road Book used by travellers in the county some 200 years ago (see page 88 for detailed map)

2

would also have made mead from honey and possibly cider from the locally grown apples, and as wheat and barley were both available, some form of ale.

The break-up of the Roman Empire in England took place following the withdrawal of the Roman troops, shortly after A.D. 410, and the country descended into the Dark Ages. Although some towns doubtless kept going for a short while, it was to be several hundred years before there were any recognisable new settlements in the whole of Herefordshire. The earliest ones recorded are religious establishments such as St. Guthlac's, which was founded on the area now known as Castle Green in Hereford, and the minster at Leominster, founded by King Merewalh of the Magonsaete about 660 A.D. Shortly afterwards, the foundation of the Hereford Diocese would have encouraged the building of simple churches and the gradual provision of permanent settlements of more than a few houses. Once a cathedral had been built in Hereford on the gravel terrace overlooking the ford across the river, a small settlement would have developed outside the religious precinct. The city's first inns, little more than simple drinking houses, probably date to this period. Indeed, as early as A.D. 750, the then Archbishop of York issued a Canon 'That no priest go to eat or drink in taverns', and there were so many inns by the time of King Edgar (959-75) that he issued a decree limiting their number to one per village.

By the 10th century Hereford had become one of the most important towns in the country—mainly because of its ford and its strategic position on the Welsh border. Immediately after the Conquest the Normans parcelled out their new kingdom and the Domesday survey gives a first indication of the size and importance of the towns and villages in the county. The Welsh were still a real problem and the whole of north Herefordshire was protected by a series of strategically placed castles, initially of timber, but, as their importance grew, they were fortified by stone. The remains of the border castles at Wigmore, Weobley and Richard's Castle, and many others that are now mainly earthworks, testify to this turbulent period. However, the castles generated settlements outside their walls and this would inevitably have resulted in a sizeable increase in the number of inns and taverns throughout the county.

3

Following the Conquest there was a gradual growth in the population of the country, as settlers from Normandy were encouraged, and with this increase came various measures to limit the numbers of drinking houses and to protect the customer. One of the most important of these was the 'Assize of Bread and Ale' in 1266. This enactment accepted the principle that both bread and ale were necessities of life and, for a period of some 300 years, it ensured that the retail price of ale was fixed according to the price of grain. At that time, ale was usually made from malted barley, or occasionally wheat, which was steeped in water and then fermented with yeast.

During the 13th century there was a gradual increase in the sale of wine, and a separation came into being between 'taverns', which sold both ale and wine, and 'alehouses' which sold only ale. In addition to these there were the wayside inns or 'hostels' that provided accommodation for travellers as well as food and drink.

Outside the towns, the principal hospitality for travellers during the medieval period was provided by monasteries—it was only along the more important pilgrim routes that guest houses and wayside inns were established, and these would have been well beyond the purse of all except the richest of travellers. In north-west Herefordshire the Augustinian Canons were initially at Shobdon, but then moved to Wigmore Abbey, where they had one of the largest monasteries in the county. They had smaller cells at Limebrook and at Wormsley and all survived until the dissolution in 1538-9. There were also two small alien priories (cells of French monasteries) at Titley and Monkland, but they did not survive the continual wars with France and both closed around the end of the 14th century. During the 14th and 15th centuries, a gradual change occurred as merchants began to travel and the influence of the church started to wane. Wayside inns became features of the countryside and hotels providing accommodation and food began to appear in the market towns.

For perhaps 1,000 years ale had been the basic drink for practically everyone, but a fundamental change occurred during the early 15th century. This was due to the introduction of hops, described by the authorities in Shrewsbury at that time as that 'wicked and pernicious weed', and the resultant manufacture of 'beer'. The hop not only gave the new drink a more bitter flavour, it was also of

4

considerable importance for its preservative properties enabling the beverage to be kept much longer than ale before 'going-off'. Of course, there were the adherents of ale:

> Though I go bare, take ye no care,
> I nothing am a-cold:
> I stuff my skin so full within
> Of jolly good ale and old
>
> Back and side go bare, go bare;
> Both foot and hand go cold:
> But, belly, God send thee good ale enough,
> Whether it be new or old.
>
> (part of a 16th century drinking song by William Stevenson
> 'Jolly Good Ale and Old')

Hops have been grown in Herefordshire for many years and the round and square oast houses, with a swinging cowl above, used for drying the hops, are a common sight in the countryside. Charcoal was used for heating, and during the drying process sulphur was added to destroy insect life and fungal and bacteriological infections. Dried hops are still pressed tightly into jute sacks called pockets. These pockets had to be marked with the name and address of the grower to identify who's was the tax liability. Hops have other benefits—a bine of hops hung next to the ceiling in the kitchen or in the public bars of many an inn in Herefordshire keeps the smoke and smells down, whilst if you can't sleep at nights try a pillow stuffed with hops.

For well over 100 years brewers produced both ale and beer, but the popularity of the former gradually declined and beer eventually became the national drink—apart from in Herefordshire where cider reigned triumphant for many years. It was early in the reign of Henry VIII that cider orchards became a branch of the rural economy, but it was the Redstreak, the famous cider apple developed by the first Viscount Scudamore on his Holme Lacy estate near Hereford before and after the Civil War, that revolutionised the trade. It was recommended that the Redstreak 'was to be preferred for your Plantation to any other apple whatsoever, especially remote from your House. First, because it yields the best of British Drinks. Secondly, because the fruit is harsh and unpleasant, not tempting the Palates of lewd Persons'. The poet, John Philips, who died in 1709 aged 32 and is buried in the entrance to the north transept of Hereford Cathedral, wrote of the Redstreak in his poem *Cyder*:

> Of no regard till Scudamore's skilful hand
> Improv'd her, and by courtly discipline
> Taught her the savage nature to forget,—
> Hence styl'd the Scudamore plant.

John Philips' brass in
Hereford Cathedral
shows a branch of
an apple tree

For many years, a coaching inn on the north side of Hereford's High Town, where the Butter Market now stands, was called the Redstreak Inn or Redstreak Tree Inn. So important was cider to Herefordshire that, in the 14th century, when Nicholas de Hereford was helping Wycliffe to translate the Bible into English, he changed the warning given to the mother of the still unborn Samson which read 'Now therefore beware, I pray thee, and drink not wine nor strong drink' to read 'drink no cider' (Judges, Ch. 13 V. 4). Surely the translation, in the well known 'Cider Bible', was no more the worse for it.

Change was gradual—it was not until the end of the 17th century that there was any serious competition to ale, beer and cider in the retail market. Even then, the cost of the new beverages, coffee and tea, was prohibitively expensive for the next half-century or more.

Although there had been previous attempts at curtailing the number of drinking houses, the first formal licensing law came at the end of the 15th century. It empowered Justices of the Peace to obtain sureties for good behaviour from the landlords and, if necessary, to close alehouses. Some 50 years later the Justices obtained the power, which they still retain, to both licence and suppress alehouses—hence 'licensed premises'.

Legislation continued and 1553 saw an Act of Parliament that curtailed the number of 'taverns', and thus limited the sale of wine. Indeed, the Act also prohibited the sale of French wines. The limits on taverns provide an indication of the size and importance of the towns at that time—London was allowed 40; York, nine; and Bristol, six. Hereford was limited to three, the same as Lincoln, Worcester, Southampton and Oxford. This did not mean that the population of the country was being deprived of places in which to drink—there were approximately 44 alehouses for every tavern in the latter part of the 16th century. This was equivalent to more than one drinking establishment for every 200 persons, a far higher ratio than exists today. These early alehouses were probably little different to the timber-framed and thatched houses that surrounded them. The larger ones would have had sheds at the rear where brewing was carried out and possibly cellars in which to protect their brew from temperature variations.

Taverns, being of a higher status, were probably of a superior construction. This may well be the reason why the more important towns and cities in the country tend to be well-endowed with substantial stone cellars of a late medieval date. They were obviously designed for public use and usually had well-constructed vaulted roofs and entries leading directly from the streets.

Throughout most of recorded history it was a legal requirement that a sign should identify all drinking establishments. Poles, which

An evergreen bush indicating an inn, from a 14th-century manuscript

7

16 **99**

Whereas by the Laws and Statutes of This Realm

NOTICE

IS HEREBY GIVEN TO ALL

INN KEEPERS, ALEHOUSE KEEPERS, SUTLERS, VICTUALLERS

and other Retailers of

ALE and BEER

AND EVERY OTHER PERSON or PERSONS KEEPING A PUBLIC HOUSE
IN ANY
CITY, TOWN CORPORATE, BOROUGH, MARKET TOWN, VILLAGE, HAMLET, PARISH,
PART or PLACE IN THE *Kingdom of England*

That, as from the **24th** *day of* JUNE, **1700**

THEY SHALL BE REQUIRED TO RETAIL and SELL THEIR ALE & BEER

by the **FULL ALE QUART** or **PINT**

According to the Laid Standard

IN VESSELS DULY MARKED *with* W. R *and* CROWN
be they made of

WOOD, GLASS, HORN, LEATHER or **PEWTER** *etc.*

Any Person Retailing Ale or Beer to a **TRAVELLER** or **WAYFARER** *in Vessels not
signed and marked as aforesaid will be liable to a* **PENALTY** *not exceeding*

FORTY SHILLINGS

FOR EVERY SUCH OFFENCE

By Act of Parliament ~ at WESTMINSTER
In the Reign of Our Sovereign ~ WILLIAM III by the Grace of God, King,
Defender of the Faith &c

supported the signs gradually became bigger and more noticeable. In the case of a tavern, there would also be an evergreen bush, which represented the vine and indicated that wine was for sale. Alfred Watkins, in an article published in the *Transactions of the Woolhope Naturalists' Field Club*, also mentions a 'chequers' sign, which was apparently common in Hereford and elsewhere. This consisted of alternate diamonds or lozenges of green and red painted on the doorframe on each side of the entrance to the inn. Watkins suggested that the sign originated in the counting board (like a chess board, but used for counting money) and that it was an indication that the innkeeper kept one of these boards for the benefit of his customers. He discovered such a sign at a couple of inns in Hereford.

Various attempts were made during the Civil War to levy duty on both the manufacture and the sale of beer and ale—attempts which were consolidated following that war and still apply to this day. This was when beer was brewed in three different qualities: strong, table, and small, and each variety attracted a different rate of duty. It was not until the late 19th century that the duty levied became based on the original gravity of the beer. The specific gravity (density) of the liquor before fermentation gives an indication of the amount of sugars present and therefore the likely alcoholic content of the final brew. Prior to the use of a hydrometer other methods were used to judge the strength of the beer, one of which was for the examining officer to don a pair of leather breeches, pour some of the beer to be tested upon a stone step and then to sit on it. If, at the end of a specified time, he found that he was stuck to the step, then the beer was deemed to be strong!

Although there was a duty on beer, spirits were exempt and towards the end of the 17th century and well into the 18th there was what Monckton in his *History of the English Public House* described as 'one of the biggest orgies of over-indulgence our island history has ever seen'. Every small alehouse in the country was in a position to sell cheap brandy and in particular, gin. The result was that consumption of spirits increased from half-a-million gallons in 1684 to over eight million gallons in 1743—an increase of well over one gallon per person per year! The various 'Gin Acts' that followed, together with increased duties and a strengthening of the powers of the justices, rapidly changed this trend and by 1758 excise duty was paid on less than two million gallons per year. The 'gin era' was over.

However, means of regulating public houses continued to attract government interest and from 1729 licence renewal had to be made at annual Brewster Sessions, originally held in September, but moved later to February.

Following the closure of the monasteries in the late 1530s, inns began to provide food and accommodation for travellers, the latter often in rooms on several levels around galleried courtyards. By the 18th century most of these establishments had lost their earlier reputation for being rat-infested hovels and were becoming orderly and well-equipped. However, there was still room for improvement as Viscount Torrington's experiences around 1790 show—'I look upon an inn, as the seat of all roguery, profaness, and debauchery; and sicken of them every day, by hearing nothing but oaths, and abuse of each other, and brutality to horses ... all town inns are so noisy by low company and intemperance'.

However, James Boswell in his *Life of Samuel Johnson* gives a totally different picture. 'There is no private house', said Johnson, 'in which people can enjoy themselves so well as at a capital tavern ... The master of the house is anxious to entertain his guests; the guests are anxious to be agreeable to him; and no man but a very impudent dog indeed can as freely command what is in another man's house as if it were his own. Whereas, at a tavern, there is a general freedom from anxiety. You are sure you are welcome; and the more noise you make, the more trouble you give, the more good things you call for, the welcomer you are. No servants will attend you with the alacrity which waiters do, who are incited by the prospect of an immediate reward in proportion as they please. No, sir, there is nothing which has yet been contrived by man, by which so much happiness is produced, as by a good tavern or inn'.

Inns were the base for carriers who delivered goods between the market towns and the surrounding rural areas. As with stage coaches, each carrier had his own arrangement. The early 19th century was the culmination of coach travel and inns were then at the height of their prosperity. They had an enviable reputation which is well expressed by Washington Irving in *Travelling at Christmas*: 'As we drove into the

Destination.	Name of Carrier.	Days.	Depart from
Aymestrey	John Bywater	Friday	*White Hart*
Bircher Com. ...	Ann Bailey	Tues. & Fri.	*Broad street*
Bircher Com. ...	Mrs. Leek	Friday	*Hop Pole*
Bodenham	John Prosser	Friday	*King's Head*
Bodenham	Thos. Gravenor	Friday	*Elephant & Castle*
Byton..............	Mrs. Holder	Friday	*Livery Stables*
Byton	Mrs. Taylor	Friday	*White Horse*
Canon Pyon......	Mrs. Griffiths	Friday	*The Oak*
Canon Pyon......	Mrs. Poyner	Friday	*The Oak*
Canon Pyon......	Mrs. Shuker	Friday	*Black Swan*
Dilwyn.............	Mrs. Edwards	Friday	*King's Head*
Dilwyn...	John Evans	Friday	*White Horse*
Docklow	Mrs. Childe	Friday	*Lloyd's Stables*
Grendon Bishop	Mrs. Childe	Friday	*Lloyd's Stables*
Hatfield	Thomas Garbett	Friday	*The Chequers*
Hope-u-Dinmore	Thos. Gravenor	Friday	*Elephant & Castle*
Hope-u-Dinmore	John Prosser	Friday	*King's Head*
Kingsland.........	John Bywater	Friday	*White Hart*
Kingsland.........	John Griffiths	Friday	*King's Head*
Kingsland.........	Mrs. Holder	Friday	*Livery Stables*
Kings Pyon.......	Mary Edwards	Friday	*King's Head*
Laysters	John Jones	Friday	*The Anchor*
Lucton	Mrs. Crump	Friday	*Blue Boar*
Lucton...........	Mrs. Reynolds	Friday	*Blue Boar*
Luston	Ann Bailey	Tues. & Fri.	*Broad street*
Luston	Margaret Heapy	Tues. & Fri.	*Blue Boar*
Puddleston	Mrs. Parsons	Friday	*The Bell*
Puddleston	Thos. Griffiths	Friday	*The Bell*
Shobdon	John Griffiths	Friday	*King's Head*
Shobdon	Mrs. Holder	Friday	*Livery Stables*
Shobdon	Mrs. Strangward	Friday	*White Horse*
Weobley..........	John Evans	Friday	*White Horse*
Weobley	Mrs. Walton	Friday	*Bull's Head*
Wigmore..........	John Bywater	Friday	*White Hart*
Wigmore..........	A. Hall	Friday	*Bull's Head*
Yarpole........ ...	Mrs. Fox	Tues. & Fri.	*Broad street*
Yarpole............	Mrs. Worthing	Friday	*Blue Boar*

Leominster carriers in 1890

great gateway of the inn, I saw on one side the light of a rousing kitchen fire beaming through a window. I entered, and admired for the hundredth time, that picture of convenience, neatness, and broad honest enjoyment, the kitchen of an English inn. It was of spacious dimensions; hung round by copper and tin vessels, highly polished, and decorated here and there with a Christmas green. Hams, tongues, and flitches of bacon were suspended from the ceiling; a smoke-jack made its ceaseless clanking beside the fireplace, and a clock ticked in one corner. A well scoured deal table extended along one side of the kitchen, with a cold round of beef, and other hearty viands upon it, over which two foaming tankards of ale seemed mounting guard. Travellers of inferior orders were preparing to attack this stout repast, while others sat smoking or gossiping over their ale, on two high-backed oaken settles beside the fire. Trim housemaids were hurrying backwards and forwards under the directions of a fresh, bustling landlady; but still seizing an occasional moment to exchange a flippant word, and have a rallying laugh with the group round the fire'.

Apart from earlier attempts to regulate the marking of drinking vessels to show the capacity, it was during the 19th century that most of the legislation that affects the present-day consumption and sale of alcoholic drink was enacted. The Alehouse Act of 1828 meant that the licensee no longer had to find sureties for his behaviour. However, he was bound to use the legal, stamped measures, not to adulterate his drinks, and not to permit drunkenness on his premises. The Beerhouse Acts of 1830, 1834 and 1840 followed—the first allowed premises to open for the sale of beer, but not spirits, on payment of a simple excise licence; the second differentiated between 'on' and 'off' licences and made 'on' licences more difficult to obtain; whilst the third ensured that licences were issued only to the occupier of the premises. Throughout the country as a whole there was a proliferation of beer-houses following the first Act, many in the country areas.

At that time there were few restrictions on licensing hours. As a whole, the only non-permitted hours were during Divine Services on Sundays, Christmas Day and Good Friday. Beer houses could only open between 4 a.m. and 10 p.m. The 1872 Licensing Act tidied up and tightened the complex legislation, but at the beginning of the 20th century public houses were, in general, still allowed to open for some 20 hours each day.

Towards the end of the 19th century and in the early years of the following one, considerable efforts were made to close down inns and public houses by refusing to renew licences, even though this resulted in the payment of compensation to the owners and landlords. This was more common in the towns than in the countryside and in Hereford, by 1919, the Compensation Authority had approved the closure of no less than 35 public houses at a cost of some £16,000.

It is not often realised that the regulations concerning licensed houses, alcohol and children are mainly of 20th century origin. Although the 1872 Act made it an offence to sell spirits to those using licensed premises under the age of 16, it was not until the Children's Act of 1908 that children under the age of 14 were prohibited in licensed premises. It was only in 1923 that it became, in general, an offence to serve alcoholic drinks to those under 18.

Regulations brought in at a time of war often have a habit of staying. It was on 23 November 1914, during the First World War, that limited opening hours were instigated—in Hereford this meant that closing time was 9 p.m.! Warnings were common and in the *Hereford Times* for 12 February 1916 Mr. Wallis (the magistrate) warned landlords that '... great as were these difficulties, they should set their faces against any drinking by soldiers. To see soldiers about the streets under the influence of liquour was a very sorry sight. The bench also regarded with much displeasure any encouragement of women to spend the money they received from the Army in the public houses of the city. They knew that in the great majority of public houses this would not be allowed'.

The Licensing Act of 1921 regularized this situation by defining 'permitted hours' as being eight hours between 11 a.m. and 10 p.m. except for Sunday, which was limited to five hours. In 1934, there was a slight improvement—an extension could be granted to 10.30 p.m. during the summer months, especially in rural areas where evening work was necessary.

The 1920s were a time of the Temperance Movement and their activities occupied many pages in the *Hereford Times*. Typical is a letter from Charles Smith of Sheffield, included in the edition of 17 July 1920: 'Herefordshire devoted over 30,000 acres to the growth of barley, hops, and cider apples wherewith to produce a poison which intoxicates; which lands carters in the street drunk, wounded, and helpless, and leaves the horses straying; and men reeling on horseback, drunk, clamouring for more beer, creating a disturbance, and ending in custody. All this is evil for the community, however profitable to the brewers. I observe that your Herefordshire Fruit Company are using

£50,000 value in early fruits, only two-fifths of which are obtained in the county and three-fifths from outside. Why are not the 30,000 acres mentioned above given to the production of fruit wherewith to feed the people, instead of to the production of a drug wherewith to poison them?'

After the Second World War there were several minor Acts, which culminated in the one of 1961 that provided for 'restaurant' and 'residential' licences. It also gave the customers' grace—the ten minutes of 'drinking-up time'. A late 20th century Act restored the situation to more or less what it was at the beginning of the century by allowing inns to stay open throughout the day if they so wish, most commonly any times between 11 a.m. and 11 p.m., with a somewhat shorter 'window of opportunity' on Sundays. A new millennium has brought new thought and it is most probable that restrictions upon public houses will be further reduced leading to the possibility of 24 hour opening once again.

Say, for what were hop-yards meant,
Or why was Burton built on Trent?
Oh many a peer of England brews
Livelier liquor than the muse,
And malt does more than Milton can
To justify God's ways to man.
Ale, man, ale's the stuff to drink
For fellows whom it hurts to think.
(*A Shropshire Lad*, A.E. Housman, 1896)

CHAPTER TWO

Brewing and Breweries

When Daniel Defoe passed through Herefordshire at the beginning of the 18th century he noted that the populace were 'diligent and laborious people, chiefly addicted to husbandry, and they boast, perhaps, not without reason, that they have the finest wool, the best hops, and the richest cyder in all Britain'. As far as cider was concerned, he went on to say 'here it was, that several times for 20 miles together, we could get no beer or ale in their publick houses, only cyder; and that so very good, so fine, and so cheap, that we never found fault with the exchange; great quantities of this cyder are sent to London, even by land carriage tho' so very remote, which is an evidence for the goodness of it, beyond contradiction'. The importance was that both cider and ale were safe to drink at a time when most water supplies were at the best suspect and often could cause serious illnesses.

Until relatively recently cider was made on almost every farm in Herefordshire. It was sometimes produced as a cash crop, but was usually made to be used by the farmer's family and labourers. Cider is made from bitter-sweet apples, which are richer in sugar but rather unpleasant to the taste as they contain a lot of tannin. After crushing the apples and pressing to extract the juice, farm cider was produced without the addition of cultured yeast, fermentation relying upon the natural yeasts in the apples to produce a still, cloudy, acidic, invigorating and thirst-quenching drink. This was much appreciated during the heat of the next summer when the farmer would provide bread, cheese, and cider for those helping with the hay-making, a practice that continued into the 20th century. These delights of making hay, and possibly others, are described by Laurie Lee in his best-selling book *Cider with Rosie*.

Where apples grow so do pears, which when processed in the same manner as cider apples are converted from unpalatable varieties of that fruit into a pleasant, heart-warming drink called perry.

Farmhouse cider was not universally acclaimed. In *Hereford in 1892*, the author comments: 'Those who have seen the wretched looking farm-house cider-mills in various parts of the country, the uncleanly surroundings, and the rough-and-ready methods used in the production of this beverage, can only wonder at the good luck that so often favoured the cider maker. All sorts and conditions of apples, some green, some over-ripe, and some half-decayed windfalls, all mixed without care or selection and crushed up in a dirty, lumbering old mill, and the juice left to ferment or mature in something like superannuated water casks or wash tubs, covered with old sacks. Such was frequently the method of making home-made cider'. Rumours also abound of the addition of dead rats and cats and the use of water from particularly noisome duck-ponds!

Late in the 19th and during the first half of the 20th centuries, cider was made by several firms in Herefordshire including W. Evans and Co., H. Godwin & Son, and H.P. Bulmer & Co. all in Hereford. In 1892, William Evans and Co.'s Cider Works on Widemarsh Common were said to produce 'two favourite beverages, namely cider and perry, in greater perfection than any other town in England'. They continued to produce cider in Hereford

THE

Dinmore Cider Works,

:: :: **DINMORE,** :: ::

BODENHAM, R.S.O., HEREFORDSHIRE.

Makers of

Telegrams : SMITH, BODENHAM,
HEREFORDSHIRE.

HIGH-CLASS 🥀

CIDER AND PERRY.

Guaranteed Pure Apple or Pear Juice, and Free from any Adulterations.

SUPPLIED IN LARGE AND SMALL BOTTLES, AND CASKS OF ALL SIZES.

ALL KINDS of FRUIT BOUGHT.

:: **BEST PRICES GIVEN.** ::

GENERAL PRODUCE BROKERS.

Proprietor : C. S. SMITH.

Dinmore Cider Works advertisement 1914

until well after the end of the Second World War, but eventually closed and the buildings were all demolished by 1975. Godwin & Son had premises at Holmer, but they have also been closed for many years. Bulmer's was founded in 1887 and initially centralised their operations in Ryelands Street, but more recently in Plough Lane. They are now the largest cider producers in the world. Half way between Hereford and Leominster the Dinmore Cider Works near Dinmore Station was active in the early years of the 20th century. They also produced cider and perry 'in large and small bottles and casks of all sizes'. Apart from the cider works mentioned above, there are some 30 cider makers listed in the 1913 Herefordshire trades directory. They included J.M. Parry and Co. of Leominster, Yeoman Bros. of Canon Pyon, and Thomas Aldridge and William Bowder, both of Wellington. The manufacture of cider by small firms continued well into the 20th century and the 1937 trades directory records Gwilliam and Jay of Wellington, H. Langford and Sons of Cobnash, Kingsland, M.E. and A.P. Quarrell of Marden and Yeomans Bros., who by that time had moved from Canon Pyon to Leominster.

As well as the cider manufacturers, cider continued to be made by a few farmers and inns using the old methods, the **Exchange** in Leominster being one that continued to make cider until the middle of the 20th century. However, nearly all cider is now made in plants resembling chemical engineering factories but, technology aside, the process has not changed much and most cider is only made when apples fall off trees, although some are picked and then left to ripen; now the natural yeasts are generally destroyed and replaced by cultured ones, but fermentation is still a batch process and is continued to complete dryness and an alcoholic content of over 8%. This results in many vats, each containing a slightly different cider, the cider-maker's art being in blending quantities from many vats to produce a consistent product. Alcoholic content, sweetness, and colour is adjusted by the addition of water, glucose, and natural colour, the resultant blend being filtered, pasteurised, and carbonated before being marketed under an appropriate brand name and logo. Ciders produced by organic methods do not go through all these processes.

Many processes produce waste-products and by-products: the beer industry amongst other things produces spent malt that may be used as animal food and 'Marmite', that famous 'you either love it or you hate it' by-product. The residue left after pressing the juice from apples is called pommace and may be used in animal feeds or ploughed into the land as a fertiliser and conditioner, but may also be used to produce pectin, a natural gelling agent used in the food industry. Bulmers used to produce much of the world's requirement for pectin from the residues of Herefordshire apples, but in a global economy things change and pectin can now be produced more cheaply from the residual pulp from the citrus fruit juice industry, meaning pectin is now produced in South America near the sources of its raw material. Thus Herefordshire has lost its pectin plant and its brownfield site in Ryelands Street is giving birth to over a hundred houses.

Until the middle of the 19th century most landlords made their own ale and beer in small brewhouses behind their inns. Thus in an 1832 sale catalogue for the **King's Head**, then in South Street, Leominster, the ground floor of the inn included 'two front parlours, good kitchen, back kitchen or brewhouse'. Very few of these small breweries survive in a recognisable state today—they have either been demolished or converted to become part of the main buildings of the inn.

However, many of the smaller inns and beer-houses that opened during the first half of the 19th century had no brewing facilities what-soever and were totally dependent on other inns or on the growing number of breweries for their supply. This change accelerated as brew-eries bought public houses whenever they came onto the market, a process that resulted in a substantial decrease in the number of 'free houses' and of independent breweries. This was followed by a series of mergers and takeovers until only a few of the largest breweries survived.

ALMELEY

WHOLESALE & FAMILY

BREWERY,

ESTABLISHED, 1853

BY

HENRY BAIRD, Proprietor,

For the purpose of supplying Families and the Trade with
Genuine Home Brewed Ales, Brewed purely with Malt and
Hops, guaranteed free from the slightest adulteration, or
deleterious ingredient of any description.

H. B. superintends the brewing of his own Ales, and having
no Agents' or Travellers' expenses, he is, therefore, in a position
to offer to his Customers a superior article at a moderate price.

CARRIAGE FREE.

IN CASKS FROM 9 TO 54 GALLONS.

Orders by Post punctually attended to.

ALMELEY BREWERY,

NEAR

LETTON, HEREFORD.

*The New Inn at Almeley advertising
in an 1876 directory*

By the end of the Second World War, the long tradition of inns producing their own beer had completely ceased in Herefordshire.

One that did try to expand was the Brewery attached to the **New Inn** at Almeley. The proprietor, Henry Baird, started his brewing business in 1853 and was taking full-page advertisements in local directories well into the 1870s. This was no small operation; as with many of the larger manufacturers he was quite prepared to supply his beer in hogsheads—casks containing 54 gallons, a staggering 432 pints!

It was during the 1870s that Charles Blundell opened the Britannia Brewery in his extensive premises at 38 South Street, Leominster where he produced ales, stout and porter. This was an extension to his main business which was the supply of coal, coke and lime. The brewery business lasted longer than Mr. Blundell, for in 1905 it had become Paxton and Co. At that time there were two other brewers in Leominster, John Job Biddle at the **Chequers Inn**, 61 Etnam Street and Charles Reynolds at the **White Swan**, 28 School Lane. The **Chequers** was probably the last pub in Leominster to continue brewing its own beer and making cider, with Harold Job Biddle as brewer and landlord in the late-1930s, also showing the inn was still in the same family.

LEOMINSTER.

BRITANNIA BREWERY,

SOUTH STREET.

CHARLES BLUNDELL,

Having recently erected a Brewery upon his extensive premises, solicits the patronage of his Friends and the Public, and begs to assure them that he purposes producing

MILD AND STRONG ALES, STOUT AND PORTER,

Brewed from the best selected

MALT AND HOPS ONLY,

IN

9, 18, 36, AND 54 GALLON CASKS,

All Orders for which will receive strict and prompt attention.

C. BLUNDELL

ALSO CONTINUES HIS

COAL, COKE, AND LIME TRADE

AT HIS SEVERAL DEPÔTS AT

LEOMINSTER AND OTHER STATIONS

OF THE DISTRICT.

Prices and particulars of which can be supplied from the Head Offices,

SOUTH STREET, LEOMINSTER.

Leominster's Britannia Brewery—an 1876 advertisement

The first brewery of any size to be built in the county belonged to J.C. Reynolds. He had originally started his business at Fownhope, but moved to a new site in Bewell Street, Hereford, in 1834 where he established himself as a brewer, maltster and wine and spirit merchant. In 1845 the whole establishment was bought by Charles Watkins, who was landlord of the Imperial Inn in Widemarsh Street. Watkins had previously brewed his own beer in a small brew-house at the rear of the Imperial, but this new acquisition enabled him to put his creative energy to work in increasing output and in finding new sales outlets. He started his new business by changing the name of the firm to the much more imposing Imperial Brewery, capitalising on the name of his inn. The beginnings of his fortune came when he transported vast quantities of his beer a few miles to the north of the city, where the navvies were digging a tunnel underneath Dinmore Hill for the Shrewsbury to Hereford railway. Within a few years he was producing 'Imperial Household and Pale Ales', described as 'pure and sound, and unrivalled for excellence of quality and value combined'. Mild and bitter beers were available at 1 shilling a gallon and pale ale at 1 shilling and 2 pence; all being supplied in 9, 18, 36 and 54 gallon casks, delivered free. The brewery grew rapidly and with the profits Charles Watkins was able to buy or lease several public houses in Herefordshire and the surrounding areas. By the end of the 19th

The Hereford Brewery about 1840

21

century in north-west Herefordshire the Imperial empire included the **New Inn** at Almeley (no longer brewing its own beer), the **Balance Inn** at Luston, the **New Inn** at Wellington, and the **Bannut Tree Head Inn** and the **Carpenters' Arms Inn**, both in Marden. These, and other purchases provided him with the main outlets to sell the beer he was brewing in ever increasing quantities. He also grew his own hops and farmed at Marden, Holmer and Burghill.

The brewery included a vat room with a beer cellar underneath, fermenting and racking rooms, and a large, partially covered area used for washing and storing casks. Adjacent buildings contained the cooper's shop, the wheelwright's shop, stables and harness rooms. The water used in all the processes came from the famous Bewell Spring by means of an artesian well some 40 feet deep.

The Imperial Brewery was put on the market in 1898. Included in the sale was the brewery with its plant and all the other buildings on the site; 35 hotels, public houses and beer houses in the city and neighbourhood; and branches in Birmingham, Cardiff and Swansea. The sale was held in London, and according to the city library copy of the sale particulars £64,000 was the highest bid for the lot. The new firm became the Hereford and Tredegar Brewery Co. but, by 1950 changes were again in the air.

These changes were also to affect the other main brewery in Hereford, which had been founded in the latter part of the 19th century. This was the City Brewery situated on the south side of Maylord Street. Here, Arnold Perrett & Co., although on a more restricted site than the Hereford Brewery, produced beer for consumption in the gradually growing number of inns, both free houses and those belonging to the company. Arnold Perrett & Co. were eventually associated with the Stroud Brewery, and in 1924 the Maylord Street premises were transferred to the Cheltenham Original Brewery Co. Ltd.

The amalgamation of the two Hereford breweries in 1950 produced the Hereford, Tredegar & Cheltenham Breweries Ltd., although it continued to make use of the trade names such as the Stroud Brewery and Arnold Perrett & Co. Brewing continued in Maylord Street until May 1948 after which the site was just used for storage and distribution. In 1951 it was put up for sale because the firm

HEREFORD.

OF

The Hereford Brewery,

FITTED WITH A

25-QUARTER PLANT,

RESIDENCE AND PREMISES,

AND

50-QUARTER MALTINGS,

HEREFORD,

TOGETHER WITH

35 HOTELS, PUBLIC & BEER HOUSES

AND OTHER PROPERTY,

SITUATE

In the City and Neighbourhood;

ALSO

BRANCHES AT

BIRMINGHAM, CARDIFF & SWANSEA,

AND THE VALUABLE

Trade Marks and Goodwill of the Concern,

WHICH INCLUDES A

CONSIDERABLE TRADE IN WINES AND SPIRITS, BOTTLED BEERS AND MINERAL WATERS.

Which will be Sold by Auction by Messrs.

COLLIER and BOWDICH

At the Auction Mart, Tokenhouse Yard, London,

On MONDAY, the 27th day of JUNE, 1898,

At Two o'clock precisely, in One Lot.

UNLESS PREVIOUSLY DISPOSED OF BY PRIVATE TREATY.

The Property may be viewed, and Particulars (with Plans) obtained of Messrs. GWYNNE JAMES & SON, Solicitors, Hereford ; and of

Messrs. COLLIER & BOWDICH, Brewery Valuers & Auctioneers,
24, *Coleman Street, London, E.C.*

The 1898 sale of the Hereford Brewery

23

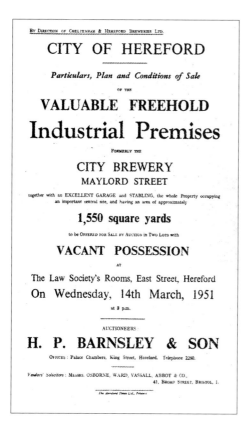

CITY OF HEREFORD

Particulars, Plan and Conditions of Sale

OF THE

VALUABLE FREEHOLD

Industrial Premises

FORMERLY THE

CITY BREWERY
MAYLORD STREET

together with an EXCELLENT GARAGE and STABLING, the whole Property occupying an important central site, and having an area of approximately

1,550 square yards

to be OFFERED FOR SALE BY AUCTION in TWO LOTS with

VACANT POSSESSION

AT

The Law Society's Rooms, East Street, Hereford
On Wednesday, 14th March, 1951

at 3 p.m.

AUCTIONEERS

H. P. BARNSLEY & SON

Offices : Palace Chambers, King Street, Hereford. Telephone 2280.

Vendors' Solicitors : Messrs. OSBORNE, WARD, VASSALL, ABBOT & CO.,
43, BROAD STREET, BRISTOL, 1.

The Hereford Times Ltd., Printers

The 1951 sale of the City Brewery,
its site now part of Maylord Orchards

was concentrating all their brewing operations in the city 'at their other extensive premises in Bewell Street'. The purchase price was £7,600 and the whole area is now part of the Maylord Orchards development.

Subsequent to the acquisition of the firm by Whitbreads, brewing operations also ceased in the Bewell Street works. After a few years all the buildings were demolished. In 1967, a small part of the brewery site disappeared underneath the Relief Road. Eventually, the Tesco supermarket was built on the remainder of the site, the extensive basement car park replacing in part the cellars belonging to the brewery.

Following the closure of the Bewell Street brewery, there was a period of some 30 years when beer for public consumption was no longer produced in Herefordshire. Indeed, throughout the country, beer brewed at individual inns almost ceased, with only a few notable examples such as the **Three Tuns** at Bishop's Castle surviving. Convenience beers, in pressurised barrels that did not depend on the skill of the landlord, flooded the market. For a time, it looked as though the old-fashioned beer-engine, used to draw the beer up from the carefully racked barrels in the cellars, would be a thing of the past.

A welcome change has occurred in recent years and locally produced beer and cider is again available. The Wye Valley Brewery, based at the **Barrels Inn** in St Owen's Street, now has its beer in inns across the county. In north-west Herefordshire 'Specialist beers' are produced by firms such as The Brew House at the **Queen's Head**,

24

Kington, Marches Ales in Leominster and the Woodhampton Brewery at Aymestrey. As a result the beer-engine has made a welcome return on most bar counters. In addition, locally-made 'single-apple' and 'vintage' ciders and perry have also made a welcome return in north-west Herefordshire with firms such as Dunkertons at Luntley near Pembridge—now an important stop on the 'cider route' through some of the more pleasant parts of rural Herefordshire.

I often wonder what brewers buy
One half so precious as the goods they sell

(Anon.)

I feel no pain dear mother now
But oh, I am so dry!
O take me to a brewery
And leave me there to die.
(Parody of *The Collier's Dying Child*, E. Farmer)

O Beer! O Hodgson, Guiness, Allsopp, Bass!
Names that should be on every infant's tongue
(*Beer,* C.S. Calverley, 1861)

North-western Herefordshire showing the area covered by this book.
The grey lines and numbers indicate the extent of each chapter

CHAPTER THREE

Hereford to Eardisley

The main road leading westwards from Hereford towards Hay-on-Wye and Brecon is the A438, in part of Roman origin, but for over 1,000 years one of the main roads leading into Wales. It keeps to a course that is just to the north of the river Wye for the whole distance to the Welsh border, often almost touching the river where once fords and ferries provided crossing points. This was one of the Hereford turnpike roads, and it leaves the city proper at the White Cross where the A4112 road to Knighton bears off to the right (See chapter 8).

When this was a simple Y-shaped junction, the White Cross used to stand on the right hand side of the Kington road, but road improvement works some years ago left it perched precariously in the middle of a traffic roundabout. The Cross was built by Bishop Charlton in 1362, during the second outbreak of the bubonic plague—the dreaded Black Death. The two outbreaks probably halved the population of the city. His predecessor, Bishop Trilleck's, attempt to curtail the original outbreak of the plague by carrying the shrine containing the relics of St. Thomas Cantilupe around the streets of the city had proved rather ineffectual, so Bishop Charlton built his cross and arranged for the market and the exchange of goods to be held there rather than in the streets of the city. This was where the country people, who were not suffering from the plague, brought their goods for sale, and where the afflicted townsfolk left their coins, doubtless suitably disinfected in vinegar, to pay for them. The pedestal and steps are original, but the rather-too-long shaft and cross were added during restoration works in 1864. This is still within the city limits, for the Liberty of Hereford includes the Township of Huntington and the boundary extends all the way along the northern side of King's Acre Road, past the **Bay Horse**, almost as far as the King's Acre itself.

27

For the first ten miles or so the main road from Hereford towards Hay-on-Wye seems to make an effort to by-pass all the village settlements. To its south are the villages of Breinton, Byford and Monnington and, a short distance to the north, there are Stretton Sugwas, Kenchester and Bishopstone. The reason may well be almost 2,000 years old—the original road leading into Wales was a continuation of Hereford's Roman Road. This long straight road forms the northern boundary of the Liberty of Hereford as it arrives from the direction of Worcester and continues westwards into Wales. It passes through the Roman town of *Magnis* at Kenchester, eventually to join the A438 at Portway, some eight miles west of Hereford.

It is reasonably certain that one of the earliest 'inns' in the county would have been at *Magnis,* for the town is included in the *Antonine Itinerary*—a road book prepared for the information of official travellers giving the names of places and staging-points, with distances between, along all the major routes throughout the Roman Empire. *Magnis* is included in Itinerary XII, which covers the 168 miles from Carmarthen to Caerleon in South Wales and then northwards through Usk, Abergavenny, across an early Wye bridge to Kenchester and then

The Roman town of Magnis *from the air, looking west*

to Leintwardine, finally to terminate at Wroxeter, the important Roman settlement a few miles south-east of Shrewsbury. The Roman road that leads westwards from *Magnis* was not considered important enough to be included in the *Itinerary,* so there are no details of other stopping points on this road leading into Wales.

Magnis was a frontier town with the military zone to the west and the full civilisation of mighty Rome to the east. It survived as a town for well over 300 years, with fine stone buildings containing elaborate mosaic pavements and hypocausts for heating. Now nothing remains above ground, but excavations early in the 20th century exposed the foundations of several buildings with wooden and stone porticoes fronting the wide main street. Some of these buildings would have provided accommodation for travellers, others would doubtless have served alcoholic refreshment.

The road from Hereford to Hay has always been of considerable importance to travellers heading for Wales and for the residents of Hay-on-Wye who needed to visit Hereford. As early as May 1776, Hill's flying diligence travelled from Hay to Hereford on Wednesday mornings for the market, returning later in the day. The fare was 5 shillings single and 8 shillings return, provided the return was on the same day. To get to market in time it would hardly have had time to stop off at any of the wayside inns, but perhaps on the homeward journey ...?

More recent travellers heading towards Wales would have needed sustenance just as much as their Roman and Georgian forebears, and the A438 road leading from Hereford was reasonably well supplied for much of its length. Only a mile or so from Hereford's boundary is the **Kite's Nest** at Sugwas Pool just past Swainshill. Swainshill is a roadside settlement in Stretton Sugwas parish, which, because of its position on the main road, seems to have become more important than the original village. Indeed, in 1880 the parish church was totally demolished and rebuilt at Swainshill, some three-quarters of a mile south-west of its original site.

The **Kite's Nest** has been a roadside inn for many years and at the beginning of the 19th century was the home for one of the many Friendly Societies that functioned in Herefordshire. Such Societies, usually based on inns and taverns, were an early expression of self-help. For a small weekly subscription, members, after an introductory period usually of three or five years, would obtain sick pay should they be ill or suffer from an accident. The money invested was, on occasion, also used to provide mortgages for members.

A deed of sale of a property in Breinton, now in the Hereford Record Office, refers to a mortgage from an old Friendly Society known as 'The Coach and Horses Society' which was 'formerly held at the house of Morris Jones, but then of William Hancocks situate in the parish of Breinton ...', which was transferred to the 'Benefit Society or Club now held at the dwelling house of ... George Davies called the **Kite's Nest** and situate in the parish of Stretton Sugwas'. The Coach and Horses Friendly Society was in existence in 1801 and the rules were revised in 1830. The **Coach and Horses** may have been the inn of that name that was described as being in Huntington Township, but there was also an inn of the same name in Breinton. In 1817 the Huntington **Coach and Horses** was the venue for a cock-fight between the Gentlemen of the City and the Gentlemen of the County. Its precise whereabouts is uncertain.

It would seem likely that the **Coach and Horses** closed around 1830 and that its Friendly Society was the predecessor of the Stretton Sugwas Friendly Society which was formed in 1832 at the **Kite's Nest**. The rules were quite complex, but were designed to ensure that all

The Kite's Nest in the 1970s

members received sick pay of six shillings per week after three years membership and eight shillings if they had been a member for five years. In addition there were pension rights of five shillings a week and from seven to ten pounds was allowed for a funeral.

The **Kite's Nest** has had a long-standing reputation for first class hospitality, for it is one of the very few inns mentioned in *Cassey's Directory* for 1858 where the editor make a personal comment. He describes the **Kite's Nest** as 'an old-established and good inn, which is kept by Mrs. Kearn'.

A curious event occurred in 1876 which involved the **Kite's Nest** and **The Volunteer** at Marden. A Settlement was made on 28 March 1876 by Thomas Lloyd, 'late of King's Acre ... but now of the parish of Stretton Juxta Sugwas, Tailor'. He had been 'committed for trial at the next Assizes to be held for the County of Hereford for having shot at one Thomas Webb with intent to do him grievous bodily harm'. It appears that Thomas Lloyd was a man of considerable means, and that he was assigning all his 'real and personal estate' to Thomas Prosser of the **Cambrian Arms**, White Cross Street, Hereford and William Ashburner of the Barton, Railway Yard, Foreman, to be held by them in trust before the court case. His properties included 'All that

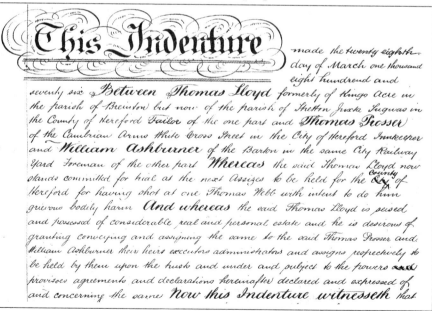

Part of Thomas Lloyd's assignment, made before he went to gaol

31

messuage or Public House called the **Kite's Nest** situate and being in the parish of Stretton Sugwas ... in the occupation of Ann Hill', and 'all that messuage or tenement now used as an Inn or Public House and known as **The Volunteer Inn** with the cottage and several pieces and parcels of land ... in the Parish of Marden'. Thomas Lloyd was sentenced to 15 years in 1876 and served time in Pentonville, Dartmoor, Wormwood Scrubs and Chatham. By 1887 Thomas Lloyd, then 62, had been released and was landlord of the **Kite's Nest**. He must have been quite an unusual landlord, for he was described as being 'the King of Herefordshire Poachers'. Perhaps poaching was lucrative, or he had other good fortune, for in 1887 he was described as owning the **Kite's Nest,** a row of houses nearby and other property in Hereford. At the very least, he must have had his property returned from the friends with whom he left it in trust. Was his release from prison the reason for the executor of the late Mrs. Ann Hill to sell all the household furniture in the premises?

THE KITE'S NEST INN,
STRETTON SUGWAS, Near HEREF RD,
One Mile from Credenhill Station.

MESSRS. F. H. SUNDERLAND & Co.
Have received instructions from the Executor of the late Mrs. ANN HILL, to Sell by Auction, upon the above Premises,

On TUESDAY, the 8th of FEBRUARY, 1887
THE WHOLE OF THE USEFUL HOUSEHOLD

FURNITURE
RICK OF PRIME HAY,
N.W. Cart. Spring Pony Cart, Pony Harness, Poultry, Hogsheads, and Casks. Tools, and other Out-door Effects.

SALE AT TWO O'CLOCK SHARP.

PROSSER, PRINTER, HEREFORD.

Part of the poster advertising the sale of all the household goods at the Kite's Nest in 1887

CATALOGUE

OUT-DOOR.

Lot
1 to 6 Farm tools
7 to 15 Tuts and casks
16 Cooler
17 Eighteen gallon cask
18 Fifty-six ditto
19 Hogshead
20 Ditto
21 Ditto
22 Ditto
23 Ditto
24 Ditto and cider
25 Ditto
26 Tun pail
27 Hop seive
28 Hay knife
29 Corn bin
30 Bread trough
31 Pig bench
32 India-rubber tube
33 Long ladder
34 Short ditto
35 Bench
36 Ditto
37 Tramming
38 One set of short gears
39 One ditto pony ditto
40 Narrow-wheel cart
41 Spring pony cart
About 30 head of poultry, at per couple
Rick of prime hay

SCULLERY.

42 Large meat safe
43 Small ditto ditto
44 Stand
45 Saucepans
46 Ditto
47 Large pot
48 Boiler
49 Box and brushes
50 Frying pan, &c.
51 Knives and forks
52 Scales and weights
53 Racking tap
54 Copper fountain
55 Table
56 Copper preserving kettle
57 Sundry ware
58 Bench

KITCHEN.

60 Oak table
61 Elm do.
62 Settle
63 do.
64 Six spittoons
65 Trays
66 Lamps
67 Brass candlesticks
68 Muller
69 Steel yards, up to 3 cwt.
70 Copper kettle
71 Iron do.
72 Brass trippet
73 Fender and fire irons
74 Home-cured ham, at per lb.
75 Do. Flitch of Bacon, at per lb.
76 Two chairs

BAR PARLOUR.

77 Table and cover
78 Ditto 2 leaf
79 Ditto small and cover
80 Eight-day clock
81 Pier glass
82 Pewter measures
83 Half-dozen spirit bottles
84 Ditto ditto
85a 3 Spirit jars
85 Fender
86 Fire irons
87 4 cane seated chairs
88 Sundry trays
89 A set of tea service (green)
90 Sundry tea ware
91 Sundry desert
92 Hot water plates
93 Cruet stand and bottles
94 Cheese dishes
95 Hot water jugs
96 Jugs (in lots)
97 Half dozen plated spoons
98 2 Pair sugar tongues
99 2 Plated spoons
100 Old china
101 Vases
102 Metal Coffee pot
103 2 Tea pots
104 Small copper kettle
105 Writing desk
106 Ink plated
107 Oil cloth
108 Sundries
109 Mahogany table, two-leaf
110 Ditto two table
111 Round table
112 Ditto
113 Ditto
114 Six chairs (new)
115 One easy chair
116 Arm chair
117 Carved oak cupboard
118 Hair-seated chair
119 Couch and cushions
120 Rug
121 Carpet
122 Sofa
123 Long deal table
124 Three forms
125 Long table (board)
126 Six cane-seated chairs
127 Oil lamp
128 Oil cans
129 Ornaments
130 Fender
131 Fire irons
132 One pair pictures
133 Ditto
134 Ditto
135 Work box
136 Worked cushion
137 Two lamps
138 Matting
139 Hearth rug
140 Two scale weights
141 Ditto
142 Curtains and blinds
143 Three hassocks
144 Two clothes baskets

BEDROOM, NO. 1.

145 Bedstead
146 Feather bed, at per lb.
147 Bolster
148 Bedstead
149 Washstand
150 Ware
151 Toilet tables
152 Ditto glass
153 Towel rail
154 Large chest
155 Table
156 Ditto small, with drawer
157 4 Chairs
158 Bench
159 Carpet bag (new)

BEDROOM, NO. 2.

160 Bedstead, brass mount, and hangings
161 Feather bed, at per lb.
162 Hair Mattress
163 Washstand
164 Ware
165 Toilet table
166 Ditto glass
167 Mahogany chest with 5 drawers
168 Small toilet glass
169 Tray (papier machie)
170 Butter tray and stand
171 Carpet
172 Washstand
173 Ware
174 Towel rail
175 Ditto
176 3 Chairs
177 Box
178 Oak Chest
179 Fender
180 Sundries

BEDROOM, NO. 3.

181 Bedstead
182 Feather bed, at per lb.
183 Ditto ditto ditto
184 Washstand
185 Ware
186 Toilet table
187 Ditto glass
188 Towel rail
189 Carpet
190 Pieces of carpet
191 Three chairs
192 Round mahogany table
193 Clothes box
194 Curtains
195 Warming pan
196 Commode
197 Clock

LINEN.

198 to 205 Eight pairs of cotton sheets, at per pair
206 Three new blankets
207 One do. do.
208 White counterpane
209 Do. do.
210 Do. do.
211 Five coloured quilts, (in lots)
212 Four table cloths (in lots)
213 One do. do. long
214 Towels (in lots)
215 Sundries.

This Catalogue of the Household Furniture at the Kite's Nest gives an excellent picture of a Herefordshire country inn in the latter part of the 19th century

The Kite was once a relatively common bird and in the 15th century, although primarily a raptor (bird of prey) it also scavenged the rubbish that was thrown out in the streets. Even so, its numbers diminished, possibly through inbreeding and, although it had special protection, it had ceased to breed in London by 1777. In Herefordshire it had become quite rare by the latter part of the 19th century. One of the last records was of one nesting in Brampton Bryan Park: 'The keeper, by patient watching, managed to shoot the male bird; the female found a new mate and returned to suffer the same fate!' In the 1860s they were still to be seen in the Wye Valley between Ross and Monmouth, but they were 'rapidly disappearing under the ruthless persecution of the gamekeeper'. Capt. H.A. Gilbert, in his *Herefordshire Birds*, published in 1954, classified it as extinct as a breeding bird, but commented that it was still occasionally to be seen in the county. In 1957 he released a young pair in Radnorshire, having obtained them from Spain. They are slowly making a come-back and red kites are once again present in the valleys of mid-Wales and gradually spreading east. The kite is famous for stealing rags and other materials to make its nest. In Shakespeare's *The Winter's Tale* (Act 4, Scene 3) Autolycus remarks 'when the kite builds, look to lesser linen'.

In 1891, Mrs. Eliza Skyrme had taken over the management of the **Kite's Nest** and in 1937 Thomas Stalvies was landlord.

The Boat Inn at Breinton in the earlier part of the 20th century
(Photograph : Derek Foxton Collection)

Breinton is a scattered parish between the main A438 and the river Wye. It includes small centres at Upper Breinton and Breinton Common, but the parish church is at Lower Breinton where there is a small area of National Trust land that includes a spring of cool clear water a few yards from the Wye. There is now no pub in Breinton, but *Slaters Directory* of 1850 includes a mention of a **Coach and Horses**, possibly the one with the Friendly Society mentioned above. It was still in existence in 1858 when the county directory described Samuel Peglar as 'mine host'. This could have been one of the several inns that were close to a ford, for there was once one that crossed the river in the Lower Breinton area. The Breinton **Coach and Horses** presumably closed well before the end of the 19th century, for there is no mention of it in either the 1879 or the 1891 directory.

There is a small part of Stretton Sugwas parish that adjoins the Wye between Breinton and Kenchester. Here the river is gravel-bottomed and shallow and a ferry was still operating in the 1920s connecting the **Boat Inn** on the left bank with Eaton Bishop on the right bank. This was presumably the **Boat Inn** that was otherwise entered under Breinton parish. Lamont, in his 1922 paper 'Fords and Ferries of the Wye' in the *Woolhope Club Transactions* points out that 'There was here also, up to quite recent times, a horse boat for conveying animals and vehicles and a boat ferry for passengers still plies regularly. All evidences indicate the strategic importance and antiquity of this river crossing, the road leading to which comes off the old Roman road from *Magna* near the **Traveller's Rest** inn and passing over the present railway line, goes by Stretton Sugwas church, crosses the Hereford to Hay highway and on down through a double row of stately oaks, past Judge

The fading sign for the Boat Inn at Breinton

Ingham's house, to the river'. The road from the highway almost to the river is now part of the Wye Valley Walk. The landlord of the **Boat Inn** in 1879 was George James; he was still there in 1891. The inn, which closed in 1948, was close to Breinton Manor, and a trace of it still survives in a rapidly disappearing painted sign on the wall of a barn, opposite the old inn.

A collection of deeds from the late 18th century refers to the **Bull's Head.** In the mid-18th century the property was described as 'All that Messuage or Tenement, Dwelling House and Inn commonly called or known by the name of the **Bull's Head** with the barns, stables, outhouses, folds, and garden thereunto belonging ... in the Parish of Breinton'. Other deeds record that the inn was sold several times, but this was not a long lived or particularly successful inn for in the sale of April 1822 it was described as being 'formerly called ... the **Bull's Head**'.

ELIGIBLE SMALL FREEHOLD INVESTMENTS.
MR. J. H. SUNDERLAND will SELL by AUCTION, at the NELSON INN, BRIDGE SOLLARS, on FRIDAY, the 27th of JULY inst., at Four o'clock in the Afternoon, subject to conditions of Sale, all that substantially Brick-built COTTAGE RESIDENCE, with good Garden, Yard, Barn, Stable, and Outhouses, with about 3½ Acres (more or less) of highly productive Orcharding, the whole in a compact Ring Fence, and situate in the Parish of BISHOPSTONE, 5½ miles from Hereford, and within 100 yards of the Road leading from the Old Weir to Bishopstone, now in the occupation of Mr. George Gardiner. The House is in good repair, pleasantly situated, has good underground Cellaring throughout, two comfortable Sitting-rooms, three Bed-rooms, and one Dressing-room, with usual Offices and convenient Arrangements. The Fruit Trees are in their prime, and the Land in good condition.

Also, all those TWO stone-built LABOURERS' COTTAGES, with good Gardens attached, situate below the above-named Lot on the same Road, and now occupied by Jenks and another, the same being FREEHOLD and offering a good investment for small Capital.

For particulars, apply to WM. HUMFRYS, Esq., Solicitor, or to the AUCTIONEER, Hereford; and for a view, to the respective Tenants.
Hereford, July 6th, 1855. [6183·

A sale at the Nelson Inn in 1855

It is always pleasant to travel along a road that includes an inn or public house, set back slightly from the roadside, every two or three miles or so. The A438 is one such road that still lives up to full expectations all the way from Hereford to the Welsh border. Were all these regular stops set up for the benefit of thirsty Welshmen bringing their goods to the markets in Hereford?

The Lord Nelson in 1999

Just over two miles from the **Kite's Nest** is the **Lord Nelson Inn**, always described as being at Bridge Sollers, but actually in Bishopstone parish. Named after England's great hero, it is no accident that Admiral Lord Nelson is commemorated on more inn signs than any other person. The famous admiral came to Hereford in 1802 and was promptly made a freeman of the city. Lord Nelson was also commemorated with a monument that was erected in 1809 in the middle of Castle Green in the city. It was originally intended to place a statue of the hero of Trafalgar at the top of the column; funds, however, only admitted the urn which is still there today. In 1851, Thomas Jackman was landlord of the **Nelson**; by 1858 it was John Perkes, by 1879 Miss Ann Jones and by 1891 Frederick Bywater. This is a roadside inn of long standing, but there was another one only a short distance away, but in Bridge Sollers parish.

This was the **Salmon Inn** which was on the left bank of the river adjacent to an historic ford across the river Wye. This was not just an ancient ford that was well used, there was also a licensed toll ferry for use when the river was in flood. The lane leading to the ford is still apparent on the left bank and the cottage that was the **Salmon** is now a private house.

Bridge Sollers, like Canon Bridge further downstream, is not named after a bridge crossing the river, but for the wharf on the river-bank where goods from the Wye barges were unloaded. The present bridge—the first bridge to be built at Bridge Sollers—was opened on

The Salmon at Bridge Sollers adjoining the ford across the river Wye. This photograph was taken by John Henry Knight about 1880. He was an inventor and photographer from Farnham in Surrey who travelled widely taking photographs such as this one of the Prosser family

6 August 1896 having cost £3,600. The costs were met partly by public subscription (especially from the Davenports of Foxley who contributed £900) and partly by the County Council (one-third of the cost). It is reputed that some of the stone for Hereford

The Salmon in retirement as a private house

Cathedral came from the aptly-named Bishopstone Hill quarries (below the main road at Bridge Dingle) and was shipped down the river by barge from the wharf at Bridge Sollers.

Apart from being an important river crossing, the western boundary of Bridge Sollers parish, adjacent to Bridge Dingle, follows the line of Offa's Dyke, the ancient 9th century boundary between England (or Mercia at that time) and Wales. It may well be that an ancient predecessor of the **Salmon Inn** was, at one time, the last inn in Mercia! Once the bridge was completed, the ferry ceased to operate and, it would appear, the **Salmon** went into retirement. Uvedale Lawrence was the landlord in 1850 and 1858, Mrs. Mary Lawrence, presumably his wife, in 1879, and William Prosser in 1891.

The next parish to Bridge Sollers along the northern bank of the river Wye is Byford where there was yet another ford that connected the north bank to the village of Preston-on-Wye. At one time there was a punt for foot passengers, and a wide flat-bottomed boat that could transport a carriage and pair across the river when it was too deep to ford. This must have been a thriving part of the river-bank when fords were the accepted (and, indeed, in many areas the only) means of crossing the river. Several deeds concerning properties in Byford include details of the ferry. Thus in June 1790 William Price Esq. sold to John Geers Cotterell Esq. considerable lands that included 'all that messuage, tenement or Public House together with the barns, stables, and Cooper's Shop and the privilege and advantage arising from the ferry over the River Wye commonly called and known by the name of the **Ferry Tenements** now or lately in the tenure possession or occupation of ... Henry Watkins as tenant thereof'. There was also an orchard of some three acres called Boat Orchard that was attached to the property. Apart from being called **Ferry Tenements**, the public house was also appropriately called the **Boat**. It stood at the top of the slope in the river-bank that led down to the dock where the ferry vessels normally lay. The landlady in 1850 and 1858 was one Mary Baker. After the bridge at Bridge Sollers was opened in 1896 these vessels gradually fell into disrepair and the inn closed to become a simple smith's shop.

The cover for a letter dated 18 March 1832 sent by the vicar of Turnastone to Sir George Cornewall at Moccas. It has a Hereford TOO LATE mark and was forwarded the following day, doubtless being left at the Portway Inn for onward transmission

Although the inns that were associated with trade up and down the river during the 18th and early 19th centuries had little chance of survival once the railway from Hereford to Hay and Brecon was opened in 1864, those that depended on passing trade on the A438, continued to prosper. One such was the **Portway Inn**, one of the three inns within the parish of Staunton-on-Wye. It stands at what is now a minor crossroads where, on the south, is the lane that winds down through the apple orchards that surround the rather remote village of Monnington-on-Wye. Having crossed the main road, the lane continues

The Portway in 1999

up the hill to the equally small village of Mansell Gamage and from there towards Moorhampton where there was once a railway station. In the past this minor road would have had more traffic, for a mile to the west of Monnington village along the splendid Monnington Walk was a boat ferry. One of the main reasons for the ferry was to convey letters to the Cornewall family at Moccas Court which lies on the south side of the river. Each day the letters for Moccas were left by the mail carrier at the **Portway** for collection. This system was only just satisfactory and, following the acquisition of the Monnington estates and the opening of the Hay and Brecon railway, Sir Velters Cornewall, at his own expense, built a toll bridge complete with roads and toll cottages. It was opened in 1869 and was described around 1900 as an elegant iron bridge of three spans. It survived until the great flood of 1960-61, when it was badly damaged by a tree and shortly afterwards had to be demolished.

The **Portway** is a roadside inn of long standing, for the Hon. John Byng, travelling on the road from Hay to Hereford on Friday, 10 August 1787 noted, 'I did intend to have breakfasted at Letton or at the **Portway**, both neat public houses, ... but kept going; by ten at Hereford and put up at the new **New Inn**, a house of noise and bustle ..'.

Elizabeth Baker was the landlady of the **Portway** in 1850, and during repairs in 1852, the wooden floors were lifted and three rows of horse skulls were found fastened to the undersides of the boards. Apparently they had been fixed there to make the floors more resonant when country dancing took place in the inn. The Baker family were still there in 1858 with William Baker listed as both landlord and farmer, and in 1879 when Mrs. Baker was once again licensee.

Towards the latter end of the 19th century, this must have been quite a bustling area, for the buildings on the road junction included a blacksmith's shop, also run by William Baker, and a post, money and telegraph office that also dealt in annuities and insurance. Tracy Preece was the sub-postmaster and a machinist. In 1891, in keeping with the rest of the activities in this busy roadside settlement, William Adam Williams was not just the landlord of the **Portway Commercial Inn**; he also advertised his abilities as a monumental sculptor, marble, wood & stone carver, engraver etc!

The **Portway** is at the eastern end of Staunton-on-Wye parish, and it is here that the Roman road and the main A438 take up the same alignment with a long straight stretch of road leading westwards, totally ignoring the isolated parish church on the rise to the right and passing several recent fruit farms. On the right again, at the far end of the straight, the imposing buildings of the Jarvis Charity Foundation catch the eye of all travellers. Originally comprising a large residential school, a house for the clerk to the charity, another for the medical officer—there was free medical care for all parishioners in Staunton, Letton and Bredwardine (the beneficiaries of the charity) for many years before they had to contribute to the National Health Service!— and 12 almshouses for six aged men and women.

Part of the Jarvis Trust School building was used as a Youth Hostel from the early part of the 1960s until the early 1990s. This was one Youth Hostel that for several years could boast of having its own drinking establishment, for one room in a rear courtyard was licensed and was open each evening. Alas, the hostel and its inn closed several years ago and this part of the old school has now been empty and neglected for several years.

A turning to the right off the main road leads up the hill, past the present village school entrance, to the village road, and right again brings the traveller to the **New Inn**. A much-altered 17th-century building, this was for many years a beer house run by the Longford family. It only obtained a 'full' licence by transfer when the Moorhampton Hotel closed. In the 1960s, when Cyril Kinsey was landlord, the barrels of beer were kept on wooden racks or 'trams' immediately behind the bar, for there is no cellar. On hot summer days, the occasional visitor who strayed off the main road, would see the barrels liberally swathed with wet tea-towels so as to keep the beer cool. Woe betide anyone who complained about the temperature or the quality of the beer! The rather spartan public bar, with old 'bus seats and heavy iron-legged tables, has long since been converted into a lounge bar and the barrels have been banished to a back room where they are presumably kept cool by much more modern methods.

The New Inn at Staunton-on-Wye in 1999

Returning to the main road, the traveller is faced with the heights of Oakers Hill, with a side road leading off to the left towards Brobury and the fine brick bridge leading across the river to Bredwardine. From the top of Oakers Hill there is a good view down to the Letton flood plain and, in the middle distance across the river, the heights of Merbach Hill. In the further distance the Black Mountains stand out against the skyline, with a glimpse of the Brecon Beacons beyond.

Letton is a small village with a few half-timbered buildings set along the main road next to the **Swan Inn**, and, a little further along, a narrow turning to the left leading down to the parish church. All is not as it appears, for the inn and its surrounding buildings are in Over Letton, which is still part of the long, straggling parish of Staunton-on-Wye; the **Swan** being the third inn within the parish boundary.

Described by Byng as a 'neat public house' in 1787, the building has had several additions and many internal alterations since that time. By 1850, it was **The Old Swan** with James Nicholas as mine host, John Nicholas in 1858, but by 1879 it had reverted to an ageless **Swan** under Mrs. Elizabeth Probert, and was still such in 1891 when the landlord, John Sandford, was also the local builder.

Penny post letter sent from Letton in 1847

There was also an early post office at Over Letton, estab-lished on 1 May 1835. This was part of the 'penny post' operating in the Hereford area a few years before the introduction of Rowland Hill's uniform flat rate of one penny, irrespective of the number of sheets of paper, providing the weight was below half-an-ounce. It was probably based at the **Swan** which was a posting house. In the 1850s post arrived from Hereford at 8 o'clock in the morning with the return at 10 minutes past 4 in the afternoon, giving sufficient time for the mail to catch the 6.30 p.m. train to the north.

It was in the early 1970s that John and Jessie Knight, looking for something to keep them occupied following their retirement from full-time work, took over the **Swan Inn**. They converted it from a rather dowdy roadside inn, only just surviving on a limited trade of local worthies, into an up-market establishment providing excellent food for the increasing number of travellers on the A438 and for those Herefordians who were prepared to take their cars out for an evening drive and meal. I well remember about 1973 helping Jessie (and John) to drink the proceeds from her first state old age pension!

The Swan at Letton in 1999

There are few buildings on the road that winds tortuously across the Letton plain on its way to Eardisley, for it is prone to flooding whenever the Wye rises appreciably. From the top of Oakers Hill this can then appear as one vast lake, winding round the base of the hill to the north until it reaches Little London and World's End, two remote parts of Staunton parish. A turning to the right, shortly after passing the **Swan**, leads northwards to Kinnersley. On the right again, a short distance along this road is the old Letton vicarage. One dark night, as the flood waters rose, the vicar made his way, rather hesitantly, back home from a rather long stay in the **Swan**. He soon had to wade, and eventually ended up in the roadside ditch, almost up to his neck in muddy river water. He eventually made it home, but the plaintive phone call came the following morning whilst the floods were still in force—would someone please get a canoe out and take him a packet of cigarettes to replace those lost during his watery activities the previous evening!

The floods along this stretch of road can be quite deep and it is not unusual for heavy lorries to have to make long diversions around this low-lying area. The course of the Roman road, ostensibly leading towards Hay and the Roman fort near Brecon, is somewhat problematical in this area. Did they suffer similar weather conditions and the associated flooding that we have now? Did they succeed in building a road across the flood plain, or did their road bear off to the left to cross the Wye at a ford and ferry crossing at Bredwardine and then continue westwards on the southern bank?

The present road winds through the plain for some two miles, before it rises slightly as the A438 bears off to the west and the A4112 Leominster road leads off to the east on the edge of Eardisley village.

CHAPTER FOUR

Eardisley to Hay

When the road from Hereford has completed its winding course across the Letton flood plain, the Kington road (A4111) goes straight ahead towards Eardisley village whilst the Hay to Brecon road, the A438, takes a turning to the left towards Winforton and Willersley. According to an 1858 directory, there was a **New Crow Inn** in Eardisley with Charles Rudd as landlord. Presumably this was at what is now the Crow Farm on the corner where the Hay road turns to the left. There is a second turning off the Kington road before it arrives at Eardisley—this is the A4112, which takes a north-easterly course through Kinnersley towards Leominster.

Crow Farm
Was this the 1858 New Crow Inn?

The approach to Eardisley is by a bridge that takes the main road over the now defunct Hereford, Hay and Brecon railway as it approaches Eardisley station just to the left of the bridge. This was not the only railway line here, for Eardisley was a junction, with a branch line leading northwards through Titley to Kington and Presteigne. The branch line had a relatively short life, opening in 1874 and closing as part of wartime economies in 1940.

The main line survived for almost 100 years, finally falling a victim to the Beeching closures in 1962. The station building is now a private house.

Two hundred or more years ago roads in Herefordshire were poor at the best of times and often totally impassable during the winter months. Alternative means of transport were sorely needed and the first 'railway' was built in Herefordshire when steam trains were some time away—Eardisley was then an essential link in the scheme.

When the Brecon and Abergavenny Canal first opened in 1800, it provided a cheap means of transport for coal, iron and manufactured goods for the people of Brecknockshire, and an effective means of exporting their farming produce. The next stage was to improve communication between the canal and the rural areas of western Herefordshire and Radnorshire. A 'feeder' railway or tram road was proposed with horses pulling wagons on iron tracks. The first Parliamentary Act, approved in 1811, gave powers to construct the railway from Brecon through Hay as far as Parton Cross in Eardisley. By May 1816 it was open to Hay and the extension into Herefordshire was started. It was completed by December 1818. Meanwhile the Kington Railway—a similar proposal to run from Eardisley to Kington—had its Act approved in May 1818, even before the line from Hay to Eardisley had been completed. Work started rapidly and the line was completed to Kington in May 1820 where a celebration was held at the **King's Head**.

From Brecon to Eardisley the distance was 25 miles; from Eardisley to the lime kilns at Evenjobb, a short distance beyond Kington, an additional 12 miles. The final part to Evenjobb was opened on 7 August 1820, providing a welcome return cargo for the trams on their way back to Brecon.

Apart from the horse-drawn carriages, there was an ingenious machine made in 1841 which two men propelled by means of cog wheels set in motion by a winch, the handles of which were turned by the men seated on top of the contrivance. On its first journey it travelled at about 6 miles per hour and made the journey to Brecon and back as far as Eardisley, but they had to push it for the latter part of the return journey as some boys had broken a cog. The horse-drawn Kington tram road passed Eardisley on a long low embankment just to the east of the village.

It was this Kington Railway that passed close to the **Tram Inn**, the public house that stands on the left of the main road towards the northern end of Eardisley village, and a complete tram plate from the original railway is still preserved at the inn. The importance of the horse drawn tram is indicated in an 1850 directory where the **Tram Inn** is described as being at 'Tram Railway Station'. The Kington horse-drawn railway was finally closed in 1874 when it was replaced by the Kington and Eardisley Railway which took a slightly different route.

The **Tram Inn** is basically a 17th-century building with a slightly later extension on the south side, but it has had many alterations throughout its life. The building was already an inn in 1750 when it was bought by George Lloyd from Benjamin Yeates. Lloyd died about 1768 and three years later his wife married a Mr. Turner. The Turner family were associated with the inn for well over half a century, eventually in association with Thomas Hatton. By the late 1840s James Watkins had taken over as landlord—the Watkins family were to be involved in the inn for many years, Mrs. Ellen Watkins being there in 1879. Previous to 1890 it was described in deeds as:

All that messuage and Public House known as the 'Tram Inn' in the Village of Eardisley in the County of Hereford with the garden orchard stables and outbuildings belonging thereto No. 729 in the Tithe map and containing One rood and ten perches now in the occupation of the said James and Ellen Baird. And all that Cottage with storehouse and garden adjacent to the above described property and numbered 728 in the Tithe Map now or late in the occupation of Mr Charles Haynes with the exception of the storehouse which is held with the said Tram Inn. ...

A timber wagon outside the Tram Inn in 1907

In 1891 the **Tram Inn** and several adjoining fields were sold by the Trustees of William Perry Herrick. In 1918 the inn was sold to Ellen Baird for £1,250. The description gives a much better impression of the working of a country inn during the early years of the 20th century:

> All that messuage or tenement known as 'The Tram Inn' ... including detached Brewery and Brewhouse, Corn and Coal House with other buildings and large garden. And also the adjoining building used as Stables and Forge, Store, Trap House with storage lofts over and cart shed.

Also included in the sale was:

> All that piece of orchard land containing about one acre and twenty perches with a building thereon used as a Cider Mill with Press and Loft over situate in the village of Eardisley ...

Ellen Baird at the Tram Inn. She was the daughter-in-law of Henry Baird, who was the proprietor of the New Inn Brewery at nearby Almeley.

As part of the agreement the purchaser was to block up a doorway and some windows in the stabling that apparently overlooked a property to the left of the inn that had been sold separately to a Mr. Povey.

Ellen Baird continued to run the **Tram Inn** for many years, and in 1932 she agreed to purchase certain rights from Alfred Morris Baker, a solicitor of Kington, who was apparently Lord of the Manor of Eardisley Borough and Eardisley Foreign. The Lord of the Manor had certain rights and privileges and 'whereas there has been held in the Village from time immemorial the yearly Eardisley May Fair or Pleasure Fair held on or about 15th May each year on land adjacent to the **Tram Inn**, the Lord of the Manor has been accustomed to take and receive tolls upon all stalls roundabouts and other erections at the said fair'. The Lord of the Manor agreed to sell 'the fair and tolls and all other fair rights (if any) over the said land for £20'. In 1941, the register of Local Land Charges recorded 'Tram Inn and Yearly Fair, held on land being waste of the manor of Eardisley adjacent to the Tram'.

The Tram Inn in the early 20th century

The **Tram Inn** is the home of the mythical Fox Pie which has its origin in the infamous radio broadcasts of Lord Haw-Haw during the Second World War. William Joyce, to give him his correct name, was born in Brooklyn of Irish parents, but spent his childhood in Ireland. He falsely obtained a British passport and founded the British National Socialist Party, having been expelled from Moseley's Fascist Party. Before war broke out he fled to Germany and from 1939 until 1945 his broadcasts of German propaganda, threats and abuse were beamed towards the British Isles. Each programme was always prefaced by the characteristic 'Chairmanny calling', spoken in an upper-class and rather plummy voice. His broadcasts were intended to strike despondency and gloom into the British people, but the reverse was the case and his transmissions were often eagerly followed, to be greeted with derision and merriment. It was during one of his broadcasts that he described how the English were starving, and that the poor people in Herefordshire had even had to resort to eating foxes!

Lord Haw-Haw

This allegation led to a marvellous idea! The **Tram Inn** would include this mythical fox in its menu and would hold an annual fox pie supper! This celebrated meal continued for several years after the end of the war, and long after Joyce had been tried at the Old Bailey, convicted and executed. He claimed that he was an American, but his illegally obtained British passport was his downfall, for it was valid until July 1940—he was guilty of treason. After a few years' break the fox supper was re-introduced by the licensees of the **Tram**, Gordon and Phyllis Parker, on 6 February 1959. Mrs. Parker described the event to the *Hereford Times* reporter many years later in 1997, when she was 86:

> When the Wales and West of England television company heard about the supper, they thought it would be perfect to add to the promotional video of Herefordshire they were making. The video was to be shown in other countries, and the impact it had was tremendous. We had letters and visitors from all sorts of places like Canada, America and even Australia.

Mrs. Parker and the fox pie

It is apparent that the 1959 fox pie supper was a very special event—the Chief Constable of Herefordshire was one of the local dignitaries amongst the 70 guests! The famous pie, with the crusty pastry crowned by a fox's head, was brought in by Mr. Wynn, the local butcher who had made it. The words on everyone's lips: 'Is it really fox?' The last word must go to Mrs. Parker. 'I've made a solemn vow that I would never discuss what was in the pie. The recipe was a secret between me and Mr Wynn and I shall take it to my grave!'

It was during the evening of 12 May 1959, not long after the famous fox pie supper, that a violent thunderstorm caused massive flooding through Eardisley and the surrounding villages. Without any doubt it was the worst flood within living memory. Water came down the

Floods at the Tram Inn

Woodseaves road, the Almeley road and the Kington road sweeping mud and destruction throughout the village. There was 4 feet of water in the square between the **Tram Inn** and its facing neighbour, the **New Inn.** According to one writer, the indomitable spirit of Eardisley youth triumphed once again. The challenge was simple—to swim from one pub to the other for a free pint!

The Tram Inn, 1999

The **New Inn** faces the **Tram** across the square. Its appearance and name (as with many a **New Inn**) are both deceptive—there has been an inn here for many years. It was the home of two Friendly Societies: the rather grandly named 'Friendly Society of Gentlemen, Farmers, Tradesmen and Others' founded in 1798, which was followed

The New Inn before the fire

by the more prosaic 'Royal Oak Club' of 1825. In 1850 the landlord was Thomas Whitehouse.

The Woolhope Naturalists' Field Club was founded in 1852, and on 24 July 1855 they held a Field Meeting based on Eardisley. They met at the **New Inn** at 9 a.m. for breakfast. The day's route took them by Willersley and Letton to Bredwardine Bridge and thence up Merbach Hill to Arthur's Stone. From Merbach point, they delighted in the magnificent panorama and discussed the geology of the region before making their way to the Clock Mill Ferry where they crossed the river once again and returned through Letton to Eardisley. At the **New Inn**, 'Mr Bryan, the attentive host, being mindful of the great truth that even philosophers must dine, had a well-prepared dinner awaiting them; and the party betook themselves to the discussion of the different "formations" placed before them'. After dinner Mr. Banks of Kington gave a talk and the party finally broke up at 9 p.m. William Bryan was still mine host in 1858, mixing his duties as landlord with some farming.

1930s advert for the New Inn

The New Inn after the fire in 1900

In 1881 the population of Eardisley was 862—in Herefordshire terms a considerable parish and village. In 1879 Francis Poulton was landlord; in 1891 John Batts was the licensee—was he still there in 1902 when the present building was built? It was resurrected from the original which was burnt down in 1900.

For several years the inn was called **The Mountie**, but it has since been restored to its old, **New,** name and now operates as **The New Strand,** a second hand bookshop, coffee house and, yes, it still has a licensed bar.

The New Inn in 1999

Thomas Hatton (born 1779) started his adult life as a butcher in Kington. He eventually became an ale-house keeper in Eardisley and was involved with the **Tram Inn** for some time. He was apparently none too successful in his enterprises, for he died in Kington

Workhouse in 1854. There were two other beer retailers listed in Eardisley in 1858—John Morgan and Thomas Philpotts—and one at Woodeaves—William Price. The road from Eardisley to Kington is totally without hostelries, so it is back over the old railway bridge to the road junction (Crow farm) and a turn to the west on the A438 towards Hay and Brecon.

The Sun Inn at Winforton in 1999

After a mile or so the well kept **Sun Inn** at Winforton appears on the right hand side of the road. Although not mentioned in the 1850 directory, it is hidden under 'Farmers' in the 1858 one with Thomas Green as farmer/landlord. It has all the appearance of having been a haven for travellers for many years. Of course it may well have been a beer house, as was the case with many of the country inns, and may not have been sufficient to provide an adequate living for a family. Thus, in the 1879 and 1891 directories the landlord, James Philpotts, was also a farmer. It is likely that his wife ran the inn as well as all the household and farming chores. In the days of Punk Rock, visiting punks were outdone by the locals. Challenged to a strip tease, the punks, used to causing embarrassment, became embarrassed themselves when failing to go the whole way—not the locals though!

The regular sequence of public houses along the Hereford to Hay road continues as the road approaches the Welsh border. Beyond Winforton, the river Wye approaches the road again in a long loop that

The original Boat Inn. The edge of the stable block to the left, which still survives, identifies the position of the replacement building

curves into the parish of Whitney; the next to the last parish in Herefordshire on the north bank of the river. Here, set as close as possible to the river bank is the **Boat Inn.** The present building is of early 20th century date, but there was an earlier **Boat Inn**, an unassuming building with a central entry and a room on each side with shuttered windows and end chimneys in a typical Herefordshire style.

At one time the **Boat** was a roadside as well as riverside inn. However, the main road was straightened some 25 years ago and the **Boat Inn** is now rather lost along a loop of what was the A438. In the early 19th century this loop was followed by the Hay

The Boat Inn at Whitney in 1999, with the stable block to the left

and Kington horse-drawn tram which ran on the side of the road, just outside the door of the **Boat Inn**. It is not just the road that changes its position in this area—the river has a long reputation for devastating floods and for changing its course as a result. One of the most notable was in 1730 when the old church and the ruins of the castle at Whitney were swept away. The site of the old church was in a field on the left bank of the river, a short distance downstream of the **Boat Inn**, but as a result of the change in the course of the river the site is now on the right bank. It is reputed that the foundations of the castle can be seen in the river bed when the water is clear and the level is low. The new church, dedicated to St. Paul, was built on slightly higher ground in 1740. The only parts of the old church to survive the flood were the font, the monument to the Williams family and some tracery re-used in the east window. However, early in the 20th century, a table, surmised to be the communion table from the old church, was discovered in the **Boat Inn,** where it was being used for serving beer. It was not returned to Whitney church, but in the 1930s was presented to the Chapel of St. John in Hay.

There has been a ferry and ford at Whitney from at least the beginning of the 15th century, for it was used by Owain Glyndwr on his way to attack Clifford and Hay castles after he had ravaged the Whitney area. The ferry was between the present bridge and the **Boat Inn**—the inn does not seem to have had any connection with it. In 1858 the landlord was John Mann—he was also a farmer and was still there in 1879.

1960s advertisement.
At this time the inn was part of a small group including the Green Man at Fownhope and England's Gate at Bodenham

In 1774 a Bill was presented to the House of Commons to build a bridge to join Whitney with the parish of Clifford on the opposite bank of the Wye. The bridge had to be kept in repair by the owners, tolls were to be charged, it was to be free from rates and taxes—present or future, and was not to be considered as a County Council bridge. Whitney Toll Bridge still enjoys all these privileges—but it has been a constant expense on the owner, for the present bridge is the fourth since 1774.

And, in order the better to enable the said Undertakers, their Heirs and Assigns, to defray the Expence of building and supporting the said Bridge; **Be it further Enacted** by the Authority aforesaid, That as soon as the said Bridge shall be made fit for the Passage of Travellers and Carriages, it shall and may be lawful for the said Undertakers, their Heirs and Assigns, or such Person or Persons as they shall by Writing under their Hands and Seals appoint, from Time to Time, and at all Times hereafter, to demand, collect, and receive, to and for the only proper Use and Behoof of the said Undertakers, their Heirs and Assigns, before any Person on Foot, or any Horses, Cattle, or Carriages, shall be permitted to pass over the said Bridge, such Tolls as they the said Undertakers, their Heirs or Assigns, shall think proper, not exceeding the respective Sums following; (that is to say) For every Foot Passenger, the Sum of One Halfpenny; for every Horse, Mare, Gelding, Ox, or other Beast, drawing any Carriage, the Sum of Three Pence; for every Horse, Mare, Gelding, Mule, or Ass, laden or unladen, and not drawing, the Sum of One Penny; for every Score of Oxen, Cows, or Neat Cattle, the Sum of Ten Pence, and so in Proportion for any greater or less Number; and for every Score of Calves, Hogs, Sheep, or Lambs, the Sum of Five Pence, and so in Proportion for any greater or less Number: Which said respective Tolls shall be, and are hereby vested in the said Undertakers, their Heirs and Assigns, and shall be paid to them accordingly; and if any Person liable to pay the said Tolls, shall, after Demand made thereof by the said Undertakers, their Heirs or Assigns, or any of them, or any Person or Persons to be appointed the Collector thereof as aforesaid, refuse or neglect to pay the same, that then, and in every such Case, it shall and may be lawful for such Collector or Collectors to stop and prevent the Passage of the Person so refusing or neglecting, or of the Horses, Cattle, or Carriages for which such Tolls ought to be paid, until full Payment be made thereof.

The original toll rates for crossing Whitney Bridge

The first two were rapidly washed away, but the third lasted until 1795 when a record flood destroyed the three centre spans of the stone bridge. The two end arches were utilised in the fourth bridge, but the remainder is of timber. The Eardisley to Hay tramroad laid its tracks across this bridge and paid tolls for the horses and tramcarts that crossed. When the Hereford, Hay and Brecon Railway was constructed in 1863, a new iron bridge was built slightly upstream of the toll bridge. Even then, the toll bridge owners asserted their rights for exclusive crossing at that point and from 1863 until the closure of the railway in 1962 the tolls had to be guaranteed by the Railway Company up to £345 per year. It seems surprising that there was no inn either at the approaches to the bridge or at the ferry, but no trace has been found—perhaps the **Boat Inn** claimed the same exclusive rights in the area as did the Toll Bridge Company!

There was another Public House usually considered as being in Whitney, but actually in the Parish of Winforton. This was **The Old Stowe Inn** which faced south across the river Wye. It was probably the beer house recorded in 1879 at Stowe with Thomas East as licensee. In 1953 it was for sale, together with nine acres of ground, by G.W. Millichap of Brecon. He was fulsome with his praises, describing it as being half-timbered and dating in parts to the 13th century with later additions. A reasonably large building, it had four reception and five bedrooms. However, it had one feature which Mr. Millichap could, quite reasonably, describe as being unique 'in that it is a private house which has a beer licence if anyone wished to take advantage of that. It is understood that previous occupiers took advantage of the licence, but the present occupiers do not'. In 1953 the freehold asking price was £5,000.

PARTICULARS OF PROPERTY FROM

G. W. MILLICHAP

F.R.I.C.S., F.A.I., F.I.Arb., M.R.San.I.

Chartered Surveyor, Chartered Auctioneer and Estate Agent, Agricultural Valuer and Compensation Specialist.   Building Surveyor's Department.

OLD BANK CHAMBERS, BRECON (Tel. 67).
and at 6, Imperial Square, Cheltenham (Tel. 2641).

THE OLD STOWE INN,

WHITNEY-ON-WYE,   HEREFORDSHIRE.

15 miles Hereford, 5½ miles Hay, 3 miles Kington.

9 ACRES. 5 BEDROOMS. BATHROOM. 4 RECEPTION ROOMS. CLOAKROOM.
MAIN ELECTRICITY. GOOD WATER SUPPLY. OUTBUILDINGS.

Details of the 1953 sale of the Old Stowe Inn with handwritten amendments

1883 sale of the New Inn at Brilley

In the hills above Whitney is the scattered parish of Brilley. Here was the **New Inn,** which was advertised for sale by auction on the premises on Monday, 28 May 1883 at 4.30 p.m., sufficiently late to allow potential purchasers to sample and establish the quality of the stock as well as examining the building. It belonged to John Probert and was described as being 'on the roadside between Brilley and

Rhydspence, and forms a convenient Hostelry for persons going to and returning from Whitney Railway Station which is about ten minutes walk'. If the only trade was from the inhabitants of Brilley going to the railway station, it must have suffered rather hard times! There was an orchard and meadow-land adjoining the inn with 'fruit trees in full bearing, and the Land is exceptionally good, lying in the eye of the sun, on elevated ground overlooking the Wye Valley'. In the 1858 directory John Probert was landlord; before 1879 he had been replaced by John Pugh and Andrew Rollerson followed him by 1891.

The **New Inn** was for sale again on 29 April 1920 when the accommodation was described as 'Serving bar, Tap room, large cellar, 2 sitting rooms, kitchen, wash-house, and 5 bedrooms'.

ALL THAT

LOT 3.

FREEHOLD FULLY LICENSED INN

KNOWN AS

THE NEW INN

TOGETHER WITH

Orcharding and Pasture Land and Buildings

EXTENDING TO AN AREA OF ABOUT

4 ACRES

Situate in the PARISH OF BRILLEY, in the County of Hereford, and being on the Road leading from Hay to Kington, and about ¾ mile from Whitney Station on the Midland Railway.

The ACCOMMODATION consists of—
Serving Bar, Tap Room, large Cellar, 2 Sitting Rooms, Kitchen, Wash-house, and 5 Bedrooms.

The OUTBUILDINGS consist of—
Two-Stall Stable and Fowl-house, Cider Mill with Press, Barn, with Mixing Shed, 2-Tie Cow-house, Coach-house and Store Room.

This House has been doing an excellent trade for many years, and is in very good order and repair.

———

For further Particulars apply to the Auctioneer, Palace Chambers, King Street, Hereford, or to Messrs. Gwynne James and Son, Solicitors, St. Peter Street, Hereford.

The 1920 sale of Brilley's New Inn,
which took place at the Crown Hotel at Hay-on-Wye

The New Inn in retirement, but the small sign by the gate is a reminder of its use by drovers on the way to Brilley

The outbuildings, which included 'Two-stall stable and fowl-house, cider mill with press, barn, 2-tie cow house and coach house', indicates that the establishment was still relatively self-sufficient. Indeed, the auctioneer felt able to state that 'this house has been doing an excellent trade for many years, and is in very good order and repair'.

A sale notice of June 1906 refers to the fully-licensed public house known as the **Red Lion Inn,** Brilley. It is only when the small print is read that it is appreciated that this inn, adjoining the main road from Kington to Hay, is actually in the parish of Michaelchurch-on-Arrow

---

All that Messuage or Tenement and

FULLY LICENSED PUBLIC=HOUSE,

Known as the "RED LION" INN, BRILLEY,

Situate in the Parish of Michaelchurch-on-Arrow, in the County of Radnor, with Garden, Blacksmith's Shop, Stable and Buildings, containing **3 roods 8 perches,** in the occupation of Mr. Benjamin Thomas Howard, at the annual Rent of **£16.**

The Property adjoins the main road leading from Kington to Hay, and is suitable for carrying on a profitable trade, including a good Blacksmith's business.

The Apportioned Tithe Rent Charge is 1s. 11d., the value for 1906 being 1s. 4d. The Land Tax is 7s.

The 1906 sale of the Red Lion, Brilley (Michaelchurch)

The Red Lion, Brilley, but on the western side of the main road from Kington to Hay, and thus in Michaelchurch-on-Arrow parish

and therefore in the County of Radnor and not in Herefordshire at all! However, the paradoxical description is sufficient for it to be given honourary membership of this volume.

On the northern side of Michaelchurch, but back again in Herefordshire, is Huntington, once the home of a major border castle, but now a remote village that still supports the **Swan Inn**. In 1879 Evan Thomas combined the jobs of landlord and blacksmith, as did John Burgoyne in 1891. The building, which is of 17th-century date, has

The Swan at Huntington has more the appearance of a private house than an inn

been a public house for at least 150 years. The east wing and the north end are later extensions.

Brilley parish stretches down to the river and here, on the boundary between England and Wales, between Herefordshire and Radnorshire, stands the historic **Rhydspence Inn**. This border inn adjoined the main road as it followed a tortuous set of bends across the Cwm Brook which formed the actual boundary, but the road was straightened some years ago and the inn is now tucked away in a loop to the north. It was substantially extended some years ago, but the main timber-framed building of 16th-century date still catches the eye of the traveller along the main road. Much of the close-set timber-framing is still exposed and on the front is a two-storey porch. The upper storey of the porch projects on three sides and the outer and inner entrances have segmental heads. There are several original windows containing mullions and transoms. The upper storey of the main building projects at the west end where it is supported by shaped brackets with shaped pendants to the angle-posts.

This, the first and last inn in England (at least on the A438!), was at one time known as the **Cattle Inn** for it lay on one of the drovers' roads from Wales. The

The Rhydspence Inn in the 1950s with, inset, an enlargement of the sign with its 'seven days' licence

cattle came from the shoeing station at Painscastle, where two strong men turned the cattle onto their backs and attached a two-part shoe to each hoof for the journey over Clyro Hill and into England at Rhydspence. On Monday 8 July 1872 Kilvert noted in his *Diary*:

> reports coming in all day of the mischief done by yesterday's flood. Pigs, sheep, calves swept away from meadow and cot and carried down the river with hundreds of tons of hay, timber, hurdles and, it is said, furniture. The roads swept bare to the very rock. Culverts choked and blown up, turnips washed out of the ground on the hillsides, down into the orchards and turnpike roads. Four inches of mud in the **Rhydspence Inn** on the Welsh side of the border ...

In 1858 the licensee was Ann Palmer; in 1879 Philip Clark was the landlord, but by 1891 John Williams had taken over.

There always seems to have been an element of confusion about the inn's relationship to the border, and some writers have suggested that the border ran through the middle of the inn! For many years the **Rhydspence Inn** was an important visiting point for Welsh drinkers from Hay-on-Wye and beyond. It was not just the 'first house in England', it was the first public house

The Rhydspence Inn from the main road
with the new extension on the right

The 1965 sale of the Rhydspence Inn

approached from Wales that was open on Sundays, when the whole of Wales was dry! It is not surprising that for many years the sign above the porch proudly stated '7 Days House!'

In the 1970s and 1980s the then landlady was concerned at whether she felt her customers were able to handle the Robinson's Winter Ale that she served. If there was any doubt in her mind, she refused to serve more than half a pint at a time!

The drovers' road and particularly the shoeing station meant that Brilley was a bustling village in the early 19th century. The **Brilley Green Arms Inn** with Richard Penny as landlord and the **Travellers Rest Inn** with William Pany as mine host are both mentioned in the 1858 directory, but had disappeared by the end of the century and their positions in this straggling parish are now uncertain.

From the **Rhydspence** the A438 enters into Wales, but the roadside inns continue with the same regularity with the **Baskerville Arms** at Clyro just before the turn to Hay.

CHAPTER FIVE

Hereford to Kington

There are two ways of getting to Kington from Hereford—the first is along the A438 as far as Eardisley and then over a long ridge of ground before dropping down into Kington. The second route also initially leaves Hereford on the A438 before bearing right on the A480—the road through Yazor, Norton Canon and Lyonshall to Kington. Once past the military camp at Credenhill, this becomes an increasingly quiet and pleasant country road, meandering through the undulating hills of north-west Herefordshire as though in no hurry to get to its destination.

For all its modern day quietness, this is an historic road, for just before Kington it connects with the A44—one of the main routes from England leading into mid-Wales.

The Hereford to Kington road served two purposes—providing the means to get to the county town and its market for the inhabitants of Kington, and as a feeder to one of the main roads leading to the Welsh coast. But it is not just this main thoroughfare that is favoured with historic roadside inns; on each side there are small villages and townships that have provided local services for hundreds of years. Indeed, the road often seems to have been designed to deliberately by-pass some of the villages such as Credenhill, Brinsop and Mansel Lacy. Larger villages such as Almeley and Weobley are also well off the beaten track.

Although the A480 crosses the old Hereford, Hay and Brecon railway line shortly after leaving the Brecon road, there was no station there and no inn, the first hostelry along the road being on the right hand side after a further quarter of a mile. Well named as the **Travellers' Rest**, this inn, which is in Stretton Sugwas parish, sits on the junction of the A480 and the long straight road that forms the northern boundary of the City of Hereford—the 2,000 year-old Roman military road that led from the Worcester direction first to the Roman town of *Magnis* at Kenchester, then to a Roman fort near Brecon, before eventually passing into the wilds of central Wales.

The Traveller's Rest on the corner of the Roman road in 2000

The **Travellers' Rest** has lived up to its name for many years, but its Roman predecessor would doubtless have been found further to the west within the walled town of *Magnis* rather than in the open countryside. Even so, the countryside around *Magnis* was not wild territory—there were Roman villas and farms scattered around the area, providing employment, producing crops and other essential agricultural produce. This would not have been just for those who lived in *Magnis*, but for the many Roman soldiers who, after being stationed at remote forts in the highlands of Wales, doubtless spent their well-earned leave in the brothels, public baths and inns of the Roman town.

There is no mention of the **Travellers' Rest** in the 1858 directories, but it is included in 1891 when Mrs. Isabella Jenkins was the landlady and in 1937 when Mrs. Dawe had the licence.

As the A480 curves gently round to the west, it passes the front entrance of the Air Force camp at Credenhill, recently taken over by the SAS, and then shelters underneath the edge of the hill itself. Now called Credenhill Park Wood, this is the site of a 50 acre hill fort—the largest in Herefordshire—in use for several hundred years before the Romans even arrived. This must have been the predecessor of the Roman *Magnis*, which, in turn was replaced by the modern Hereford.

Also running underneath the hill and crossing the A480 almost at right angles, is the line of the Roman Watling Street—the main road following the whole length of the Welsh border from Caerleon to Chester. To the north-east it heads towards Tillington and in the opposite direction it passes through Credenhill village on its way to *Magnis* and what was doubtless a bridge crossing of the river Wye.

Although reasonably large now, at least by Herefordshire standards, Credenhill was a small parish with a population of only some 220 people in 1858. As such, it managed to attract a post office and a railway station, but did not rate an inn.

An effort has recently been made to improve the situation, although some way outside Credenhill village. A mile further along the A438 is a minor junction with a turning leading off to the right towards Brinsop. Here, a hundred yards up the road and before the turning to the church, is that rarity in Herefordshire, a totally new hostelry. The **Dog and Duck**, which until recently was the White House Farm, but now provides food, accommodation and drink—all the necessities of a wayside inn.

The A480 continues in a west-north-westerly direction, past the Mansel Lacy turn and the slim spire of Yazor church on the right. Only a bare half-mile further along the road, and this may once have been the Welsh border. Here the A480 crosses the line of the Dyke built by King Offa

The Dog & Duck at Brinsop, described as a bar and bistro

over 1,200 years ago to form the western boundary of his Kingdom of Mercia. However, the border gradually moved further westwards and now a long stretch of this great earthwork is in Herefordshire. No longer a frontier here, and no wayside inn for weary travellers! However, there was apparently one in the latter part of the 18th century for the *Hereford Journal* records an auction at the **Red Lion** at Yazor on 28 November 1792, and, some three weeks later, a note that Margaret Legas was carrying on business there.

A short distance further along the road is a minor turning to the left that eventually connects with the Hereford to Hay road near Mansell Gamage. Just a short distance from the Kington road is Moorhampton, a railway hamlet. Here was Moorhampton Station—or to give it its full name 'Moorhampton for Weobley', for this was the nearest station to Weobley, a few miles to the east. However, the station served another purpose, for it was the nearest halt to two important Herefordshire mansions, Garnons (the home of the Cotterell family) to the south and Foxley (the home of the Davenports) to the east. Now the hamlet rests on past glories, for the Hereford to Hay railway has long been closed, but the Victorian railwaymen's houses remain as does the imposing building that was once the **Moorhampton Hotel**.

The Moorhampton Hotel from an early 20th century picture postcard

The Hereford, Hay and Brecon railway was opened for goods traffic as far as Moorhampton on 24 October 1862 and the whole line was opened almost two years later, on 19 September 1864. The promoters, of what to all intents and purposes appears to have been a rather remote rural line, were not looking at a simple local railway—their main ambition was to provide a connection from Birmingham and the West Midlands through to Swansea and South Wales as an alternative to the line through Hereford and Abergavenny. This was sufficient to encourage some potential entrepreneurs to set up public houses near to the railway. However, the grand plans were not to be, and although the line did take some through traffic, essentially it remained a local service. Yet by the late 19th century it had become well established with four passenger trains daily each way, and a special market train leaving Hereford on Wednesdays at 5.25 p.m. to bring traders back to Hay and the intermediate stations. From time to time there were also overnight goods trains between Birmingham and Swansea. There were five stations between Hereford and Hay: Credenhill, Moorhampton, Kinnersley, Eardisley and Whitney. The journey time from Hereford to Hay averaged about 50 minutes.

In August 1888, some 50 members of the Woolhope Naturalists' Field Club left Hereford in horse-drawn brakes intending to visit Brinsop, Wormsley and Weobley. The weather turned for the worse and at Weobley 'the examination of the interesting old borough was only

The Moorhampton Hotel in 1999

attempted by a few of the most determined; yet not withstanding the persistence of the rain, the seats were again resumed in carriages most punctually, and a Mark Tapley spirit pervaded their respective occupants as they drove through a drenching rain to the hotel at Moorhampton, upon reaching which they were ultimately rewarded by a temporary glimpse of sunshine, and an excellent dinner, well served'.

According to the 1891 Kelly's Directory, the licensee, Thomas Price, was also a farmer and in addition was responsible for the posting house. There was not enough local trade to support the **Moorhampton Hotel**, travellers using the train to visit Weobley tending to go there directly, rather than stay at Moorhampton and the hotel eventually closed. But another inn was the beneficiary, for the spirits licence was transferred from the **Moorhampton Hotel** to the **New Inn** at Staunton-on-Wye, which previously had been a simple beer house.

According to Slater's 1850 directory there was a **White Lion** in Yazor parish with Thomas Bevan as proprietor. It was still there in 1858, but by then it had become a simple **Lion**, with Edward Davies as landlord. There is no further mention and the building has not, as yet, been identified.

The railway takes a direct west-north-westerly course from Moorhampton through the scattered village of Norton Canon on its way to Kinnersley. Surprisingly there was no station to serve Norton Canon, but perhaps one was intended, for hidden down the back road that joins Norton Canon to the A438 at the **Portway Inn,** and on the left just over the old railway bridge before arriving at Upper Norton Farm, was the **Railway Inn**. In 1891 Henry Powell was the landlord

The one time Railway Inn at Norton Canon

there and also a machinist. It is now a private house, but memories of its hospitable past must remain, for it is now called Brewery House. Presumably, at the end of the 19th century, Henry Powell was brewing his own beer.

Norton Canon still retains one inn, the **Three Horseshoes**, a little way out of the village at Eccles Green, further along the main road towards Kington. Whilst Norton Canon as a whole was the 'north settlement of the Dean and Chapter of Hereford', the name Eccles Green, which was certainly in use in the 14th century, is thought to indicate a one time Celtic Christian settlement. In the later 19th century the **Three Horseshoes** is where James Rude was both landlord and village blacksmith. For many years it was a simple beer house, perhaps satisfying the thirst of weary travellers waiting for their horses to be shod. The **Three Horseshoes** is a popular inn name relating to the blacksmithing trade, even though horseshoes normally come in sets of four! The usual, semi-humorous suggestion is that horses were normally brought to the blacksmith because they were minus one shoe. This has led to several inn signs showing a horse squatting on its haunches, plaintively holding up one shoe-less hoof for inspection. The Norton Canon **Three Horseshoes** has a more prosaic inn sign that just includes three simple horseshoes, but it brews its own beer for which it has won awards.

In the middle of Norton Canon parish, before reaching Eccles Green, there is a turning to the right, the B4320, that leads towards Weobley. The road curves to the north-east around Yazor Wood before dropping past the grounds that once belonged to Garnstone House and so entering Weobley village from the south. Weobley's pubs are dealt with in chapter 8.

The Three Horseshoes at Norton Canon in 2000

The next hostelry involves yet another diversion off the main Kington road. In this case the diversion is to the left at the Sarnesfield crossroads, along the A4112 towards Eardisley. There was once a public house at Sallies, where the lane to Logaston is on the right. This was the **Halfway House Inn**, where, in 1858, Robert Morley was landlord. Perhaps it was half-way between Weobley and Eardisley, or was it for the more long distance traveller, being roughly half-way between Leominster and Hay-on-Wye? Although it was a considerable distance along the main road to another inn, the **Halfway House** could not have been very successful—it must have failed in the latter part of the 19th century for it is not mentioned in the 1891 Kelly's Directory. However, the memory remains, for the house is still called 'The Old Cider House'. Almost opposite the **Halfway House** there is a group of cottages in one of which Winnie, the current long-serving landlady of **Ye Olde Tavern** in Kington, was born and brought up.

Go past the drive to Kinnersley Castle and then take a left turn once again along a long, low-lying road that eventually finds its way to the A438 a few hundred yards from the **Swan** at Letton. Well before this and just over the railway bridge, on the opposite side of the road to what was once Kinnersley Railway Station, is the **Kinnersley**, known for many years as the **Kinnersley Arms Hotel**. James Smith was listed in the

Halfway House—the Old Cider House at Sallies

76

	a m	p m	p m	p m	p m	p m		
HEREFORD dep.	9 22	1245	3 45	5 25	8 15	...	...
Credenhill ...	9 34	1258	4 2	5 37	8 27	...	...
Moorhampton ...	9 41	1 6	4 9	5 45	8 34	...	...
Kinnersley ...	9 49	1 13	4 17	5 53	8 42	...	...
Eardisley ...	9 52	1 17	4 20	5 57	8 45	...	...
Whitney ...	10 0	1 24	4 28	6 5	8 53	...	...
HAY ...	10 8	1 33	4 36	6 14	9 1	...	...
Glasbury ...	1021	1 44	4 48	...	9 13	...	...
Three Cocks J. ar.	1025	1 50	4 52	...	9 17	...	...
Talgarth ...	1054	3 5	0	...	9 23	...	...
Talyllyn Junc. ...	1046	2 15	5 12	...	9 35	...	...
Dowlais ...	2 25	3 35	6 20	...	...	...	...
Merthyr ...	2 32	3 45	6 29	...	...	...	...
Cardiff ...	4 19	5 38	8 24	...	...	...	...
NEWPORT ...	3 35	4 57	7 45	...	...	...	...
BRECON ...	11 8	2 35	5 30		9 48	...	...

	p m	p m	p m	p m	p m		
BRECON ... dep.	7 15	1032	110	5 50	...	...
NEWPORT ...	...	8 25	1110	2 5	...	...
Cardiff ...	...	7 50	1090	1 10	...	...
Merthyr ...	...	9 38	1210	2 50	...	...
Dowlais ...	...	9 35	12 5	1 10	...	...
Talyllyn Junction ...	7 27	1046	1 25	6 1	...	...
Talgarth ...	7 38	1057	1 85	6 11	...	...
Three Cocks Junc. ...	7 49	1111	1 52	6 20	...	...
Glasbury ...	7 54	1116	1 56	6 25	...	...
HAY ...	8 1	1124	2 5	6 33	...	...
Whitney ...	8 12	1136	2 15	6 44	...	...
Eardisley ...	8 19	1145	2 23	6 52	...	...
Kinnersley ...	8 24	1150	2 29	6 58	...	...
Moorhampton ...	8 31	1157	2 85	7 4	...	...
Credenhill ...	8 39	12 4	2 45	7 12	...	...
HEREFORD ...	8 52	1217	3 0	7 25	...	...

MARKET TRAIN leaves Hereford for Hay and intermediate stations
WEDNESDAYS at 5 25 p.m.

directory as landlord in 1891. Was he the same James Smith who was a farmer at Upper Newton Farm in the same parish? Before this rather grand name was invented, this was the simple **Station Hotel**, reflecting its position and perhaps the aspirations of the original railway builders to provide a main route from the Midlands to South Wales. It was a well placed inn—the more energetic train passenger could sit in the bar and, on hearing the train coming from the Hay direction, still have time to consume his pint and run across the road to catch the 11.45 a.m. or 2.23 p.m. train into Hereford! Stations such as Kinnersley served a very wide area and not just the local parish. Thus Francis Kilvert, when vicar of

The Kinnersley in 2000

Bredwardine, caught the train at Kinnersley, his nearest 'main line' station, some three miles from his home.

Kinnersley means 'Cyneheard's clearing' an appropriate name for an area that would have been well wooded up to and beyond the Norman Conquest, and situated on the edge of what is still known as Letton Lake, from its habit of flooding practically every winter.

In Upper Ailey, only a short distance to the west of the **Kinnersley Arms** was another inn—the **Mason's Arms**. This was presumably the establishment that belonged to Mrs. Margaret Evans in 1891—she was a beer retailer and shop-keeper. The dual role

The one time Mason's Arms at Upper Ailey still sports a sign, but as a 'private', not 'public' house

continued, and in 1934 it was serving the community as a post office as well as an inn. It is not particularly obvious why the trade of the Mason should be associated with this inn; perhaps it was an association of name rather than profession.

The Lion at Ferney Common in the late 19th century

The **Mason's Arms** was built late in the 16th century on an L-shaped plan with wings to east and south, but there have been various modern additions. On the north front there is a moulded eaves-beam with shaped brackets below it. Adjoining the east wing is a weather-boarded building. The owner decided not to renew the licence in 1946, but the building still survives and has a sign outside to remind passers-by of its historic past as the **Mason's Arms**.

This was not the full tally of public houses in Kinnersley parish a century and a half ago, for in the 1858 directory the two professions of beer retailer and blacksmith were once again merged in the figure of Richard Huxley at an otherwise unnamed establishment.

The Ferney Lion near Woonton

Returning to the main road junction at Sarnesfield and the road leading towards Kington once again beckons. On the right, well before the village of Woonton, is the **Lion Inn**, at Ferney Common. In 1891 it served a useful dual purpose, being also the village shop with Thomas Winney as landlord. This was a simple roadside inn until the early 1980s when it was extended. Marital and financial problems then forced its closure for some time until a new landlord, who had previously been at the **Bell** at Yarpole, took over. The lion—the king of beasts—comes in a variety of colours on inn signs, with 'Red', 'White', 'Black' and 'Golden' being common. However, being known locally as the **Ferney** makes this **Lion** unique.

The loss of the **Buck Inn** in the middle of Woonton is a great pity. This building, now a private house, is of 17th-century date but has been re-fronted in stone. It was an inn for many years, and a note in the *Hereford Times* for 18 August 1857 records the death at Lower Stocks, Almeley, of Ann, relict of the late John Hall of the **Buck Inn**, Woonton. The following year saw William Jones as landlord. By 1891 the licensee was George Williams. The name was presumably a reference to a male deer, although it could refer to a spirited young man— a dandy!

Jenkins, a farmer who lived between Hereford and Bromyard, was said to have power over witches. He was renowned for his ability to remove spells. He also had second sight, and people travelled long distances to see him. Once he visited the **Buck Inn**. After the meal he called for the reckoning, and the landlady replied 'Fourpence for eat, fourpence for drink, eight pence on the whole'. Thinking the charge exorbitant, the farmer put the money on the

Until recently this fine building was the Buck Inn in the middle of Woonton

80

table and drew a circle round it in chalk. When the landlady came to pick up the money she began to go round and round the table, repeating her request for payment. The servant came and tried to reach the money, but the same thing happened to her. The ostler came in and tried: then there were three people circling the table. Another servant went out into the yard where the farmer was preparing to depart, and quietly asked him what was to be done. 'You take the money with a pair of tongs', he said. 'That will stop them'.

In 1946 the licence of the **Buck Inn** was transferred from Harold Ward to Mr. Joseph Bromage who moved down the road from the **Maidenhead Inn**, at Lyonshall. There is still one indication of the inn's importance not just in the village, but for travellers passing along the road. Hidden amongst the attractive creeper that covers much of the stone face of the building is the AA village sign for Woonton, recording the distances to Hereford and London.

A **Bridge Inn** at Woonton is mentioned in Slater's 1850 directory with William Jones as landlord, but there is no further mention. At about the same time there was also a **Plough Inn** at Woonton, where Samuel Watkins acted as both landlord and wheelwright. Just north of Woonton, at Hopley's Green, Edward Davies was a retailer of cider in 1891.

Woonton, although liberally served with inns, beer and cider houses, is not a parish in its own right, it is simply a township within the larger parish of Almeley. The village centre is almost a mile to the west of Woonton and is approached from all directions by side roads. In the centre of Almeley is the **Bells Inn**, a pleasant, traditional hostelry that makes no pretensions to be

The Bells at Almeley

anything else. In the 19th century it is described as the **Bell Inn**, the multiple bells seem to have arrived rather recently! In 1850 Thomas Williams was landlord; in 1891 Thomas East was a farmer as well as having the responsibility of licensee. Once a Marstons house, the landlord in the 1970s and 80s managed to combine a living with a milk round. Nowadays the milk round has gone, but instead the inn doubles as the village shop.

Once the New Inn at Almeley

The **New Inn** at Almeley, only a few doors down the main street from the **Bells**, has been closed for some years, but the rather gaunt stone building still stands on the corner of the road leading from Woonton. Although just a simple beer house, it was the home of the Almeley Brewery, founded in 1853. It was here, during the latter part of the 19th century that Henry Baird, the proprietor, was also chief brewer and maltster. Vestiges of the

The New Inn was included in the Imperial Brewery sale of 1898

brewery remain, with a doorway at the bottom of the garden to the cellar. Before the end of the 19th century it had been taken over by Watkins' Imperial Brewery of Hereford and was included in the brewery sale of 1898. It was then rather grandly advertised as being convenient for those travelling by train on the Kington and Eardisley branch of the Great Western Railway. Before 1898 the Imperial Brewery must have closed down the brewing operation at Almeley, for according to the sale catalogue across the yard was 'the old brewhouse'. Interestingly, the front garden was described as having cellarage underneath it. This may suggest that the cellars belonged to an earlier building that fronted directly onto the road, the existing building being described in the sale details as 'modern'. In 1898, the landlord, Mr. Rooke was paying a rent of £25 per annum—quite a high figure for a simple beer house. In an attempt to change the image the name was changed to the **Pheasant**, but this was not successful and it has now been closed for many years. The **New Inn** stands opposite the earthwork remains of Almeley motte and bailey castle, just south of the church and churchyard.

Returning to the A480 at Woonton, the road begins to wind again as it heads through Holmes Marsh before dropping down into Lyonshall, a rather curious village in two separate parts. What appears to be the village centre is where the A480 road does a sharp double bend, but then, almost half-a-mile northwards is the old village centre, complete with ruined castle and church, where the A480 finally meets the main A44 Leominster to Kington road.

An early 19th-century road book notes that Lyonshall contained 128 houses with 678 inhabitants. There seems to have been a variety of inns and beer houses in and around the village, some of which are

The Royal George—the last remaining inn in Lyonshall—in 2000

now hard to trace. Some say that there was as many as eight! The 1891 Kelly's Directory notes that 'Lyonshall is an extensive parish and village bounded on the north by the river Arrow with a station on the Kington and Eardisley branch of the Great Western railway'.

The one surviving hostelry, in the middle of the present village, is the **Royal George Inn**, which was built around 1600. The upper storey formerly projected on the south-west side, but like many others has

ROYAL GEORGE

been under-built. It has been suggested that the name of this inn was changed in 1792, when the flagship *The Royal George* sank at Spithead with the loss of some 900 lives—the name change being to commemorate the bravery of the sailors. However, this was not the case, for the prefix 'Royal' seems to be a relatively new addition to the name. Early deeds only refer to the **Old George Inn**. Also, in 1858, when Sarah Kinnersley was land-

1961 advertisement

lady, and again in 1891, when Daniel Price was licensee, it was simply the **George**. Even as recently as 1932, when the Royal Commission examined the building as part of their county-wide examination of historic buildings, it was still just the **George**. When did it finally achieve royalty?

Directly across the road from the **Royal George** was the **Maidenhead Inn**. In 1932 it was described by the Royal Commission together with the adjoining house. 'They have been much altered, but incorporate in the west part a 15th-century building. The upper storey of this building projects on the east side with a moulded bressummer and close-set framing below, all now included in the central passage-way of the house. The east part of the house is 16th-century with a 17th-century addition'. In 1850 William Lloyd was licensee and on 27 March 1855 the *Hereford Times* recorded the marriage of Harriett, daughter of William Lloyd of the **Maidenhead Inn**, Lyonshall, to William Price of the Mill Half, Whitney. By 1891 George Davies was landlord. According to *Lyonshall 2000* the building next to the **Maidenhead** was at one time the **Stone House Public House**.

The Maidenhead in Lyonshall was only a few yards from the Royal George

Originally the horse-drawn tramway from Eardisley to Kington, and latterly the Eardisley to Kington Railway, both passed through Lyonshall and were both recorded with inns. The earliest must be the **Wharf Inn**, opposite the church next to the Lodge leading into Lynhales, for the various stops on the horse-drawn tramway reflected their origin as feeders for the Brecon Canal and were called wharves. It was mentioned in 1850 with John Hatton as landlord, but was absent in 1891. The inn was where the tramway crossed the main road, then to pass to the east of the church and the castle on its way to Kington. The author of *Lyonshall 2000* notes that it was also called the **Weymouth Arms**. Did it change its name once again to reflect the new steam trains and become **The Railway Inn**? The *Hereford Times* for 5 February 1890 refers to charges of gambling and allowing gambling on the premises being brought against Cornelius Cowles, the landlord of the **Railway Inn**, Lyonshall. He must have survived, for according to the Kelly's Directory for 1891 he was still the landlord a year later.

There were three stops on the Eardisley to Kington line—Almeley, Lyonshall and Titley, the latter being at the junction with the

The sign on the building in 2000 indicates that this was the Old Weymouth Arms, but earlier it was the Wharf Inn

Leominster to Kington line. Towards the end of the 19th century trains were running reasonably smoothly. The first train left Kington at 9.10 a.m. and arrived in Eardisley some 25 minutes later, turning round and returning to Kington by 10.20 a.m. It made three more journeys during the day, ending up at Kington at 7.35 p.m. after a full working day. However, this rural line was not a complete backwater. From Eardisley there were connections through Hay and Brecon to South Wales, and through Hereford to Bristol, Gloucester, London and the south of England. From Kington, branch lines led to New Radnor and Presteigne, whilst the main line took passengers to Leominster where they could travel through Bromyard to Worcester or on the main line to Shrewsbury and the North. This was certainly the age of the train, and the inns and hotels close to the stations made the best of the trade.

Two other inns are mentioned in Lyonshall in the 19th century. In the centre of the village was the **Greyhound Inn**, which had Thomas Lloyd as landlord in the 1858 directory. Was he related to William Lloyd at the **Maidenhead**?

At Nextend, well to the north of Lyonshall castle and church was the **Holly Bush** which was described as adjoining the old railway, in this case the Leominster to Kington line, just south of Titley Station. The holly with its red berries, which is now associated with Christmas, was used by the Romans during their Saturnalia—the period of riotous celebrations and great debauchery also held in December. In 1879 Thomas Morris was a farmer at The Rise and George Watkins was a beer retailer at Nextend. By 1891 Thomas Morris had moved and was the landlord at the **Holly Bush**. It has been closed for many years.

Once the Hollybush at Nextend, this is now a private house

The A44 from its junction with the A480 through to Kington is without any roadside inns. The thirsty traveller has to await the great variety to be found in Herefordshire's north-western market town.

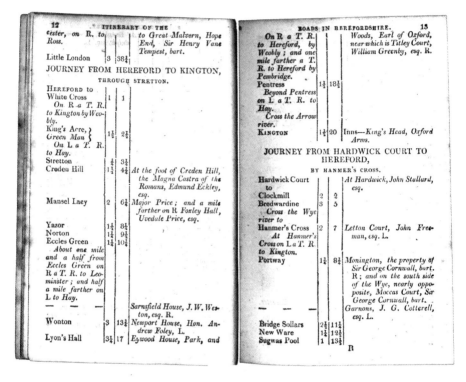

The Hereford to Kington road from an 1805 road-book

CHAPTER SIX

Kington—South and East

Kington is a busy market town in the north-western corner of Herefordshire. Despite a canal that was abandoned on its way from Leominster and a railway that closed down in 1955, Kington continues to function as a commercial and shopping centre for north-west Herefordshire and the neighbouring parts of Radnorshire.

An 1820s road book provides an early description. 'Kington or Kyneton is a small market town situated on the Arrow, at the north-western extremity of the county, near the borders of Radnorshire. The town is well built, and is inhabited chiefly by clothiers, who carry on a considerable trade in narrow cloth'. In 1801 there were 1,404 inhabitants in 311 houses of which 644 were men and 760 women.

A much more personal description is derived from Parry, writing his *History of Kington* as 'from an eminent writer' in 1845. 'In former days this town was awake only once a week, and that was on a Market-day. If you had passed through it at any other time you may have seen the shops open, and the houses open, and a few persons walking about the streets with their eyes open; but the shops, and the houses, and the people therein were all asleep; the few persons who walked about, looked as if they did not know whither they were going, or what they were doing. The shops were cold for want of glass in the windows, and the articles exposed for sale appeared as if they had been in that state ever since Noah's flood, and old-fashioned enough to have come out of his ark: the shop-keeper was often standing at his door, not looking for customers, for that would have been vain employment, but merely gaping for some-thing to fill his eyes; and if a neighbour happened to be sauntering

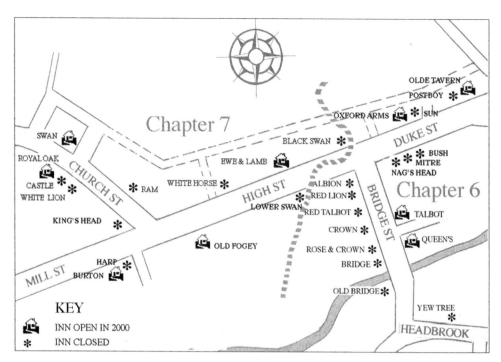

Kington, showing the positions of inns described in the text

NAME CHANGES

Many pubs in Kington have changed their name over the years. The name on the left is the current, or last used name; the names in the right-hand columns being other names by which the inn has been called over time

CHAPTER 6

Rose & Crown	Lord Nelson	Nelson
Bridge Inn	New Bridge Inn	
Talbot	White Talbot	Lyon
Oxford Arms	Salutation	
Olde Tavern	Railway Tavern	House in the Fields
Postboy's Arms	Waggon & Horses	

CHAPTER 7

Ewe & Lamb	Lamb	
Lower Swan	Swan in Chain	White Swan
Old Fogey	Wine Vaults	Spirit Vaults
Harp	Millwright's Arms	
Burton Hotel	Milner's	Gorely's
Ram Inn	Prince of Wales	
Swan	Upper Swan	
Royal Oak	Oak	

by he had a bit of a chat with him; these two persons, propping their backs against a wall, and thrusting their hands into their breeches pockets, talked for a time about things in general, and when tired they parted; the one lounger walked down the street to seek for someone else to gossip with, and the shop-keeper returned into the shop to keep himself awake by killing flies and wasps. Whenever a coach came into the town, and changed horses at an Inn, all the indolent, gaping, staring and yawning population of the town, came out to look at the said horses, and the coach, and the coachman, and watch the interested process of taking off one set of horses and putting on another; the very horses themselves appeared to wonder what the people could be staring at, and when the coach left, the town became so quiet again that the quacking of a duck or the squeaking of a pump-handle, could be heard from one end of the town to the other'.

Parry goes on to state that, besides the **Oxford Arms**, the **King's Head** and the **Castle**, there were 13 inns and public houses licensed by the magistrates in the town, together with ten beer and cider houses in the town and its vicinity. The 13 other inns included: **Bridge Inn**, **Upper Swan**, **Sun Inn**, **Harp Inn**, **Royal Oak**, **Mitre Inn**, **Talbot Inn**, **White Horse Inn**, **Prince of Wales** (previously named **Ram Inn**), **Rose & Crown Inn**, **Queen's Head Inn**, and **Nag's Head Inn** and one other.

To balance this excess of public houses, Parry explained that Kington had a teetotal society founded in February 1842. The members had to declare 'We agree, by divine assistance, to abstain from the use of intoxicating liquors, except for medicinal purposes and religious ordinances'. There must have been a lot of converts, for by May 1842 it had about 70 members!

In 1858 the two posting offices at Kington were in the **Oxford Arms** and **Milner's Hotel**. The mail coach left the **Oxford Arms** at 9.10 a.m. for Aberystwyth, Duffryn Castle and Penybont. At 3.20 p.m. the returning mail coach left the **Oxford Arms** for Hereford and Gloucester, whilst the *Arrow* left at 10.00 a.m. for Hereford returning at 5.15 p.m.. The journey took two-and-a-quarter hours. The **King's Head** was the main base for carriers to Hereford, Builth and Rhayader.

An 1891 Trades directory provides a fresh picture of the importance of Kington as a centre for the whole of north-western Herefordshire. 'Kington is a market and union town, head of a county court district and petty sessional division, 20 miles north-west-by-west from Hereford. Kington stands in a fertile valley beneath sheltering hills, on the borders of Radnorshire, and on the roads leading from Hereford to Aberystwyth; the town is nearly surrounded by water, the river Arrow (famous for its fine trout) running on the south side and the Back Brook on the north and east sides, the latter falling into the Arrow about half-a-mile below the town. It consists of four well built streets. with many modern houses of stone and brick, and is lighted with gas, by the Kington Gas Company Limited, from works at the east end of the town, and water is supplied from works in a picturesque glen a short distance from the town, the property of a limited company, formed about 1886, and is conducted through cast-iron mains to a reservoir at the Wyche, 100 feet above the town, and holding 31,000 gallons. The town is now undergoing a very complete system of sewerage by the Commissioners.

'The town is chiefly supported by agriculture, but there is an iron foundry, a nail manufactury, a tan yard, a small woollen mill, and extensive corn mills and malt houses. An extensive trade is also carried on by the Old Radnor lime works, the offices of which are in Kington; the works of the company, at Dolyhir, are furnished with the most improved machinery for drilling and crushing the limestone rocks.

'The market is held on Tuesday, a great business being transacted on that day in eggs, butter and poultry, this being the mart to which the Welsh send their produce, to meet dealers who gather here from all quarters. The horse show on September 19 has attained great importance and is attended largely by breeders and dealers from all parts of the kingdom. The market for the sale of agricultural produce and for butter and poultry is held at the Upper Cross, High Street, and in Church Street. There are two hotels and several inns'.

At the Kington Licensing Sessions in February 1916, the police reported that there had been 10 convictions for drunkenness in 1915 against 17 in 1914.

*Late 19th century Bridge Street. A Temperance Hotel on the left (now the
post office), the Talbot and Queen's in the distance on the left
and the old Albion on the right*

Bridge Street and Headbrook

The southern part of Kington is centred on Bridge Street, which leads
southwards from the area called Lower Cross to cross the river Arrow
into the Headbrook district. The eastern part of the town starts from
Lower Cross and is based on Duke Street and its continuation, Victoria
Road. Here it meets the by-pass, with the Sunset district on the further
side centred on Waterloo Road.

Starting at the top end of Bridge Street on the west side, the
Albion Hotel, at number 2 is described in the Schedule of Listed
Buildings as being of 18th-century date. There is no other mention of
this establishment which may well have been a private hotel.

Continuing down the west side, the **Red Lion**, mentioned in
1783, is considered to be the present number 6, whilst the **Red Talbot**
was at numbers 8 and 9. Number 9 was included in the 1934 Royal
Commission on Historical Monuments Volume 3 as being a 17th-
century building of two stories with attics that was much altered in the
18th century. Parry notes 'The **Red Talbot** in Bridge Street was one of

6 Bridge Street,
probably the Red Lion

8/9 Bridge Street,
probably the Red Talbot

the most ancient inns in the town, and ceased to be a public house about the year 1772. The house is now [1845] occupied by Thomas Lewis Esq., the proprietor'. The Talbot was a hunting dog, white with black spots, bred by the Talbot family in the 15th century. There were several branches of the family in Herefordshire. However, a talbot is simply a dog in heraldry. The arms of the Wolseley family of Wolesley are argent, a talbot passant gules (that is a red dog on a silver shield). There is no record of Wolseleys in Herefordshire, so perhaps an early landlord who had been a servant of the Wolseleys chose the name to honour his old master.

The **Crown Inn**, which closed some time before 1778, was apparently at numbers 11 and 12 Bridge Street. There was also the **Rose and Crown**, described as being at 16 Bridge Street. This was mentioned in 1845 when Thomas Stokes was landlord, followed by John Meredith in 1850. An earlier name for this inn was the **Lord Nelson,** or simply the **Nelson,** for which Pigot's 1824 Directory has Samuel Savigar as licensee. On 5 May 1877, Skarratt noted in his diary

'The furniture of S. Morris of the **Rose and Crown**, was sold by Ball and Blakeley, he having decided to leave Kington for Birmingham. Corbett of the **Queen's Head** has taken the premises'. The inn was probably closed some time in the 1880s.

The **Bridge Inn** was apparently at number 22 Bridge Street, on the western side close to the bridge. It was mentioned as early as 1707.

The captions on p.95 should, of course, refer to Bridge Street, not Broad Street

11-12 Broad Street,
'he site of the Crown Inn

...has been a change to John Tringham. The *Hereford Times* for 25 October 1856 records the marriage of Margaret, eldest daughter of John Ross of the **Bridge Inn**, Kington, to George Price, at Eardisley. On the assumption that 'new' refers to the inn and not the bridge, there appears to have been an element of rebuilding of the inn about this time, for in 1858 John Ross is recorded as being at the **New Bridge Inn.** He did not stay for long, for in the

16 Broad Street,
once the Rose and Crown or the Nelson

Hereford Times for 24 July 1858. John Bedford, a boy from Pembridge, was charged at Kington Petty Sessions with stealing a leather strop from James Watkins, landlord of the **Bridge Inn**. This was considered to be a serious offence and he was committed to the House of Correction for 14 days and then to the Reformatory School for 5 years.

There seems to be an element of confusion with the **Old Bridge Inn**, also described as being in Bridge Street—in one description it was at number 23, next door to the **Bridge Inn**. It was not mentioned in 1824, but in 1845 Margaret Griffiths was the landlady. By 1850 John Griffiths was landlord and he was again entered in Kelly's Directories for 1858 and 1863.

The inn continued in use until after 1891, when Richard Davies was landlord. However, it was then described as being in Headbrook, suggesting that it was on the far side of the river from the town. At the Kington Licensing Sessions in February 1916, all the licences were renewed with the exception of the **Old Bridge Inn**, which had recently been sold, and no application had been made for the renewal of the licence.

There is no mention of the **Bridge Inn** or **New Bridge Inn** in the 1891 directory and it may have been closed. However, there are conflicting stories about when these two inns closed. One reference states that the **Bridge Inn** was closed 'by Miss Foot in 1913', whilst another states that 'it was moved to Church Bank in the 1930s'. However, other references suggest that it was the **Red Talbot** that was moved to Church Bank. Presumably it was just the licence that was moved.

On the eastern side of the street and still surviving after many years of operation as public houses are the **Talbot** and the **Queen's Head**, on either side of the lane that leads to the market and its car park.

The **Talbot Hotel**, or **White Talbot** as it was known in the 19th century, or even earlier as the **Lyon**, is at 52 Bridge Street. It is a listed

1876 advertisement for the Talbot

The Talbot in 1999

building and the Royal Commission described it as having been 're-fronted in stone. It is of two storeys with attics and forms a T-shaped building with the cross wing at the west end. Inside the building are some original moulded ceiling-beams and a doorway in the east wing has a moulded frame and an ornamental head with foliated spandrels. The staircase is original and has half-newels with moulded angles surmounted by tall diminishing shafts with panelled faces and moulded terminals; the balusters are turned and the risers are panelled'.

Parry mentions Philip Holman, who was appointed High Sheriff of Herefordshire during the reign of Charles I. He writes: 'he resided at a house then called the Lyon, in Bridge Street, now the Talbot Inn; and according to tradition King Charles I, in the year 1633, slept at his house. The Arms of the founder of the Hall are therein sculptured in brown oak, with his initials (P.H.) over the same, surrounded by a wreath. The house is otherwise much ornamented, and has a male figure of the same material on the east side. The Arms are a Chevron between three arrow's-heads, or spear-heads, reversed'. Later in the book he calls this inn the **White Talbot** and mentions that it had been 'until lately in a very dilapidated state'. He recorded that the Court Leet and Court Barn are said to have been held here 'from time immemorial'. In 1845 there was a high brick wall at the rear enclosing

97

a yard for ball playing—presumably a fives court, although there was also a cockpit.

It was in Bridge Street in 1817, near the **White Talbot Inn**, that one Thomas Langslow, an idle and dissolute youth, took a knife and 'inflicted many desperate wounds on the body of one James Green, a clerk in the office of James Davies, Esq., a solicitor in the town'. Although Green was saved by prompt medical attention, Langslow was tried and sentenced to death. He was executed on Saturday, 12 April 1817 in Hereford. Apparently the bells of all the parish churches in the city tolled during the awful ceremony and for about four minutes after the platform dropped he appeared convulsed, and frequently exchanged a handkerchief which he held from one hand to another. The execution probably took place on the platform above the main doorway of the Nash-designed County Gaol in Bye Street (now where the cinema stands in Commercial Road). Executions were 'fully exposed to the general view of all spectators without the walls, and of all the prisoners within, who should be ranged round the general court for that purpose—and in the hope of preventing crimes by making a due impression on all who witness these melancholy examples'.

In 1844 the Oddfellows opened a second Lodge in Kington, the earlier one being at the **Lamb Inn**. This was a lodge of the 'Wolverhampton Order of Loyal Odd-fellows' and was in the **Talbot Inn** where the landlord was William Pitt. There were 35 members initiated on the opening day and, after attending divine service, all returned to the **Talbot** where they 'sat down to an excellent dinner. The loyal toasts were drank by the parties afterwards, and the company separated, highly delighted with the festivities of the day'.

There is some confusion about the landlords at the **Talbot** in the 19th century. One reference has members of the Hatton family there in the mid-1850s, but *Pigot's Directory* of 1824 has Joseph Meredith, followed by John Meredith in 1863. The latter seem to be more likely for on 6 October 1877 it is recorded in the *Diaries of Thomas Carleton Skarratt* that Mrs. Meredith, late of the **Talbot**, now of the **Castle**, had a paralytic stroke. This followed the entry in the *Diary* on 7 May 1877 where Skarratt commented that 'Mr. Cook, late of the **Nag's Head**, a few days ago purchased the **Talbot**' and, on the 15 August 'Mrs. Foster, late Miss Cooke of the **Nag's Head**, removed to the **Talbot**'. In 1891 Mrs. Rachel Foster was landlady and in 1913 William Wishlade was mine host.

There is a note in the *Woolhope Club Transactions* for 1914 that 'The **Talbot** barn, in which Mrs Siddons performed her début, is now used as a pigstye'. This is presumably the barn at the rear of the **Talbot** that was described by the Royal Commission as being of 'one storey and two bays, partly of stone and partly weatherboarded'. Sarah Kemble, eldest child of Roger and Sarah Kemble, was born on 5 July 1755 at the **Shoulder of Mutton**, in Brecon. Sarah Siddons, as she became, began acting very young, and it may have been when the family was in Kington in 1759, that she first performed on a stage in the **Talbot** barn. The **Talbot** had ceased being an inn by the early 1980s, but has subsequently reopened.

The **Queen's Head** public house is at 50 Bridge Street. It is a 17th-century building that has been re-fronted in brick, although it still has some exposed timber-framing. In 1845 Sarah Watson was landlady, but by 1850 it was John Fuller and in 1858 James Waters. There was

The Queen's Head in Bridge Street

another change before 1863, when Samuel Davies was licensee. The 1891 Kelly's Directory records the landlord as Thomas Jones. The Kington Curse Doll, now in the museum, was found in roof beams of the inn's barn. It has been suggested that this was the reason for there being so many publicans there during the mid-19th-century. The inn now brews its own beer.

Another inn that is thought to have been in Bridge Street is the **Angel**, where Thomas Price was landlord in the mid-1820s. It was apparently sold, and probably closed, in 1832. It was most likely on the east side of the street. There was also the **George**, with Charles Vaughan Snr. as landlord, according to Pigot's 1824 Directory. George Boulton was listed as being there in 1858, but the inn (or more probably beer house) probably closed soon afterwards. The sites are not known of the **Carpenter's Arms** and the **Bird in Hand**, both mentioned in 1851, and both probably in Bridge Street.

Crossing the bridge over the river Arrow, and Headbrook leads off to the east to the by-pass. Here, at number 31, was the **Yew Tree Inn**, open during the mid to late 1800s, probably as a beer house. Thomas Griffiths is recorded as a beer seller at Headbrook in 1845—this could well have been at the **Yew Tree**. No other inns are recorded to the south of the river.

Duke Street and Sunset

Duke Street leads eastwards from the Lower Cross, its junction with High Street and Bridge Street, and, before the by-pass was built, it led to the railway station and was the main road leading towards Titley and Presteigne.

The **Nag's Head**, was on the south side of Duke Street, at number 3, just past the Bridge Street turning. It was mentioned in 1845 when Francis Whitney was landlord. In the 1850s and '60s Henry Cook was the landlord. On 24 March 1877 Skarratt entered in his *Diary* 'Pritchard has left the **Nag's Head**, Holder, the coal agent, taken it'. A year and a half later, on 7 November 1878, Skarratt made another entry regarding Pritchard: 'Pritchard, late of the **Nag's Head**, being tired of this life, made an attempt to destroy himself by cutting his throat. The wound was a bad one, but is hoped will not prove fatal'. The habit must have been catching, or the **Nag's Head** cast a spell on its residents, for the *Hereford Times* for 4 July 1885 reported that Jane Holden, the wife

The Nag's Head was at 3 Duke Street

of the landlord of the **Nag's Head**, had been charged with attempted suicide. The case was dismissed and the chairman considered arresting the husband. The inn is not mentioned in the 1891 Trades directory, but apparently struggled on, finally to close in 1930.

Next door to the **Nag's Head** at number 4 was the **Mitre Public House**. The 'mitre', the ceremonial headgear worn by bishops, was commonly used for centuries to show allegiance to the established church. William Luntley was landlord from the mid-1820s to the 1840s, and Thomas Scull during the

The Mitre and the Bush Inn were at 4 and 5 Duke Street.
In part, the memory remains—no. 4 is called 'Mitre House'

1850s and '60s, when the inn had a bowling alley and was very popular. On 9 December 1878, Skarratt noted in his *Diary* that 'Mr Huxley of the **Mitre** died suddenly of epilepsy when about to dress himself'. His widow struggled on for some eight years, but in the *Hereford Times* for 2 October 1886 there is the notice: 'For Sale—The **Mitre Inn**, Kington, In the occupation of Mrs Huxley'. By 1891 Miss Selina Hutchins had taken over, but the inn had had its best days almost half-a-century earlier and it finally closed its doors in the mid-1930s. At number 5 was the **Bush Inn** open during the 18th century, but apparently no later.

There were two licensed premises on the north side of Duke Street, **The Oxford Arms Hotel** and the **Sun Inn**, both mentioned in the 1770s. According to *Pugh's Hereford Journal* the Commissioners appointed by Act of Parliament for repairing several roads leading into the town of Kington were to meet in the **Oxford Arms** on Monday, 3 December 1790 at 12 noon. This was presumably a meeting of the turnpike trust. Parry, writing in 1845, had no hesitation in describing the **Oxford Arms** as the 'principal Inn in the town' and 'formerly called the **Salutation**, which lets post-chaises and horses—and where the mail coach stops for the change of horses and refreshment of passengers. The excise-office is also kept here, and the Commissioners' appointed under the Kington Street Act hold their meetings here. It is a stone and timber building, three stories high, with a long frontage, and commodious in all other respects for noblemen, gentlemen and travellers. The present occupier [1845] is Mr Joseph Gardner'.

As early as 1796 a coach left the **Oxford Arms** each Friday at 5 p.m. bound, via Hereford, for London. It arrived at midday on the Sunday. By 1825 the **Oxford Arms** was described as 'the principal house of entertainment and commercial resort in the town'. At that time it was kept by Mr. Thomas Rogers. By 1835 the route from London through Hereford was extended to Aberystwyth. Also in the summer months a stage coach from Worcester arrived at the **Oxford Arms** three times a week on Mondays, Wednesdays and Fridays, returning the following day. The railways were being constructed by the 1840s and in 1841 a coach called the *Little Wonder* went from this hotel to Hereford, to carry passengers to meet the *Mazeppa* coach and catch the train at Cirencester. In 1845 a coach called the *Rover* left the **Oxford Arms** every morning at six o'clock, and arrived in Birmingham in time for the trains for all parts of England. It returned to Kington the same evening. At that time the landlord was Joseph Gardner.

A few years ago Ken Reeves, writing about the **Oxford Arms,** noted that 'one of its landlords was transported for forgery, another landlord's wife committed suicide in the Arrow, drowning her baby at the same time, and the building was severely damaged by the explosion of 1842'.

The 1850 *Slater's Directory* describes the **Oxford Arms** as a Family, Commercial and Posting House and Inland Revenue Office, with George Evans as landlord. He was still there in 1863. Was it really possible to negotiate one's tax over a pint of ale or was this just the excise office? The *Hereford Times* for 14 March 1857 observed that 'the **Oxford Arms** in Kington is having a commodious new room built on, courtesy of the owner, Lady Langdale'.

Skarratt regularly included comments on the **Oxford Arms** in his *Diary*. Thus, on 24 April 1854, he recorded that 'Bowen, ostler at the **Oxford Arms**, died after a few days illness. He formerly kept the **Sun Inn** in Duke Street'. He was presumably the father of the Mr. Bowen Jnr., who was married a few days earlier on 8 April.

Skarratt continued. On 8 August 1854 'A picnic was got up by Mrs Evans (**Oxford Arms**) and Mrs T Price. The ladies walked to Hergest Park and took tea, shaded by the fir trees, and afterwards were fetched home by four or five gentlemen—self being one of the number.

In 1876, the Oxford Arms providedf most facilities!

103

About 9 o'clock the Party re-assembled at the **Oxford Arms** and to the merry sound of the violin sported the light fantastic until 2 o'clock in the morning'. Later that year, on 20 November, he recorded that a procession formed at the **Oxford Arms**, walked to the Field, re-formed, then proceeded to **Milner's Hotel**, where there was a champagne luncheon 'all partaking thereof to pay five shillings'. In the evening there was a Ball at the **Oxford Arms**, under the patronage of Lady Langdale and James King-King Esq.

This inn was a regular stopping point for members of the Woolhope Club on their outings. Thus in August 1853 the Hereford party gathered at 6 a.m. at the **Green Dragon Hotel** in Hereford where a small coach was waiting for them. By 9 a.m. they were in Kington where they had breakfast at the **Oxford Arms Hotel**. After their business meeting they went on to examine the sandstones in the Nash quarries and then continued over the hill towards Presteigne and through Knill towards the 'igneous dyke of Stanner rocks'. By this time 'the hour fixed for the not less important duty of dining was fast

The Oxford Arms in the 1930s

approaching'. They scrambled down to the Aberystwyth road and arrived back at the **Oxford Arms Hotel** by 5 p.m. The record states that 'the dinner was an excellent one in all respects ... and upon the removal of the cloth, the Chairman gave the health of the Queen and the Royal Family, which was drunk with all due honour. After dinner there was a paper on *Colour in Plants: its Causes and Distribution* and the party finally broke up at 9 p.m. The Hereford members finally arrived back at the **Green Dragon** about 11 p.m. The **Oxford Arms** was obviously a strong favourite, for even when they went to the Kington area by train in 1879, some 26 years later (in order to visit Water-break-its-neck), they had a cold collation there before catching the 7.40 p.m. train home. It was not until their visit in 1888 that they transferred their affections to the **Burton**.

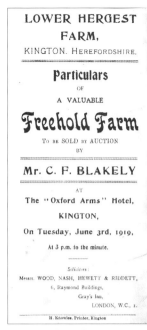

A sale held at the Oxford Arms in 1919

William Harvey was landlord in 1891. The **Oxford Arms** was largely rebuilt in 1937 with an elaborate 18th-century front and in the January 1939 *Hereford Guide* it was described as having 15 rooms and had been 'entirely redecorated and refurnished' with a 'beautiful Dining and Visitors Lounge'. It was closed for a while in 1993, but is now once again open.

The Oxford Arms in the early 20th century with a rather odd banner
(Photograph : Derek Foxton Collection)

The Oxford Arms in 1999

The **Sun Inn** was a few doors further down Duke Street at number 33. The 'Silurian Lodge of Free and Accepted Masons' was opened on 10 March 1791 at 'Mr. John Morris's house, called the **Sun Inn** and was still there in 1793', but on 21 August that same year Mr. Morris announced that the 'house was not continuing as an Inn after the last day of this month'. The Silurians then moved to the **King's Head**. However, the Lodge was not very successful and it closed about 1800. The **Sun** must have reopened, presumably in the same building, for it became a coaching inn and 'An Omnibus commenced running in 1844 from the **Sun Inn** in Duke Street to the **Maidenhead Inn** in Hereford on Wednesdays

The Sun Inn in the early 20th century

106

The Sun in 2000

and Saturdays, and returned the same evenings'. In 1825, John Bowen was landlord, in 1845 John Hollings and in 1850 James Morris. By 1863, James Morris was running a butcher's shop from the premises as well as the inn. Skarratt noted on 8 April 1854 'Was married at Kington—Mr Bowen (jnr) **Sun Inn** to Miss Stone, Market Hall. At the close of the Ceremony a little excitement took place by the arrival of the mother of the fair bride, who stormed away at a great rate and threatened to tear all the hair off her precious head, the result was she had to be turned outside'. The **Sun** closed in the 1960s.

Duke Street becomes Victoria Road as it leads towards Sunset. Here is the **Olde Tavern**, one of the three inns in Herefordshire to have an entry in the CAMRA guide to good interiors. The inn was established in 1767 when it was known as the **House in the Fields**. With the coming of the trains it became the more prosaic **Railway Tavern**. Skarratt noted on 24 February 1878 that 'A portion of the field next to Sunset Road, late in the occupancy of Griffiths of the **Railway Tavern** and adjoining the Charity [property] has been divided into garden allotments of £1 rental'. An 1891 directory has the landlord as Albert Jones. For well over a hundred years the licence of this inn has been held by just two generations of the family. The two sisters Gertrude and Mary Jones died in 1976 and 1989 respectively. Although Fred Jones is still given as licensee according to the board over the door, Winnie is the 'active' landlady. In 1928 the glass sign for **Ye Olde Tavern** cracked and was taken down. The pace of life is slow in this excellent inn—the sign was not put up again until 1985!

The Olde Tavern, once the House in the Fields, in 1999

Next to the **Tavern** on the town side was the **Postboy's Arms**, later the **Waggon and Horses**. It was closed about 1890.

The **Duke's Head** was at Sunset, but the precise site is unknown. It was an ale house that was open in 1851. On 2 September 1856 the *Hereford Times* recorded the death of Lucy (aged 44) wife of Richard Griffiths of the **Duke's Head Inn**, Sunset. In an 1858 Directory, Richard Griffiths of Sunset was a beer retailer, whilst George Bampfield also of Sunset added the trade of carpenter to his activities in selling beer. This could have been at the **Wharf Inn**, Sunset, only mentioned in 1845 when the landlord, Richard Vaughan, was described as a cider-seller. There are no other named pubs mentioned in Sunset, but Mrs. Ann Lloyd was a beer retailer at 24 Sunset in 1891.

Kington—North and West

The space at the western end of High Street is called the Upper Cross where once stood a market hall called the Butter Cross that was pulled down in 1768. At the eastern end of the High Street, at the junction with Bridge Street, is the Lower Cross; here stood another building called the Hide Market House that was demolished about the same date. Alfred Watkins of ley-line fame had no doubt that standing crosses occupied these sites before the Market Houses were built. Lower Cross now refers to a row of houses to the rear of the main street.

At the Upper Cross, the road forks with Mill Street continuing straight ahead and with Church Street, the main thoroughfare, bearing off to the right and uphill to the church. As with most streets in Kington, the north side of High Street is numbered from the Lower Cross to the Upper Cross; the south side continuing the numbers in the reverse direction.

High Street

There are deeds in the Record Office for an inn called the **Black Swan**, apparently at 2-4 High Street. It was open in 1664, but was probably closed before 1800. The 1678 deed refers to 'All that messuage and tenement the **Black Swanne** adjacent to a shop in the tenure of Thomas Gippe and the room there adjacent lying on the backside in the tenure of William Collins ... The Great Chamber lying over or being over the shop and the chamber adjacent on the backside of the said chamber ... With part of the cockloft over the said chamber and one passage or way crossing the end of another passage then lying over part of the entry and leading from the said

Great Chamber unto the said back chamber consisting in length six feet and in breadth five and thirty feet. The kitchen or brewhouse adjacent to the said back room in the tenure of the said William Collins with room and stable lying together adjacent to the said kitchen or brewhouse. All that part of the cellar now in the tenure of Mary White together with such part of the fold or backside now in the tenure of the said William Collins and also such further part of the said fold as is adjacent to the end of the said stable—all of which premises lying and being on the lower or east side of the said entry or fold. Also free ingress to the rooms and premises and use of the pump and water now being in the fold'. Mary Knight was a widow and the owner of the **Black Swanne**, and the deed involved the sale of part of the premises to her son, William, for £17. This money went towards meeting a debt to a saddler for £20. It may well be that another William Knight, who was assessed at five hearths and was valued at £5 13s. in 1664, was her husband.

The Ewe and Lamb in 1999

The **Lamb Inn** was at number 12 High Street. The building is described by the Royal Commission as being of 17th-century date, but heightened in the 19th century; inside are two original moulded ceiling-beams. In 1824 Thomas Jones was the proprietor, and in 1840, following a failed attempt some 18 years earlier at the

White Lion, another effort was made to form 'a Lodge of Oddfellows to be called the "Loyal Lord Durham Lodge", at the house of Mr Thomas Jones of the **Lamb Inn**'. This was more successful and by 1842 it had some 75 members. It acted generally as a Friendly Society and was so successful that within five years another Lodge had been opened in Kington at the **Talbot Inn**. By 1850 Edwin Powell was landlord of the **Lamb** and he and his wife stayed for many years. Skarratt noted for 16 February 1880: 'A very rainy day with strong gales which blew part of the plaster off the front of the **Lamb Inn**'. Also on 25 January 1881 the rather enigmatic entry: 'Mr. Hughes, Saddler, tired of being so near a neighbour of Mrs. Powell of the **Lamb**, removed back to his former premises next to Mr. Hall'. On 26 September 1891 the *Hereford Times* recorded the 'Sale by Auction, by order of the Trustees of the will of the late Mrs. Emma Powell of the **Lamb Inn**, now on lease to Mr. J.T. Duggan'. According to an 1891 directory, Charles Hodges was the landlord and James Thomas Duggan was a farmer. Mrs. Powell lived in Church Street. It was all eventually resolved and in the *Hereford Times* for 10 December 1892 there was an invitation to the 'Complementary dinner at the **Lamb Inn**, Kington, in honour of Corporal Joseph Lilley, who had resigned from the Kington Volunteers after 32 years of service'. The inn still survives, but lengthened its name in 1993 to the **Ewe and Lamb**, and has had several changes of landlord in recent years.

The **White Horse Inn** was at 19 High Street—a 17th-century building set back from the road. In 1824 Thomas Wilton was the landlord. John Price, who was the landlord between 1845 and 1858, was also a tailor and dyer. By 1891 Charles Price was the licensee. The inn was sold in 1945 by the Cheltenham Original Brewery Co. Ltd. with a clause in the conveyance to prevent the premises being used to sell intoxicating liquor in the future. It is now a bookmaker's office.

Probably the most important public house along the High street was the **Lower Swan Inn**, on the south side of the street at numbers 51-53. It was in existence by 1771 and had previously been known as the **White Swan** and the **Swan in Chain**. A badge of the Bohuns, Earls of Hereford, is a white swan with a chain

The Lower Swan at nos.
51-53 High Street in 2000.

The Swan in Chain still
survives high up
on the building

round its neck. Parry noted in 1845 that 'With the **Lower Swan Inn**, there was formerly connected a large assembly room, (now converted into offices by Mr. M. Sayce) with an orchestra, and every other appendage essential for promoting the pleasures of the "Mazy Dance"'. Mr Sayce was the agent for the Phoenix Fire-office. According to Parry: 'The **Lower Swan** was for many years the principal Inn in the town. In 1824 Henry Rogers was landlord. The emblems of Bacchus were eventually demolished by Mr. Sayce in 1842'.

Much of the building was then used for the Mechanics Institute, founded in 1841 as a result of the exertions and strenuous efforts of a remarkable traveller, George Egroegg Droffnor who visited the town and neighbourhood several times between 1838 and 1841. He let his beard grow long and generally slept in clean straw in a barn or cow house. He never drank spirits or beer and 'suffered the greatest privations, without ever assigning any motive for inflicting upon himself the severities he practised.' Even so he was apparently well respected

A small crowd outside the Wine Vaults at the beginning of the 20th century.
In the centre of the picture is the Market Hall
which replaced the King's Head in 1885

and in 1841 spoke to a large audience in the Swan Assembly Rooms on the physical character of man. The Mechanics Institute included a circulating library, reading room and museum. It took the *London Times* and *Sun* as well as local newspapers and leading journals. The building now includes a television shop, but the inn is still remembered with a swan in chain high up on the gable.

The **Wine Vaults** was in Upper Cross on the south side of High Street. It was called the **Spirit Vaults** in 1850 when John Welson was landlord. In the 1863 Kelly's Directory William Welson is recorded as a 'wine and spirit merchant' in High Street— presumably the same establishment. Skarratt noted on 23 February 1879 that 'Mrs. Jones

WILLIAM WELSON,
WHOLESALE AND FAMILY
Wine & Spirit Merchant.

Sole Consignee for Manders & Co.'s Dublin Stout.

Agent for Bass & Co.'s Burton and East India Pale Ales.

Wine Vaults.
37, HIGH STREET, KINGTON.

An 1876 advertisement for the Wine Vaults

113

*Customers standing outside
the Old Fogey in 1999*

(**Wine Vaults**) sister to Mr. W. Welson, who had been ill some weeks, died today'. Although this establishment was not mentioned in the 1891 directory, it has continued to serve the citizens of Kington and in 1993 had a name change to become the **Old Fogey**.

Also on the south side of High Street, in the region of Upper Cross, was the **Harp Inn**. The Harp is very much a Welsh symbol and it is not surprising to find it used in this area close to the border. About 1824 James Thomas was the landlord (although the inn was then described as being in Cross Street). It was also mentioned in 1845 with Samuel James as landlord. Rapid changes followed and by 1850 it was John Ross; 1858, Mr. Watkins; and 1863, Edward Williams. The saga continued with Skarratt recording on 7 January 1883 'Mr. Sam James of the **Harp**, was summoned from time into eternity'. The **Harp** was closed sometime in the late 1800s, but could well have become the short-lived **Millwright's Arms**, which was recorded in 1851 with James Sheldon as landlord, but never mentioned again. The sale details of the **Harp Inn** in 1883 describe it as having been a private house for several years, but observed that the licence had been retained. It was suggested that the building could be re-used as an inn because the **King's Head** opposite had closed. This was not successful and the last directory entry was in 1885. Facing the **King's**

Head, the **Harp** was next to the passage alongside the **Burton Hotel** in Mill Street, the Harp Yard being under the archway.

High Street also included the **Unicorn Hotel**, a listed building of grade II* category, apparently of 14th-century date, and formerly the Unicorn Guest House. There was also the **Virgin** in Upper Cross and the **Bull** in Lower Cross, both with unidentified sites.

The **King's Head** stood on the corner of the triangle formed by Church Street and Mill Street. Parry, writing in 1845 recorded that 'at the

The old Harp Inn still has its yard entry with a sign reminding passers by of old glories

bottom of Church Street on the west side of a site of land on which stood the old Butter-cross: for about half a century post horses and chaises were let at this house, but are not by the present proprietor, Mr John Roberts. The Turnpike Commissioners hold their meetings at this house; and also the Kington railway proprietors assemble here at stated periods to transact business. Travellers and graziers are accustomed to receive good entertainment and satisfactory treatment at this long-established inn'.

The London Mail Coach through Worcester first arrived, in the year 1821, at the **King's Head Inn**, kept by James Hayward, and afterwards by his widow, and continued running to this house for about three years; subsequently it ran to the **Oxford Arms Hotel**. Previous to the mail coach coming here, the old coach from the **Crown Inn**, in Leominster, came to the **King's Head** three days each

An 1876 advertisement for the King's Head, demolished some 9 years later

week. It was discontinued soon after the arrival of the mail coach service. To cater for all the traffic the inn needed considerable stabling. Indeed, the 1823 rent book records 'a granary over a four stall stable and coach house, a seven stall stable and open stable, a post house with eight stalls and stable and cowhouses, a barn and a wain house'.

In the mid-19th century there were several Friendly Societies in Kington. The Society of Gentlemen, Mechanics and Others was established in 1792 and met at the **King's Head**. The rules were quite strict. 'Any member who shall by fighting, wrestling, or any other wilful exercise, be disabled, so that he cannot follow his usual employment, shall not be entitled to any allowance for sickness or infirmity'. 'Political or religious discussions are not allowed'. Even more restrictive, and perhaps suggestive of considerable health problems 'no person shall be admitted under the age of eighteen, nor above thirty-five years'. The members were not entitled to any benefit until two years after their admittance. The Society, which had just over 100 members in 1845, held an Annual Meeting in August when they attended divine service and then dined together 'in the Society's-room at the **King's Head**'. The rules stated that strangers were not allowed into the room unless on business and that a box with 'proper keys' was kept in the room, but that no money was to be taken from the box unless in the presence of five members together with the landlord and landlady. There were other Friendly Societies that met at other public houses in the town but, 'owing to the neglect and mismanagement of the officers, to whose care the contributions were entrusted, these institutions, intended for the good of mankind, were discontinued about the year 1810 or 1811'. The King's Head Friendly Society was still holding its Annual Dinner in 1890 when it was described as nearly 100 years old. By that time it had moved to the **Burton Hotel**.

Skarratt again provides several revealing snippets of local life and inns in his *Diary*. Thus on 25 August 1854 he mentions the 'Club Feast Day. Weather as fine as could be wished for. 180 men and a larger number of women walked in procession through the streets, headed by the Kington band, having previously been to church. H. Miles Esq. took the Chair at the **King's Head**. After dinner at the **Oak** the fiddlers' talent was called for and they began to foot it up the middle and down the sides to their hearts content. The **King's Head** and the **Harp** also had their parties at night to enjoy a few hours recreation with the light fantastic toe'. A few days later on 6 September on a more ominous note 'Mr. Rogers of Michaelchurch died suddenly at the **King's Head Inn** and it was feared from the effect of poison.' Kelly's Directory for 1863 has Mrs. Elizabeth Roberts as licensee.

There is then a gap of several years before Skarratt returns with a view of the street on 21 December 1880. 'The dead poultry market for Xmas today was the largest I ever remember. Standings were placed side by side from Miss James, grocer, to the Burton Hall and round the front of the **King's Head**—there were also carts about the **Swan** and the **Oak**'.

By this time the days of the **King's Head** were numbered. Skarratt noted on 30 August 1881 that a 'meeting of ratepayers was called to take into consideration the advisability of building a Market Hall on the site of the **King's Head**'. By 1 December that year it had all been decided and Skarratt recorded the sale and the prices obtained:

'The **King's Head** property, divided into four lots, was put up for sale by auction:

MILNER'S
FAMILY AND COMMERCIAL HOTEL,
UPPER CROSS,
KINGTON.

J. M. MILNER,

WHOLESALE AND RETAIL

WINE AND SPIRIT
MERCHANT,
UPPER CROSS,
KINGTON.

J. M. M. announces to economists, that for the convenience of Private Consumers, he has *Imported, in Quarter Casks, direct from the Vineyards*, and has now lying in Bond, a choice selection of Fine Old PORTS and SHERRIES, of the first brands and of the most approved vintages.

An 1851 advertisement for Milner's Hotel, later the Burton

Lot 1: the Plock to Mr Bodenhem for £250

Lot 2: the barn, part of the Stable and half of the land at the back to Mr Walker for £145

Lot 3: the remaining part of the Stables and land at the back to Mr Purchase for £145

Lot 4: the two houses between the King's Head and Mr Smith's, with the Coach House and Stable at the back— not sold, £120 being the highest bidding'.

He added that 'The **King's Head** and Stable opposite **Burton House** was reserved for a new Market Hall. There was then a break for some 18 months, for Skarratt noted on 13 July 1883: 'The **King's Head Inn** being untenanted, the friendly society connected with it so many years transferred their patronage to the **Burton House**. His final note was on 21 January 1885: 'Commencement was made in the pulling down of the old **King's Head**'. Photographs taken before the demolition show a rather undistinguished looking building. The red brick market hall that replaced it was originally tower-less, the tower being added to commemorate Queen Victoria's Jubilee in 1897.

Mill Street

Just beyond the building that was once the **Harp Inn**—a short distance along the south side of Mill Street—is the **Burton Hotel**. For many years this was known as **Milner's Hotel** and before that it was called **Gorely's**. The changes of name reflected the various owners, Thomas Gorely being recorded in 1850 as running a 'Family, Commercial and Posting House', but by 1851 the landlord was John Milner.

The importance of **Milner's** is demonstrated by an entry in *Skarratt's Diary* for 1 November 1853. He recorded that 'A meeting was held at **Milner's Hotel** for the furtherance of the Scheme and adjourned to the following day, Wednesday, so as to obtain the attendance of the farmers of the neighbourhood. (Mr E. Vaughan Currier in the Chair)'. Fortunately he added the comment that 'the Scheme being a railway from Leominster to Kington, independent of any other line'. The railway from Leominster was eventually opened on 20 August 1857.

The change from Milner's to Burton House

Milner's Family and Commercial Hotel continued for some time, but Thomas Bowen took over in 1862 and it then became the **Burton House**. This change was the start of a series of disasters, well described by Skarratt in his *Diary*. On 28 December 1877 he recorded 'A very sudden death occurred to Mr Davies of **Burton House** (late of the **Swan**), between 10 and 11 p.m. He was sitting in one of the public bars of the hotel in the company of Messrs. Stanway, F. Blakeley, W. Ball (auctioneer) and Vaughan (Downfield), when all at once he put his hand to his throat and said "It's all over!" and "Oh, God!" and died. Blood at once issuing from his mouth through the rupture of a blood vessel occasioned by coughing. He had, for a long time past, been in a precarious state with a diseased heart'. On 6 May 1878 Skarratt noted 'The furniture and outdoor effects of the late Mr Davies of **Burton House**, were sold by Mr Ball—the Hotel to be let on a repairing lease for a term of years'.

The problems continued for this was followed on 26 September 1879 when 'Mr Griffiths of **Burton House**, (late of Ebbw Vale) died almost sudden from the effects of excessive drinking'. This was not all, for although the 1891 Kelly's Directory described Frank William Parameter as the landlord, he was not to last long there, for the *Hereford Times* for 24 October 1891 informed its readers that 'Frederick William Parmeter, late landlord of the **Burton House Hotel** suffered examination in bankruptcy at Leominster County Court'.

BURTON HOUSE HOTEL, KINGTON.

JOHN DAVIES,

WHOLESALE AND RETAIL

WINE AND SPIRIT MERCHANT,

AND ALE AND PORTER DEALER.

Burton and East India Pale Ales, and Watkins's Dublin Stout, supplied in Casks from 9 to 56 Gallons each.

A Market Ordinary every Tuesday.

Commercial Gentlemen and Visitors will find this Hotel spacious and very convenient.

The "Public Hall" may be hired for Balls, Concerts, Entertainments, &c. For terms, &c., apply to the Proprietor, Mr. JOHN DAVIES, BURTON HOUSE HOTEL, KINGTON.

An 1876 advertisement for the Burton Hotel

The Burton Hotel in the 1950s

The Burton Hotel sale in the 1950s.
Resident's Lounge (upper) : *Coffee Room* (lower)

122

The 1950s sale of the Burton Hotel

A series of landlords followed and in about 1950 the inn was offered for sale by Sunderlands:

By order of Mr & Mrs E Fishley, who are retiring:
The sale of this property offers an excellent opportunity of acquiring one of the Oldest-Established and Principal Hotels in the Town of Kington, charmingly situated in the Valley of the Arrow, and offers great possibilities for extensive Catering in a district which is rapidly becoming one of the most popular of Inland Resorts.

The Hotel being centrally situated in the Main Street has enjoyed great popularity for many years and it may well be said that 'he who knows Kington knows "The Burton House"'. It is within easy reach of the popular Kington Golf Club, and good fishing can be enjoyed in the River Arrow. The Property comes into the Market solely owing to the retirement of the Vendors and the Auctioneers have much pleasure in submitting for Sale this Valuable Property, the history of which dates back many years. Very few Hotels have enjoyed so great a popularity over so long a period as stands to the credit of 'The Burton House' situated on the main Hereford to Aberystwyth Road in a delightful Tourist and Agricultural Centre.

The Ratable Value at that time was £60. The ground floor included an entrance hall, comfortable bar, coffee room, dining room and billiards room, whilst the kitchen boasted an Aga cooker. On the first floor were four bedrooms, a bathroom, a dining room and residents' lounge and a spacious ballroom. The second floor had 12 bedrooms, six fitted with washbasins, and one bathroom. Also included was a productive kitchen garden including young fruit trees and a galvanised poultry house and run.

The number of bathrooms has doubtless increased since 1950, and the **Burton Hotel** continues to provide accommodation and meals, for many years being in the same ownership as the **Castle Pool Hotel** in Hereford.

Church Street

Church Street winds uphill on its way to the parish church and castle site, both towards the top of the hill. On the right side, ascending, was the **Ram Inn**. Thomas Hatton (1753-1799), a butcher of Kington, made his will on 16 October 1799, just before he died. In it he referred to having 'lately purchased of Mr John Harris the **Ram Inn** in Kington for the sum of 300 guineas'. He recorded that he had 'paid him the guinea in part' and required that if he had not paid the remainder then his executor should borrow on the premises in order to support his wife and children. His widow Mary Hatton (neé Lilwall) (1758-1839) married again to William Griffiths (1760-1832) who was then described as an ale-house keeper of Kington. William was still landlord at the **Ram Inn** in 1824. For almost 100 years the Griffiths family were associated with inns and ale houses in Kington, including the **Duke's Head** in 1856, the **Old Bridge Inn** in the 1860s, and the **Railway** in 1878.

The **Ram Inn** was mentioned in 1845 when P. Pugh combined the trades of landlord and plasterer. He may have been responsible for the name change to the **Prince of Wales**, but this wasn't a successful move and the inn had closed by 1850. It was at 7 and 8 Church Street, now the home of Freetime Picture Framers.

7/8 Church Street, once the Ram Inn

A little further up Church Street, the Square opens out on the right. Here is the War Memorial and opposite it is the **Swan Hotel**. Described as being of early 19th-century date, it probably replaced an earlier building, for the **Swan** was operating in 1794. In 1824 Charles Vaughan Jnr. was the landlord. This is the same as the **Upper Swan**, mentioned in 1845 with John Havard as innkeeper (he eventually moved to the **Royal Oak**, just across the road). During the 1850s William Green was landlord, but by 1863 the colour of the landlord had changed and Thomas White was running the **Upper Swan**. The 1891 directory listed Mrs. Jane Davies as landlady.

Skarratt recorded in his *Diary* for 29 November 1854 that 'An accident occurred at the **Upper Swan** which, if it had happened in the morning, might have been attended with great loss of life. Mr. Ball of the New House (the landlord) having had for some time workmen employed in excavating a cellar under the portion fronting the Square, had given further orders in the morning. Shortly after the Hucksters had left in the afternoon the whole side fell out with a crash covering the spot they occupy, and bringing with it bedsteads, and other portions

CHURCH ST., KINGTON.

SWAN AGRICULTURAL

AND

COMMERCIAL HOTEL.

JAMES S. MORRIS, Proprietor.

Commercial Gentlemen and Others will find good Accommodation.

EXCELLENT STABLING,
WITH LOOSE BOXES FOR HUNTERS.

HOME-BREWED AND BURTON ALES, DUBLIN STOUT, &c.

Wines and Spirits of the Best Quality.

An 1876 advertisement for the Swan

The Swan Hotel in 2000, with the war memorial in the Square

A typical 1960s advertisement

of furniture employed in the rooms'. Fortunately no one was hurt. At that time a huckster was a person who sold small goods or fruit in the street, not necessarily using aggressive behaviour. There were presumably stalls in the Square. This collapse may well have given rise to the 19th-century rebuilding of the frontage.

Several landlords in Kington failed to pay their bills and Skarratt noted, on 19 April 1877, that James Morris of the **Upper Swan**, 'having given a bill of sale to the company who supplied his house with drinkables, and not being able to meet his payments, has had to leave, and the other creditors are minus their accounts'.

There were two Friendly Societies meeting at the **Swan** (**Lower** and **Upper**). The Friendly and Loyal Society, founded in 1794, met at the **Upper Swan Inn**, whilst the 'Lower Swan Friendly Society of Gentlemen, Tradesmen and Others', also first registered in 1794, met at the **Swan Inn** in the High Street. Since then the **Upper Swan** has seen off all its feathered rivals and has reverted to being the simple **Swan**.

Across Church Street and a little further up the hill is the **Royal Oak Inn**, which announces on its signboard that it is the 'Last in England'. It is a 17th-century building that was extensively altered in the 18th century. Like many of the older buildings in Kington, it is mainly of stone, being two stories high with attic dormers. It has an attached barn to the east.

The Royal Oak in 1999

The **Royal Oak** is, of course, named after the tree in Boscobel Wood on the borders of Staffordshire that offered shelter to King Charles after his defeat at Worcester. Perhaps the inn should adorn its door with a branch of oak on 29 May each year in commemoration of the event—oak-apple day!

The **Royal Oak** was the home of the 'Provident, Loyal, and Friendly Society of Married and Single Women', which was established in 1792 at the same time as the Men's Society at the **King's Head**. The Friendly Societies paid out in cases of sickness and contributed towards funeral expenses. In 1845 this women's Society had about 95 members, and held their Annual Meeting on the Friday in Kington Feast Week (the same day as the men) 'at the **Oak Inn**, before the clock strikes ten in the forenoon, to walk to and from church in procession, according to seniority of admission— and afterwards dine together at the Inn'. The landlord of the inn was not to allow the 'matrons' to take money from the box, except for the payment of the sick and in the presence of five members. They were a little more lenient than the men, allowing entry from the age of 16, but 35 was still the upper age limit. Shortly afterwards the men of the Royal Oak followed their lead, forming the Royal Oak Friendly Society in 1794.

William Evans was landlord in 1824 and Philip James in 1845. Skarratt noted in his *Diary* for 20 January 1854: A farewell dinner took place at the **Oak** out of respect to Mr. James who is leaving and going to reside at the Llandegly Hotel. Mr. F. Parker took the Chair and the company did not break up until very late. 1 February 1854 was a general moving day for several Kington inns. Whilst Mr. James of the **Oak** moved to Llandegly, Mr. Havard of the **Swan** took on the **Oak**, and Mr. Bryan Jun. entered the **Swan**. This was a complex operation and the obvious happened. As Skarratt put it 'Through a misunderstanding between Mr. Havard and his landlord Mr. Tom Ball, (on account of a bill owed by the latter) Mr. Havard refused to give up possession or pay his rent. The result of which ended in Mr. Bell putting the Bailiffs in the house. Mr. Bryan was obliged to have a wagon load of furniture etc put at the **Castle** until matters were settled'. Sophia and John Havard continued at the **Oak** into the 1860s; the 1891 Kelly's Directory has Thomas Powell as landlord.

The last public house in England continues to thrive, but the **Castle Inn** a little lower down at 31 Church Street closed in 1992. It is an 18th-century building, described by Parry in 1845 as 'The **Castle** in Church Street, originally the **Crown** is kept by Mr. James; it is a lofty and spacious house, well suited for the accommodation of farmers of Radnorshire, and others who may be disposed to attend here on fair and market days. The establishment is well conducted by the proprietor, Mr. Thomas James'. The James family were prominent in the Kington hostelries in the middle of the 19th century with Philip James at the **Royal Oak** and Samuel James at the **Harp Inn**. There was also another Thomas James who was an innkeeper at an unspecified house

A 1876 advertisement for the Castle Hotel

in High Street. The **Castle** was still run by Thomas James in 1858, but he probably died soon afterwards for Mrs. Mary James is recorded as licensee in 1863. By 1891 the James family's tenure of the inn had ended, for the landlord was Thomas Pritchard. The inn was presumably named after Kington Castle—now a field, about 150 yards north of the church and close to Bach Brook, which is popularly known as Castle Hill. It contains an irregularly-shaped knoll that may have been shaped to include a small mound. The barony of Kington was probably created at the end of the 11th century when the castle and the outlying dependent knights' mottes and baileys would

The Castle Inn in 2000

have been built. The barony was never of any great importance. Repairs of a palisade at Kington Castle are mentioned in the Pipe Rolls for 1187, but it is likely that the castle was destroyed in August 1216 by King John and never rebuilt. Huntington Castle then became the centre of the barony.

A sign partly hidden behind plants by the door still proclaims this building as the Old White Lion

Next door to the **Castle** was the **White Lion Inn** at 32 Church Street. It was described by the Royal Commission in 1934 as being of 17th-century date, but much altered in the 18th. At the back of the yard there was a storehouse or barn, that was then weatherboarded.

Henry Hatton (1793-1843) was a butcher in Kington in 1818, but like several other members of the Hatton family he transferred to the licensed trade becoming landlord of the **White Lion Hotel** from about 1820. Henry erected a high brick wall at the inn for ball playing, but this was not the only 'sport' at the **White Lion** for there is a reference to cockfighting there in 1779. A copy of Parry's *History of Kington* has a manuscript note following the description of the wall. It reads 'The latter fives court wall was taken down 1877 and the material used in the erection of 6 cottages on the site of the Old Market Hall by the owner John Hatton'. Henry Hatton's sister, Elizabeth (1827-76) was born at the **White Lion** and eventually became a servant at the

Elephant and Castle in St. Peter's Street, Hereford. Members of the Hatton family in and around Kington tended to be butchers or innkeepers, but the family also occupied the position of Parish Clerk for well over a hundred years from 1728 to 1843.

In 1822 a charter was granted to establish a new Lodge of Oddfellows at the **White Lion Inn**, then still kept by Henry Hatton. About 10 persons became members in the first year but 'the fertile imagination of some ladies, who wished to keep their lords at home, suggested the possibility and the probability of the existence of many things in the lodges "which ought not to be", a breaking up of the lodge soon followed the circulation of the slanderous reports so extensively diffused by the fair sex of Kington'. The next attempt was at the **Lamb Inn** some 18 years later.

Henry was still at the **White Lion** in 1830 and after he died his widow, Jane, took over and stayed until about 1850. She was followed by Ann Vaughan in the 1850s and Ashton James in 1863. Was he a relative of Mrs. Mary James who was next door at the Castle? The 1891 Kelly's Directory lists William Luckett as landlord. At a later date the inn was renamed the **Eagle**, but it was not successful and finally closed in the 1960s.

In a 1992 article the **Glass and Bottle** was described as having been 'in Church Street on the corner where Holiday Hall now stands'.

The **Cock Inn** is another lost pub that was open as early as 1752. There is a mention of a Friendly Society called the Amicable Society of Married and Single Women that was first enrolled in 1797 and met at the **Cock Inn**. It was probably in Church Street. The name could derive from the inn hosting cock-fighting, or from the 'cock horse' that was needed to pull laden wagons up the adjoining hill. Dunkling and Wright provide a third alternative based on 'cock-ale'. This was apparently ale mixed with the jelly of a boiled cock and other ingredients. The authors do not make it obvious whether this drink was for pleasure or as a medicine!

At Floodgates, to the north-west of the town, John Morgan was a beer retailer in 1863. Was this the **Waterloo Inn** in Stanner Road which had its licence withdrawn in 1891? There are always a list of inns and taverns that have been totally forgotten except for name. In Kington they include the **Black Bull**, the **Black Boy's Head**, the **Three Boys Head**, **Three Horseshoes**, **Spread Eagle**, and **Pied Bull**, all of which applied for an annual licence on 30 September 1752. In addition there was the **Engine**, for which there is a deed in the Herefordshire Record Office dated 1785.

CHAPTER EIGHT

Hereford to Weobley

There are several ways to get from Hereford to Weobley, none of them particularly direct and nothing that can be classified as a main road. Following the A480 Kington road from Hereford, a signpost just a mile past the Credenhill turn beckons the driver to turn right to Brinsop and Weobley. This is a quiet, winding road that arrives in the new part of the village, passing the castle grounds on the left before arriving at the end of the High Street. Perhaps the most common way is to continue further along the A480 towards Kington and, in the middle of Norton Canon parish take the B4320 turning to the right. This road curves to the north-east, leaving the heights of Yazor Wood on the right, before dropping past the grounds that once belonged to Garnstone House and so enters Weobley village from the south-west.

For the benefit of this chapter a third route has been chosen. The main A438 road from Hereford to Hay and Brecon is left behind at the White Cross, and the Knighton road, the A4110 leading in a north-north-westerly direction is taken. This goes through Canon Pyon and Bush Bank heading towards Eardisland and Kingsland. Well before reaching these pretty villages on the rivers Arrow and Lugg (Chapters 13 and 14), the road crosses the A4112, the main thoroughfare from Leominster to Eardisley and thence along the A438 to Hay. The A4112, leads south-westwards to Dilwyn and then to the outskirts of Weobley, both just to the south of the main road. The approach road passes the rather grim building on the left that was once the Weobley Union Workhouse at Whitehill, to approach the village by the appropriately named Back Lane. Turnings to the left lead into Broad Street. This is a route full of interest, for the A4110 follows the line of the Roman Watling Street as it goes northward from the Roman Town at Kenchester (*Magnis*) to the various Roman forts in the Leintwardine area.

The earliest road book, called the *Antonine Itinerary*, dates back to the Roman period. It records the distance from Abergavenny to Kenchester correctly as 22 miles, but the distance from Kenchester to Leintwardine is rated rather highly at 24 miles rather than the correct 21. The Roman traveller equipped with this *Itinerary* would have been following the south-north road up the Welsh border, slightly west of the modern equivalent—the A49.

This Roman route starts at the White Cross junction towards the western edge of Hereford. The road crosses the Yazor Brook, that once fed the defensive ditch that ran around Hereford City, before climbing gently up the hill towards its junction with Roman Road. This is the road leading westwards towards Kenchester and forms the northern boundary of the Liberty of Hereford. Well placed on the junction, where the Tillington Road provides one of the other possible routes towards Weobley, the main road continues straight ahead, past the **Three Elms Inn**. Although officially in Hereford, the inn is actually in the Township of Huntington, a chapelry within the city boundary. It was originally called the **Three Crosses** possibly referring to the three roads that crossed in this immediate area—the Roman Road; the Hereford to Knighton Road; and the Tillington road, which until

The Three Elms Inn in 1994

recently crossed the Knighton road to run directly into Grandstand Road on its way to Hereford. However, there is an alternative derivation, for the Berkeleys who held the nearby parish of Tillington had arms that included a red shield with three gold crosses, and the Carpenters, who followed them, had three gold crosses on a blue chevron. In 1891, Richard William Mailes was licensee of the **Three Elms**. This was presumably the licensed premises at Huntington, then called the **Three Elms Pool House**, that was offered for sale by auction in October 1920.

Diversions from the main road make the whole journey much more interesting and the first is off to the left to Burghill and Tillington. Indeed the so-called Weobley road from the Three Elms leads up past the old St. Mary's Hospital (described in the 1891 County Directory as the County and City Lunatic Asylum, but following its closure in the mid-1990s, now a housing estate) into Burghill village. This is a village that is now without a pub, but this was not always the case. The records can sometimes be a little ambiguous, for Burghill is a large parish that includes the township of Tillington, a mile-and-a-half to the north-west, as well as the hamlet of Portway on the main A4110 road to the east.

The only pub entered in the 1858 directory for Burghill is the **Bell Inn** at Tillington. However, there were several cider retailers including John Wood at Burghill, James Morris at Portway, and Thomas Mellin at Tillington. They are almost certainly operating from the same buildings that are described as inns in later directories.

The 1891 directory describes the **Tow Tree Inn** as being in Burghill village with Mrs. Mary Ann Daw as licensee. But Tillington, which it described as a considerable township had no less that three public houses. There was the well-named **Live & Let Live Inn**, which was run by William Langford who was also a mason and shop-keeper. Apparently this particular inn name originated at Tillington, for there is a story about it. Many years ago, a man named Patrick kept the village shop, and another named Smith kept the **Bell Inn**. The latter decided to add to his income by selling household requirements, much to the annoyance of Patrick, who promptly asked the magistrates to grant him a licence, and on obtaining it (they were relatively easy to procure in those days) named his house **Live and Let Live**. During the 19th century the idea 'caught on', with inn-keepers in other towns, who considered that rivals had taken an unfair advantage of them using the name, to the extent that at one time there were at least 23 inns called Live and Let Live.

Also long gone is the **Bird-in-Hand Public House**, with Thomas Matthews as mine host. One author commented that in 1926 there were 174 public houses with this name in England! Presumably it follows the old proverb 'A Bird in the Hand is worth Two in the Bush', especially if there was a nearby house called the Bush! The Russian version of the proverb is also worth quoting: 'Don't promise the crane in the sky, give the tit in your hand'. Traditionally the sign for this inn, which quite often dates back to the 17th century, consists of a mailed fist on which a falcon was perched.

Tillington — The Bell Inn in 2000

Finally, and still surviving, after winning all the battles in Tillington, is the **Bell Inn**, with George Rampling as landlord in 1891and George Matthews (possibly a relative of Thomas) in 1937. There are many inns called after a single Bell, or in some cases multiples up to Twelve Bells (in Cirencester)—it is an easy and simple shape that must have always appealed to signmakers. Most signs depict church bells, or occasionally hand bells.

Back to the main road at Portway, and it was here until recently that Burghill parish had yet another inn. This was the **Royal Oak**, shown on earlier Ordnance Survey maps as a simple beer house. In

*The Royal Oak at Portway is now a
private house, but the name still
survives on the adjoining bus stop*

1891 Charles Walters was the land-lord. It was probably the house of John Tuck, described in 1937 as a simple beer retailer. It has recently closed, but the bus stop still reminds the weary traveller of a once popular inn.

From Portway the road continues over a slight rise until it drops into the long straight through Canon Pyon, a village some 7 miles north-west from Hereford. The only suggestion for the source of the word 'pyon' is 'island of the gnats'! Words similar to this are characteristically used of slight raised areas in marshy land. Canon Pyon belonged to the canons of Hereford cathedral and was worth the not inconsiderable sum of £12 10s. at the time of the Domesday survey. Before the Norman Conquest King's Pyon belonged to King Edward the Confessor, but afterwards William the Conquerer gave it to Walter de Lacy.

The first inn is the **Plough**, described in 1891 as being at the New End with John Steele as both landlord and agricultural implement

The Plough at Canon Pyon

maker. At one time this must have been a pub with a canny old land-lord, for at the end of September 1920 David Evans, then aged 83, was fined £7 10s. with £2 10s. costs at Weobley Police Court for selling whisky above the scheduled price!

A little further up the road and on the opposite side is the **Nag's Head**, also described as being at New End in 1891. In 1858 James Porter was landlord; in 1891 it was Henry Francis Patrick who was also a grocer. Was he related to the Patrick at the **Live and Let Live** at Tillington? The building is of 17th-century date and was originally L-shaped with wings to the east and north. A modern building has since been added to the angle.

Old Taylor's ghost was associated with the **Nag's Head**. The story of his eventual 'laying' was told by 'Nonagenarian' in the *Hereford Times* well over a hundred years ago. He wrote 'There was old Taylor's ghost, that used to walk about at the White Cross. He couldn't rest because he had moved a landmark [whether this was the White Cross or some other landmark is uncertain]. He used to ride

The Nag's Head, Canon Pyon in 2000

The back of a 'bus— modern day advertising

upon a little pony, and sometimes he would be seen sitting on a stile. ... at last his ghost was laid ... One stormy night a fellow whose name I have forgotten, walked into the bar of the **Nag's Head**, and said he had seen old Taylor, and had promised to meet him in the Morning Pits that night at twelve. Of course nobody believed him, and as the night wore on the others jeered him, and said "I would not go on such a night as this." He said he would not; but as the hour drew near he was obliged to go. Something forced him to run, so that he reached the Morning Pits as the clock struck twelve. There the old man was waiting. "Follow me," said he; the other followed him into some strange place, which they seemed to reach in a very short time. In the place were two immense stones. "Take up these stones," said Taylor. "I can't," said Denis (he was nick-named "Denis the Liar"). "You can," said Taylor, "try." He tried, and tilted them easily. "Now come with me," said Taylor, "and place them where I shall show you." He carried them, and put them down with ease. "Now," said the other, "I caution you never to tell anybody what you see here this night." He promised. "And now," said he, "lie down on your face, and as you value your life, don't attempt to look either way, until you hear music, and then get away as fast as you can." He lay a long time without hearing what he earnestly desired, but at last the welcome sound was heard ... He was a very different man after that, though he soon died from the effects of his fright.'

The Record Office hold deeds for the **Crown** at Canon Pyon, for the period 1755-1872, but this inn is not mentioned in the directories for 1858 and 1891. However, it was apparently still working for there is a photograph of the Thompson family standing outside apparently taken in 1904.

There may have been a **New Inn** at Canon Pyon in the early years of the 19th century for a travelling chimney sweep called William Barnet or Bennet died in a barn at the **New Inn** and was buried in Canon Pyon churchyard on 14 January 1823. However, it is not mentioned in the 1858 or later directories.

King's Pyon is a small village about half-a-mile to the west of the main road, some 2 miles north-west of Canon Pyon. However, the parish covers a larger area and in 1881 the population was 439, somewhat less than Canon Pyon which had 701 inhabitants. There doesn't appear to have been a pub in the village, the local inn being at Bush Bank, on the main road. In 1891 this was a simple beer house run by James Walton. It is shown on earlier maps as the **Corners Inn**, but has since been known as **Bush Bank**, or now simply the **Bush Inn**. This is a name of great antiquity, for a bunch of evergreens hanging over the door was used by the Romans to indicate a wine shop. Indeed, the same sign is still used in parts of Europe to signify that wine is produced on the premises. Ale houses used to have a pole outside that was decorated with evergreens such as ivy. One wonders how significant it is that here there is an inn on the side of a Roman road with a name that would have been appreciated some 1,900 years ago!

The Thompson family outside the Crown Inn at Canon Pyon about 1904

The Crown Inn has completely changed its role

The Bush Inn at Bush Bank, earlier The Corners

The Red Lion, later the Spitfire,
and now part of Sheppards

In 1946 there appeared to have been tension between a crowd of locals and the licensee of the **Corners Inn**, Mr. F. Pursey. He refused to sell Denis Evans and Geoffrey Amos any cigarettes, so, as part of a gang of five, they threw down several gates on land that he owned. They said they only did it 'for a lark', but the magistrates felt that the activity was dangerous and 'must be stamped out'. They were each fined £4 plus costs.

The contretemps does not seem to have put Mr. Pursey off running his pub, for he was granted a full licence (to enable him to sell spirits) in February 1951, an application that had been supported by a petition which indicated that the nearest inn with a full licence was two-and-a-half miles away. He had to pay £375 for the monopoly value. By this time Mr. Pursey had held the licence for 42 years and at the same time he submitted plans for some structural alterations to the property.

It is just past the **Bush** that a diversion has to be made, for a once well-known pub with a chequered history is off to the right in a rather remote hamlet called Upper Hill. Here was the **Red Lion**, officially in Hope-under-Dinmore parish. In the 1858 directory John Merrick was landlord, whilst in the 1891 directory it is listed as being a public house and shop run by Edward Harper. This was a fully licensed house that continued well into the 1950s but was eventually taken over by Sheppards. It is the older building to the right of the main store. It was closed finally on 21 February 1975 according to a notice still just inside the door and the pub sign, with its final name, **The Spitfire,** is still in the building.

A tenancy agreement with the Cheltenham and Hereford Brewery dated May 1950 is of considerable interest. Many of the conditions may well seem harsh by modern day standards:

'The tenant agrees ... in particular to whitewash the walls of the cellars, urinals, and closets once in every year and to replace all glass in the windows which shall be

The Spitfire sign is still on display inside Sheppards

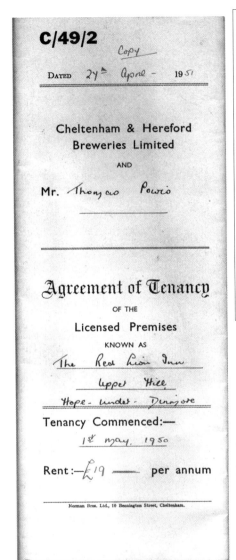

C/49/2

Copy

DATED 24ᵗʰ *April* - 19 51

Cheltenham & Hereford
Breweries Limited

AND

Mr. *Thomas Powis*

Agreement of Tenancy

OF THE

Licensed Premises

KNOWN AS

The Red Lion Inn

Upper Hill

Hope - under - Dinmore

Tenancy Commenced:—

1st May, 1950

Rent:—£19 —— per annum

Norman Bros. Ltd., 10 Bennington Street, Cheltenham.

CHELTENHAM & HEREFORD BREWERIES, LTD.

TELEPHONE:
HEREFORD 2426

TRADE MARK

TELEGRAMS:
MALT HEREFORD

BEWELL STREET
HEREFORD

Our Ref JRT/HLB.

Your Ref

11th. May, 1951.

Dear Sir,

The Red Lion Inn, Upper Hill,
Herefordshire.

We enclose herewith a copy of your
Tenancy Agreement C/49/2 relating to the
above House, for your retention.

Yours faithfully,
CHELTENHAM & HEREFORD BREWERIES, LTD.

Manager.

Mr. Thomas Powis,
Red Lion Inn,
Upper Hill,
Hope-under-Dinmore,
Herefordshire.

*A tenancy agreement for the
Red Lion from the Cheltenham
and Hereford Brewery in Bewell
Street, Hereford,
the site now occupied by
Tesco's supermarket*

broken ...', 'to cultivate and manage the garden (if any) in a good proper and husband-like manner and to keep the ground clean and free from weeds and to preserve all fruit and other trees and shrubs'.

The *Terms of Trading* included 'the Tenant agrees to purchase of and from the Landlords or their nominee or nominees, and from no other person firm or company, all the Beer, Ale, Porter and all other Malt Liquors and all Cider, Perry, Wines, Spirits, Liqueurs, and alcoholic cordials, alcoholic British Wines, and other sweets (all of which are herein referred to as "liquor") sold or consumed on the premises, or which shall be brought therein to be sold or consumed, or which shall be sold elsewhere by the Tenant under any occasional licence

144

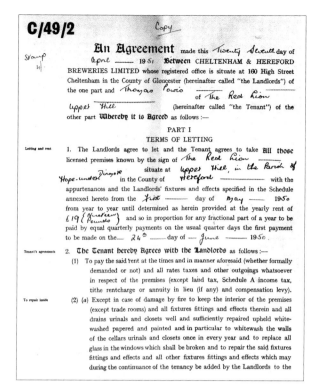

The first page of the agreement

granted to him as licensee of the premises, and to pay and settle up with the Landlords or their nominee or nominees for the same on demand at the prices ... from time to time charged by the Landlords to their Tenants in the same district ...'

And in the *Conduct of Business* 'Not to permit any money, slate, share out, or similar club or society to be established or carried on ... without the previous written consent of the Landlord' and 'not to be engaged or interested in any other trade or business than that of the Licensee of the premises without first obtaining the written consent of the Landlord thereto'.

Compliance with the Licensing Law was also included. 'The tenant agrees ... to keep the premises and all drains, privies, and urinals therein or attached thereto together with sinks, draining boards, glasses, and other utensils including beer engines and pipes, scrupulously clean and in good order and condition' and 'To supply whenever reasonably required by the public suitable refreshment other than intoxicating liquor at a reasonable price and keep the premises open for the sale of food and non-alcoholic beverages at all reasonable times (if any) at which there may in the opinion of the Landlords be a sufficient demand therefore' and 'at all times to reside on the premises'.

The licensee also had to agree that he would 'At all times keep the premises open for the sale of liquor during such hours as shall be allowed by law, and conduct the house in such orderly manner that the necessary Justices' licence may not be refused to be renewed or the removal or transfer thereof imperilled'.

One of the standard tenant's conditions caused some hilarity. It was 'to maintain the gas, electricity and sanitary and water services including all tanks stoves and boilers ...'—this for a building that was then still lit by paraffin lamps!

The road northwards from the **Bush Inn** starts off straight and after half-a-mile or so reaches Knapton Green where there is a side turning to Birley village. Here, according to the 1858 directory, was the **Three Horseshoes** with William Bengree as mine host. It probably closed before the end of the century for there is no mention of it in the 1891 directory.

The road continues to run straight and true in a northerly direction until just after a minor cross-roads, where a narrow back road from Leominster goes first through Ivington and then crosses the main road, as though it is of no significance, to continue westwards towards Dilwyn. Just past this cross-roads there is a rather awkward bend where the road crosses Tippet's Brook, and here the Pembridge road bears off to the left leaving the main road to continue directly northwards towards Kingsland, Mortimer's Cross and Wigmore. It is here

The Duke's Head at Dilwyn, now totally retired

146

that the route that is being followed in this chapter leaves the Roman road, for Dilwyn is the next port of call.

At one time Dilwyn was on the main A4112 Leominster to Eardisley and South Wales road, but it had a by-pass in the 1970s and now the general feeling of the village may well reflect its possible origin, for the name in old English could mean 'secret place'. The castle site is in the southern part of the village. It is almost circular, about 45 yards in diameter, and surrounded by a mostly wet ditch.

In 1881 there were 1,046 people living in the parish—ample to support more than the one public house remaining and there is indeed a second one in the older records. This is the rather elusive inn called the **Duke's Head**. At one time it was in the southern end of the village opposite the west end of the front railings of the Great House. A number of villagers remember the building when it was a shop with a peculiarly high counter. This may have been because the villagers were then children and so it seemed to be high, or it may have been the original bar counter. The tithe assessment calls it the **Old Duke's Head Inn.**

Previously the **Duke's Head** occupied a different building, now demolished. This was on what is now the Village Green opposite what were presumably the stables at the **Crown**. In the tithe list it is shown as 'Cross House'. However a collection of deeds in the Herefordshire Record Office includes a mention of **The Cross House**, a malthouse and public house, later known also as **The Duke's Head**. It was part of the partitioned estate of Richard Bradford of Dilwyn which was sold to Richard Dayas, also of Dilwyn, in 1794. In the bundle there is a sale poster for the **Cross House** or **Duke's Head** dated some time towards the end of the 19th century. It is not mentioned in the 1858 or 1891 directories.

A 1931 advertisement for the Crown, then rather grandly called a Hotel

The Crown Inn is of 17th-century date, but has been entirely re-fronted and otherwise much altered. The Royal Commission on Historic Buildings, visiting in 1934, noted that inside the building there was some 17th century panelling, including three enriched and arcaded panels, and one panel inscribed T.C., I.C. It is said to have come from the church during the 1867 restoration. In 1858 James Lord was landlord; he was also the village butcher. In 1891 Charles Ingram was mine host. The inn has a traditional two bar layout with the saloon on the left and the public on the right

The Crown Inn at Dilwyn

Weobley

A road book for 1801 notes that Weobley had 160 houses with 608 inhabitants (294 men and 314 women). It goes on to comment:

> Many of the houses are well built modern structures; the town having suffered greatly by fire some few years back. The town is governed by two constables; it returns two members to parliament, who are chosen by the inhabitants of houses of £20 per annum rent and upwards, paying scot and lot, and resident therein 40 days before the election.

The 1891 Kelly's Directory provides an excellent indication of the changes that took place during almost a century:

Weobley is an ancient town, borough and parish and head of a union and petty sessional division, three-and-a-half miles north from Moorhampton station on the Hereford, Hay and Brecon railway. Weobley, previous to the passing of the Reform Act of 1832, returned two members to Parliament. 1881 pop 882 which included 95 officers and inmates of the workhouse.

Another century later, and the Weobley Members of Parliament are long since forgotten. The Weobley Union is no more and the Workhouse has been closed for many years, although the building still stands. There is no longer any petty sessional division or even a police station and the railway has been closed for some 40 years. However, Weobley continues to exercise its charm as one of the prettiest black-and-white villages in the county with many ancient buildings that were never re-built or even re-fronted, for their sole purpose was to provide one of the magic votes that could return the two Members of Parliament from what was truly a 'rotten borough'.

'Rotten', it might have been in parliamentary terms, but this did not apply to its public houses, and three survive in one form or another to the present day—the **Unicorn**, the **Salutation** and the **Red Lion**. However, in 1936, Captain R.T. Hinches, Chairman of the Bench of Magistrates was moved to say that the sanitary conditions in the pubs in the Weobley Division were not up to standard. This did not apply specifically to Weobley town, but to the whole Division.

Timmins, in his *Nooks and Corners of Herefordshire,* published in 1892, has an additional comment:

The erstwhile **Bear Hotel**, from the balcony of which the worthy candidates were wont to address the electors, now shows a forlorn and sadly degenerate front to the street; its many chambers silent and deserted, and the great doors ever closed.

Some years earlier, Townsend, in his 1863 *History of Leominster,* discussed the mid-17th century Civil War and noted that Charles I spent the night of Friday 5 September 1645 at the **Unicorn** at Weobley. He goes on to explain:

> The **Unicorn Inn** at Weobley, had its name changed to the **Crowne**, in honour of Charles I's visit, and is now a private house, inhabited by Mr Palmer, Surgeon of that place. The king would, no doubt, be reminded on this occasion of the old proverb, once common in these parts: "Leominster Bread and Weobley Ale".

The Throne, once the Crowne and then the Unicorn

It is evident that the **Unicorn** was a well-established inn in the 17th century, but this is not the present day **Unicorn**. The older **Unicorn** still survives across the road, on the corner of High Street and Hereford Road. For many years it has been called the Throne, in commemoration of the Royal visit. It was built in the late 16th century on an L-shaped plan with a projecting upper storey.

According to the present inn sign, the **Unicorn** was established in 1887, but this does not agree either with Townsend or with the 1858 directory, which lists Mary Ann Lloyd as landlady of **Ye Olde Unicorn**. In 1891 William Jones was landlord and in his spare time he manufactured nails, presumably in the barn at the rear.

The Unicorn in the 1870s

The **Unicorn** was a legendary animal that was represented by medieval writers as having the legs of a buck, the tail of a lion, the head and body of a horse, and a single long pointed horn, white at the base, black in the middle and red at the tip, projecting from the middle of its forehead.

> The unicorn has but one horn in the middle of its forehead.
> It is the only animal that ventures to attack the elephant, and so sharp is the nail of its foot, that with one blow it can rip the belly of the beast. Hunters can catch the unicorn only by placing a young virgin in his haunts. No sooner does he see the damsel, than he runs towards her, and lies down at her feet, and so suffers himself to be captured by the hunters. The unicorn represents Jesus Christ, who took on Him our nature in the virgin's womb, was betrayed by the Jews and delivered into the hands of Pontius Pilate. Its one horn signifies the Gospel of Truth.
>
> *Le Bestiaire Divin de Guillaume,*
> *Clerc de Normandie* (13th century)

The unicorn is one of the supports for the Royal Arms, the other supporter being the Lion, and is so shown on the Weobley inn sign. There are many other references to this mythical animal in literature, perhaps the best known and loved being:

151

A.A. Appointed

Phone 230

Ye Olde Unicorn Hotel
WEOBLEY, HEREFORDSHIRE

*The Unicorn in a 1950 guide
without dormer windows*
(above)

*A 1950s advertisement with a full
range of dormer windows inserted*
(right)

A.A.　　　　Established 1887　　　　R.A.C.

BOARD RESIDENCE　　LUNCHEONS　　TEAS
PARTIES CATERED FOR

TERMS & BROCHURES ON REQUEST

Ye Olde Unicorn Hotel
Weobley, Hereford

FULLY LICENSED FREE HOUSE

'Phone Weobley 230　　　　　　　Proprietor: J. W. Jones

The Unicorn in the year 2000

The Unicorn Inn sign

"'Well, now that we have met," said the Unicorn, "if you'll believe in me I'll believe in you. Is that a bargain?'"

(Lewis Carroll, *Through the Looking Glass and what Alice found there*)

The **Unicorn** is at the southern end of the village, a few yards to the east of the main street. It is a 17th–century timber–framed building standing two storeys high. It was substantially improved, in the 1950s, when a series of dormer windows were inserted, making best use of what was previously attic space. The building has a jettied front and was probably built as a house, being converted later to a hostelry. There is a long wing on the north side which was used as a barn in the early 1930s, but now operates as a fish and chip shop.

Timmins' sketch of the Salutation in 1891

Inside the hostelry much timber-framing and ceiling-beams are exposed and the original staircase has shaped slat–balusters, moulded strings and newels.

In December 1951, John James, who had run the **Unicorn** for 40 years, died in Hereford Hospital. His parents had been the proprietors of **Ye Olde Unicorn Inn** in the High Street before him.

A little way down the High Street from the **Unicorn**, but on the

153

opposite side is **Ye Olde Salutation Inn,** quite a mouthful and, not surprisingly, often shortened to the **Sal.** It comprises a gable-fronted building facing down Weobley's main street with, on the right, a 16th-century timber-framed section, obviously once a house in its own right. The many changes to the buildings are well shown by a comparison of Timmins' 1891 sketch with a recent photograph. In 1858 it was listed in the directory with William Brown, who was both builder and innkeeper, whilst in 1891 Joseph Williams was licensee.

The Salutation in 2000

The inn sign is now rather non-controversial, with a young man on his knees in front of a fair damsel, but earlier religious signs for inns with this name referred to the Annunciation—the greeting and proclamation of the Archangel Gabriel to the Virgin Mary. This was a sign that was strongly opposed by the Puritans and it was then that many were changed to less contentious subjects. Of course, the name can also refer to a variety of salutes or greetings, usually where the intention is to put oneself in the power of the person saluted, such as touching one's cap, shaking hands, presenting arms, lowering of sword points, lowering the flag, and gun salutes. One could also add the kiss and even rubbing noses, although these have not as yet been seen on an inn sign!

In Bell Square, at the far end of Broad Street, the main street of Weobley, stands the **Red Lion Hotel**, a grade 2* listed building with parts dating back some 600 years. The east cross wing of the house is of 14th-century date with exposed timber-framing consisting of large square panels. The upper storey of this block originally projected on the east side and at the south, but it has been underbuilt at the southern end. On the east side it rests on curved and moulded brackets springing from shafts attached to the main posts. At the north end there is an original doorway, now blocked, with moulded jambs and an ogee head. In the upper storey are two original windows, now also blocked, each of three trefoiled ogee lights with cusped spandrels; the mullions have been removed. The upper storey of the south end of the wing retains two curved braces forming an arch in the framing. The main block has

The Red Lion Hotel

Telephone : 220   **WEOBLEY**

A historical 13th century Inn, famous these days for its Grills and Duck Suppers

The Red Lion Hotel in the 1950s

The Red Lion from Church Road

been much altered and is mainly of 17th- and 18th-century date. It has been suggested that the arched opening (now blocked) and the adjoining narrow doorway may represent an earlier shop or workshop, possibly of a craft nature, but this seems unlikely.

North of the main building there is an outbuilding which is of medieval date and includes two massive crucks in the north and south walls; the framing of the side walls is in large squares. In 1934 the outhouse was described as being partly demolished; fortunately this building, with its two heavy crucks, was repaired and still survives.

On 1 January 1794, the *Hereford Journal* recorded an auction sale at the house of John Watkins, called the **Red-Lion Inn**, in the Borough of Weobley. In the 1858 directory, the industrious landlord, William Langslow, was a maltster and farmer as well as an innkeeper. The inn was of considerable importance in Weobley by the end of the 19th century when it was the **Red Lion Hotel & Posting House.** Many other important events, such as the first local annual rabbit coursing meeting, took place here. This occurred on Thursday 4 January 1890 and was advertised as 'Rabbits free, particulars from the **Red Lion Hotel**, Weobley'.

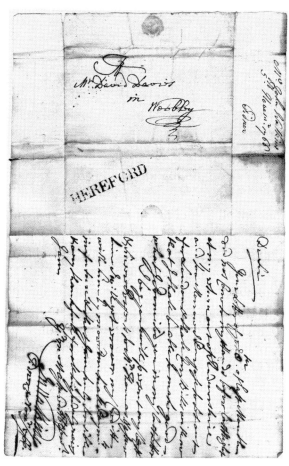

A letter sent from Hereford to Weobley on 5 November 1766 would have gone to the Red Lion as Posting House

A much more terrifying event took place a few years earlier in September 1885. A number of hop-pickers based at Homme Farm, between Dilwyn and Weobley, had walked over to Weobley to buy bread and meat. They then went to the tap-room of the **Red Lion**, where there was 'much merriment and laughter'. A little later in the evening two local men decided to join the party of hop-pickers—John Hill, known as 'Sailor Jack' and John Williams who was called 'Irish Jack'. Later that night, one of the hop-pickers, a young girl called Ann Dickson, was battered to death in a nearby field. John Hill and John

John Hill
(left)
and
John Williams
(right)

157

Williams each tried to blame the other, but the law was fully capable of dealing with this conundrum, and both were condemned to death. The public executioner, James Berry, blamed strong drink for the offence: "'In not one single instance—leaving out the case of juveniles whom I hanged—did I send to eternity a person who was a teetotaller'". He described Hill as being "'undoubtedly the worst of the two. He was an evil fellow, with a hang-dog look and bulging brow'". Hill and Williams were both hanged in Hereford Gaol on 23 November 1885.

It was in 1969 that the **Red Lion** was described as having been 'carefully restored and redecorated' by Bulmers of Hereford, the then owners. The City Guide for that year includes the prices for various meals (converted to decimal currency for convenience):

Gammon steak (Herefordshire Style)	£ 0.82
Roast duckling (façon de chef)	£ 0.98
Escalope of veal—Marsala	£ 0.98

with a choice of 100 wines from £ 0.80 to £ 5.00

The **Red Lion** is now a private hotel and is no longer open to all.

The 1891 directory mentions a Charles Morris, who was a beer retailer at Weobley Common, but there is no further reference to this inn.

At Ledgemoor, a small village just over a mile south-east of Weobley, is the **Marshpools Country Inn**. It has bars and real ales and is a rare example of a recently-formed inn in rural north-west Herefordshire.

CHAPTER NINE

Hereford to Leominster

Most people take the simplest road from Hereford to Leominster—the improved and somewhat re-routed A49 trunk road—but a quieter and certainly more attractive road is slightly further to the east through Sutton St. Nicholas, slightly to the right of Marden then northwards to Bodenham where the A412 curves back to join the A49 at Hope-under-Dinmore.

The A49 Trunk Road

The A49 is the main Welsh border road, the modern equivalent of the Roman Watling Street which, slightly further to the west, went from Caerleon to Chester. As such, it had to have had a good collection of public houses at one time to deal with the weary traveller, but now there is only one left directly on the main road—**The Old Comrade,** otherwise known as the **Pig in a Poke,** at Wellington Marsh—although there are several hidden away down side roads.

From Hereford the A49 goes directly northwards up Holmer Road with the racecourse on the left and an industrial and retail estate on the right. The northern limits of the city are where Holmer Road meets the Roman Road at a roundabout, and here on the left is the **Starting Gate,** just within the city boundary. Its licence dates from 1953 and the building now has a restaurant and an extensive hotel wing.

Just beyond the Roman Road junction is Holmer church with its detached tower and almost opposite it is Coldwells Road, a minor road leading to Munstone and Shelwick. Between these two villages on the right-hand side of the road is the **Rose Gardens Inn,** a quiet country pub less than 2 miles from the centre of Hereford. However, it has not always been quiet, for the *Hereford Times* for 9 October 1886 reported

The Rose Gardens in 2000

that Emily Johnson and Mary Plunkett, who were hop pickers from Birmingham, were accused of breaking into the **Rose Gardens Inn**. The inn is not mentioned in the 1858 directory, but in 1891 Edward Jones was the landlord. By 1937 Mrs. Harriett Florence Hughes was the landlady.

The 1858 directory mentions a **New Inn** at Holmer, but there is no further record. However, Holmer parish is quite large and includes a portion within the city of Hereford as well as that outside. It continues to the east to the Worcester road where the parish includes the **Swan Inn**, well within the city boundary.

From Holmer it is a long haul up the A49 before the next inn is reached. The turnings off to the right to Pipe and Lyde, and Moreton-on-Lugg do not offer any hospitality and, indeed the latter is a relatively new settlement for the population of the entire parish in 1888 was only 83. Even so, it boasted a station on the Hereford to

160

Leominster line, a station that never grew to the stage of having a refreshment room. Indeed, the first station office when the line opened in 1853 was in an oak tree called 'Eve'. It lost its top in a violent storm in 1839, the same storm that blew down its neighbour 'Adam'. Eve was originally used by one of the navvies as his house, and after the line opened it formed the residence and office of the Station Master! It was complete with a brick fireplace and chimney and had a thatched roof! When the station was built it became a lamp

'Eve'—the stationmaster's office at Moreton

room until 1869 when it was converted into a stable for a donkey. It was no small tree measuring 25 feet 6 inches in circumference. A party of 13 are said to have had tea within it and it was used for the occasional picnic—had it survived it could have made an unique inn!

Just beyond the turn for Moreton is the large fenced area of the now disused Ministry of Defence storage depot. It fills much of the space between the A49 and the railway and continues for almost a mile to the north, encircling an inn and a few houses on the eastern side of the main road that make up part of Wellington Marsh. This is a small hamlet that straddles the main road and has scarcely two dozen houses, but it must have been a home from home for weary travellers during the 19th century. Indeed, it is difficult to know where to start for the place was full of inns!

With rumours that most of the houses in the Marsh were inns, the Tithe Map, produced for Wellington in 1842, has been examined in detail. This shows all the different fields and properties and includes an apportionment or inventory that lists all the owners and tenants. It was, of course, designed for taxation purposes, to establish the one-tenth that had to be paid to the church in tax.

Apart from the houses along the main road, Wellington Marsh consists of a short cul-de-sac, Marsh Lane, leading off to the west with houses on each side. The Tithe Map lists one inn on the north side in plot 413. This was called the **New Inn** and was owned by Matthew Hurds and occupied by Thomas Warburton. It had apparently ceased to be an inn by the middle of the 19th century, but the building still stands, although it has had a completely new front. Although this inn has closed, the name has continued on.

Across the main road is the **Old Comrade**, the only inn to survive in Wellington Marsh. It is described in the 1842 Tithe simply as plot 432, a public house with cottage

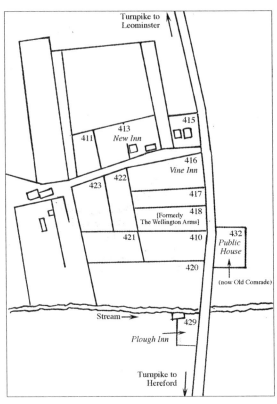

The section of the Wellington Tithe Map dealing with the Marsh

At one time this was the New Inn in Marsh Lane

and garden, and William Donovan as host. No inn name is given. In the 1876 directory the only entry for Wellington Marsh is Mrs. Maria Donovan who sold cider and in 1879 was described as a beer retailer. By 1891, this establishment is described as the **New Inn,** presumably

The sale of the New Inn as part of the Imperial Brewery in 1898

having taken its name from the one across the road. George Morgan was the licensee. At some time before 1898 it had become part of the Hereford Brewery empire and was advertised in the sale of that year as a freehold beer house with Mrs. Hannah Mace as tenant. She paid a rent of £15 per annum, a very small sum even in those days.

Eventually the **New Inn** was granted a full licence—was it then that it had another name change and became the **Old Comrade**? For many years a rather solemn bowler-hatted and bemedalled gentleman looked down from the sign, but times were to change and new signs suddenly appeared on the main road—the old sign was deposited in an outhouse. The name was changed to the rather disastrous **Pig in a Poke**, and an attempt was made to change the image. As so often with 'Pig' names, this was unsuccessful; presumably locals found it difficult to say 'I'm just going to "The Pig in a Poke" for a pint!' Another new landlord and the mistake was partly rectified, at least from the Hereford

The Old Comrade in 2000

163

Although rather battered, the Old Comrade still has an air of dignity that is totally lacking with the Pig in a Poke

direction. The bowler-hatted gentleman, now looking a little battered, was brought out of retirement and placed above the entrance. However, at the millennium, the **Pig in a Poke** sign faces travellers from the Leominster direction. The life expectancy of this sign is unknown, but long may the **Old Comrade** survive!

The Tithe Map has much more to say about Wellington Marsh, for across the lane from this **New Inn** was the **Vine Inn** and garden on plot 416. It was owned and occupied by Thomas Bayley. Once again, it did not survive for long. Part of this plot is now occupied by a row of early 20th century cottages—one of the authors resides in one of them!

The bus stop still remembers the Old Comrade

There was more, for a little way towards Hereford, just across the stream and on the west side of the road was the **Plough Inn,** shown on the Tithe as plot 429. John Pitt owned it and William Pitt was the licensee.

Also at the Marsh, and of uncertain, but pre-1875 date, was the **Wellington Arms**. This was between the **Plough** and the **Vine** in a building that eventually became the Police House. It is not described as an inn on the Tithe Map, but an abstract of deeds refers to it in 1896 as 'a Public House known by the name of the **Wellington Arms**, but since occupied as a private dwelling house ... formerly occupied by

164

*The terrace in Marsh Lane
that replaced the Vine Inn*

Marsh Farm was at one time the Plough Inn

John Wilkes and the late by Police Constable Parkes'. Until relatively recently this was still a police house, but it has since been sold and is now a private dwelling.

Wellington village itself is reached a little further up the A49, the turning for the village being at the beginning of a short stretch of dual carriage-way. This improvement to the A49 was carried out in the 1970s when it was antici-pated that the road would become a major artery to South Wales. It remains one of the few bits of dual carriageway between Shrewsbury and Hereford! Two buildings have suffered from this long-forgotten idea. One was a forge. It was in the way of the dual carriageway and had to be removed. In the end it was carefully taken down and has since been erected at the Avoncroft Museum. The other building survives, but now in very poor condition—it is the gaunt looking Georgian building facing onto the main road just beyond the turn into Wellington village. This was the **Bridge Inn**, a roadside hostelry for many years. On the 1842 Tithe Map it is shown as the **King's Arms** with Thomas Preece as landlord. There was a change by 1850 when Frederick Bishop became mine host. In 1858 it was the **Bridge Inn and Commercial House**, still with Frederick Bishop in charge. In 1876 Thomas Walwyn was landlord. The **Bridge Inn** was the only public house mentioned in Wellington in the 1858 directory, but beer houses were usually excluded.

WELLINGTON,
HEREFORDSHIRE.

TO BE SOLD BY AUCTION,

By order of the Mortgagee and under a Power of Sale

BY W. L. LEES,

AT THE BRIDGE INN, IN WELLINGTON,
On THURSDAY, the 22nd Day of OCTOBER, 1846,

At FOUR o'Clock in the Afternoon, subject to Conditions to be then produced :---

A FREEHOLD
MESSUAGE,

With the **GARDEN** and **ORCHARD** attached, containing about a Quarter of an Acre, situate at Wellington Marsh, adjoining the Turnpike Road leading from Leominster to Hereford, in the occupation of George Hornsby.

☞ For a view apply to George Hornsby, on the Premises, and for further particulars to Mr. J. G. Woodhouse, Solicitor, Leominster.

J. V. CHILCOTT, PRINTER, LEOMINSTER.

Although not named, this poster referred to the sale of the Vine Inn
at the Marsh, the sale taking place at the Bridge Inn.
The handwritten note indicates that it was a forced sale
by direction of the mortagee

In 1882 members of the Woolhope Club decided to visit Ivington Camp and hoped to go by train to Ford Bridge Station. However, they commented that 'The railway authorities are just now so happy and contented with the crowds of travellers that fill their trains that they

At one time one probably the main hostelry between Hereford and Leominster, the Bridge Inn has now fallen on poor times.

The 1926 sale of the Bridge Inn

could neither set us down, nor pick us up, at any convenient time.' Not to be beaten, the Club resorted to the old 'four-in-hand' and visited several churches *en route*. After considering the ruinous state of the Perrott Almshouses they left their carriages at the **Bridge Inn** and 'walked on the raised pathway by the brook lane to Wellington Church', but did not make use of the facilities of the inn.

By 1891 Mrs. Martha Jones was landlady and also a farmer. The **Bridge Inn** was closed by the mid-1920s and was offered for sale by auction by Stooke & Son on 30 June 1926. It was bought by a Mr. Aldridge of Wellington for £160.

A diversion into Wellington village has always been worth while, and now even more so, for it is a village that still has its church, chapel, school, village shop and post office, and, of course, village pub. The **Wellington at Wellington** is a new name for what was originally the

LOT 1.

A BRICK BUILT AND SLATED HOUSE,

FORMERLY KNOWN AS

"THE BRIDGE INN"

WITH EXCELLENT

ORCHARD AND PRODUCTIVE GARDEN

Situate in the VILLAGE OF WELLINGTON, adjoining the Main Road Hereford to Leominster, and also with a Frontage to the road leading to Wellington Village, and extending to a total area of

1 Acre   0 Rood   7 Perches

(or thereabouts), viz. :—

Ord. No.		Description.			Area.
301	..	PASTURE ORCHARDING	..	..	.743
302	..	HOUSE, BUILDINGS AND GARDEN		..	.303
		TOTAL	..	..	1.046

THE HOUSE contains—Entrance Hall, Smoke Room, Tap Room, Snug, Kitchen, Scullery, 4 Bedrooms on FIRST FLOOR and 5 Bedrooms on SECOND FLOOR.

THE BUILDINGS comprise—Stabling for 6 with Loft over, a Range of Two Piggeries, Fowl House, Wood and Coal Shed.

WATER is supplied by Pump in Back Kitchen.

The Land Tax amounts to 12s. 11d.

POSSESSION of this Lot can be given on Completion of Purchase.

According to the local newspaper, it was sold to Mr Aldridge of Wellington for £160, bidding having risen rapidly from £100.

An adjoining enclosure of rich pasture land extending to over 4 acres was sold at the same auction for £315

The 1926 sale details of the Bridge Inn

The Wellington at Wellington in 2000, earlier the Rose and Crown

Rose and Crown. In 1876 it was a beer house with Mrs. Eliza Turner as landlady. It is not mentioned by name in the 1891 directory, but Mrs. Elizabeth Turner was still working as a beer retailer, doubtless at the **Rose and Crown**, which, in 1876 was sold at auction by Alfred & Dearman Edwards. On 16 July 1902 it was again for sale and was bought by the then expanding Stroud Brewery Co. for £510. At that time it included a provision shop and was occupied by John Skeats Young who paid an annual rent of £20. With the recent new name has come sizeable extensions to provide a traditional bar and an excellent restaurant.

There was another inn in Wellington village until relatively recently. This was the **Plough Inn**, further down the village street. It was a beer house in 1876 with Abraham Aldridge as landlord. By 1891 Arthur Daniel was running the establishment and was also a

CANON PYON AND WELLINGTON,

HEREFORDSHIRE.

Particulars and Plan

—— OF A ——

FREEHOLD FARM

CALLED

"LOWER DERNDALE,"

In the Parish of Canon Pyon,

A COTTAGE & GARDEN

At Westhope Hill.

A PIECE OF MEADOW LAND,

At Wellington, and THE

"ROSE & CROWN" INN,

Wellington,

To be SOLD BY AUCTION, by

MESSRS.

ALFRED & DEARMAN EDWARDS

AT THE

LAW SOCIETY'S ROOMS, EAST STREET, HEREFORD.

On WEDNESDAY, the 16th JULY, 1902,

At **THREE** o'clock

(SUBJECT TO CONDITIONS OF SALE).

LAMBE & STEPHENS,

Solicitors, Hereford.

A VALUABLE

FREEHOLD INN

Called the "Rose and Crown" with Provision Shop, comprising a house with Garden and Orchard and Outbuildings, situate in the centre of the Village of Wellington, containing in all 1·412 acres more or less, in the occupation of Mr. JOHN SKEATS YOUNG, at the Annual Rent of £20. Tithe paid last year, 7/4. Land Tax, last payment in 1897, 6/8,

The 1902 sale of the Rose and Crown at Wellington

*The brick extension to the earlier timber-framed cottage
was at one time the Plough at Wellington*

farmer. The building still survives, although there is little indication that it was originally a pub. The inn door on the side elevation, which has since been converted to a window, is still discernible to the keen eye. The 'public bar' was to the right of that door.

Then there is the elusive **Globe Inn**, a beer house reputedly in Wellington. The 1851 census shows Thomas Lewis aged 38 and his wife aged 36 together with their four children and his sister aged 50 all living at the **Globe**. It is not named as such in the 1842 Tithe apportionment, nor are the Lewises mentioned. Nor is it mentioned in the directories for the 1850s, 1870s and 1890s. It is thought to have been down Bridge Lane, a turning off the main village road that crosses the Wellington Brook and then leads as a track up into Wellington and Dinmore Woods. It is suggested that there was a decree during the reign of Queen Victoria (or it may have been earlier during the Napoleonic Wars) that foresters should not have to travel more than a mile for their lunchtime cider—hence the many cider houses in remote cottages in the woods.

From the Wellington turn the A49 takes a direct northerly course towards Dinmore Hill. Just as the road starts to climb the hill there is a turning on the right that skirts the hill and heads eastwards to Bodenham. A short distance along the road is a typical railway settlement—Dinmore Station. The station itself closed in June 1958, but the **Railway Inn** continues to provide an excellent service. It is not just the station, now a private house, and the inn that are of interest to railway buffs—it is here that the trains disappear for some 1,300 yards underneath Dinmore Hill, with an excellent view of the tunnel entrances from the road bridge adjoining the inn. The original single line tunnel was dug in 1852/3. its construction being of some interest. Alfred Watkins recorded that his father told him that 'a great deal of beer went to the making of that tunnel, and as he had just built his new brewery (he had been up to the

The twin railway tunnels next to the Railway Inn

Great Exhibition of 1851, and there bought the newest brewing appliances, glorified under the high-sounding name of "Imperial Patent", thus providing a name for his inn [in Hereford]) he did most of the supplying'. The stone sighting tower on top of Dinmore Hill had to be a lofty structure in order to obtain the necessary clear views from the mouths of the tunnel at both ends to its top and thus establish the direction of the tunnel. It was circular and built of stone, with a stone spiral staircase inside. Doubtless much of Watkins senior's beer was used in the construction, for Alfred described the faulty construction of the stair, which had missing steps even when he was a lad. In 1927, he wrote that 'the central pillar is a separate structure, with the steps notched into it and into the wall at the outer ends. So a slight sway by tempest tends to destroy the structure. It is doomed'. Since Watkins wrote that piece, the upper part of the tower has indeed fallen, but a substantial amount remains and is visible from the public footpath that leads from the A49 towards Bodenham.

The sighting tower on Dinmore Hill

The Railway Inn next to Dinmore Station

172

When the line was doubled in 1893 another single tunnel was built. The opportunity was taken to cut the second tunnel on a less steep gradient which means that the two adjacent tunnels have the distinction of neither entrance being level with its opposite number.

The **Railway Inn** is built of the same well-cut stone as the station buildings and is obviously of the same date. It must have started its life providing beer for the navvies and then for travellers using Dinmore Station as they relaxed on their way home from Hereford or further afield. There were other events and the *Hereford Times* for 13 February 1886 notes that the 'Annual Pigeon Shooting is to be held at the **Railway Inn**, Dinmore, Proprietor E.T. Morgan'. Just over a year earlier in January 1885, Mr. Morgan was granted an extension of two hours on the occasion of his Annual Supper.

As the trunk road reaches its highest point, the Queenswood Country Park is on the western side of the road with a car park and several buildings, one of which is of considerable fascination to anyone with an interest in pubs. The building is now a café, but in an earlier life it was the **Essex Arms** in Widemarsh Street, Hereford, for during 1989 and 1990 it was carefully demolished timber by timber

The Essex Arms in Widemarsh Street, Hereford

and erected on its new site. The original **Essex Arms** may have been built as a house in 1660 and could have been named after the ill-fated Earl of Essex, a member of the local Devereux family, who was a favourite of Queen Elizabeth. However, he eventually fell so far from favour that he was beheaded on Tower Hill in 1601. His titles of Earl of Essex and Viscount Hereford were eventually passed on to his son, Robert, by James I after he ascended the throne.

The **Essex Arms** was a popular pub in Hereford in the early years of the 20th century. In 1930 it was sold by auction to the Stroud Brewery owner, A.J. Perrett, for £3,600. However, as time went by the surrounding houses were demolished and the area became mainly industrial. The inn finally closed to customers in May 1969 and for many years stood by the side of the road with its windows boarded up—a sad looking monument to a lost residential area of the city. Complex negotiations involving planning approval and listed building consent were needed before it could be moved to its new site.

The rebuilt Essex Arms in the Queenswood Country Park

Hope-under-Dinmore is the village on the northern side of Dinmore Hill and it is here that the **Royal Oak Inn** was to be found. In 1858 it was described simply as the **Oak** with Thomas Robinson as landlord, but by 1891 William Price ran the establishment as the **Royal Oak** and also acted as assistant overseer, assessor and collector of taxes. Price was the landlord on 27 September 1890 when, according to the *Hereford Times*, there was a fire at the **Royal Oak Inn**. Apparently it was started by an oil lamp in a bedroom. All was not lost, for the railway signalman telegraphed Leominster for the fire engine. The inn must have been rather unsuccessful for the licence was not renewed in 1914. However, the building is mentioned by Anthea Brian in her article 'As to the River Lugg' (*Woolhope Club Transactions*, 1994, 77-8), where she refers to the old Hampton Bridge which had disappeared by the time of the 1845 Tithe. She goes on to say 'a footbridge was built at the site of the old bridge in 1851 and then in 1864 an iron bridge to carry a tramway was built on what must have been the foundations of the old bridge, just above the weir. This tramway was used to bring stone and other materials into the sawmill'. [It

HAMPTON COURT ESTATE,
HEREFORDSHIRE.
ANNUAL SALE OF COPPICE WOOD,
The Property of John H. Arkwright, Esq.

RUSSELL AND SON
WILL SELL BY AUCTION,
On WEDNESDAY, the 29th day of JANUARY, 1862, at ENGLAND'S GATE INN, Bodenham, commencing at Two o'clock in the Afternoon, and subject to conditions of Sale, the following Lots :—
IN Tankards Walls, 229¼ Lugs in 6 Lots.
In Old Coppice, 354 Lugs in 9 Lots.
In Hack Wood, 306 Lugs, in 7 Lots.
In Hacklet Coppice (Henner Wood). 92 Lugs in 2 Lots.
In Collier's Coppice (ditto), 129¼ Lugs in 4 Lots.
In Howe Wood, 487½ Lugs in 12 Lots.
In Lydes Coppice (Dinmore Hill), 172 Lugs in 6 Lots.

On THURSDAY, the 30th day of JANUARY, 1862, at the OAK INN, Hope-under-Dinmore, at Two o'clock in the Afternoon, the following Lots :—
In Burghope Wood, 335 Lugs in 9 Lots.
In Queen's Wood, 446¼ Lugs in 11 Lots.
In Busk Wood, 302 Lugs in 9 Lots.
In Hill Pitt (Bury Woods), 243 Lugs in 6 Lots.
In Horse Coppice (Winsley), 198 Lugs in 6 Lots.
In Birches Coppice (ditto), 379¼ Lugs in 10 Lots.
In Fishpool Coppice, 259¼ Lugs in 7 Lots.
The Lots will be ticketed, and may be viewed One Week prior to the Sale. Catalogues and further information may be had of THOMAS POWELL, the Woodward, Dinmore Hill, who will show the Lots ; at the Office, Hampton Green ; or of the AUCTIONEERS, Kingsland, Leominster.

A two day sale of timber from the Hampton Court Estate took place at England's Gate Inn at Bodenham and at the Oak Inn at Hope-under-Dinmore

175

was in 1830 that the mill was extensively repaired by Richard Arkwright and the water of the Lugg was used to power newly-built saw-mills cutting stone as well as timber and used for the large-scale alterations and additions made to Hampton Court at that time]. Anthea goes on to say 'the line of the tramway is still visible as a raised bank across the fields towards what was the **Oak Inn** close to Hope under Dinmore church, this was probably the line of the old road as well. Sadly the iron bridge collapsed into the river in the summer of 1991 when a herd of cows was driven across it and only the abutments with the stone pillars that stand at either end of the bridge remain'.

There is also a mention of an inn called the **Falcon** at Hope for which there was a tenancy agreement in 1810. This may have been the establishment for which R. Blindell was a victualler in 1858.

From Hope to Leominster is some 4 miles, a journey that has always had to be taken without an inn stop for there are no wayside hostelries throughout the length.

The 'Back Road'

The 'back road' from Hereford takes a course well to the east of the A49, but eventually joins it at Hope-under-Dinmore. The Hereford end starts at the bottom of Aylestone Hill, where the main Worcester road picks up the line of the Roman Road that forms the northern boundary of the city. The road heads due north towards Sutton St. Nicholas and Bodenham, but the first stop is at the small village of Shelwick where, on a side road leading off to the right towards Munstone, was once the **Bannut Tree Inn**. It was only a few hundred yards along the road from the surviving **Rose Gardens Inn**. In 1891 William Hoskings was land-lord, and in 1937 the landlady was Mrs. Annie Elizabeth Groves. The **Bannut Tree** was in Holmer parish, about a mile north-east of the parish church. It was a 17th-century building with an 18th-century barn added at the north-eastern end and was a beer house throughout its life. A 'Bannut' is a dialect word for a 'walnut' and is also known from the rural saying 'A woman, a spaniel, and a bannut tree, the mooar ye bate [beat] them the better they be'. A walnut tree growing in front of a public house was at one time regarded as being equivalent to a signboard.

The Golden Cross Inn at Sutton St. Nicholas in 2000

Back to the northern road and across the river Lugg to Sutton St. Nicholas. Here is the **Golden Cross Inn** which was not mentioned in the 1858 directory. By 1891 it was run by John Pumphrey who was also a shopkeeper. In 1937 Alfred Jones was the landlord—the inn still survives to serve the considerable parish of the two Suttons: Sutton St. Nicholas and Sutton St. Michael. A 1937 directory also records William Jancey as landlord of the **Bridge Inn** in Sutton St. Nicholas, an inn not otherwise noted.

The road continues northwards from Sutton until at Folly it is joined by the road coming from Withington to the south-east. Here, close to the junction on the west side of the road, is the **New Inn**. It is of 17th-century origin and had diagonal framing in the two gables, but has since been extensively modernised. In 1858 James Taylor was the landlord; in 1891 it was John Griffiths. The *Hereford Times* for 7 April 1888 advertises a sale at the **New Inn**, Marden, of 'a free-hold cottage, shed and pigstye etc in the occupation of George Miles, at Tumpy Lakes'.

There were several pubs in Marden at the end of the 19th century, but the only one apart from the **New Inn** to survive to the present day

The New Inn at Marden in 1999

is the **Volunteer** at Walker's Green. This is on the road that starts on the A49 at Moreton-on-Lugg and crosses the railway and the river Lugg in quick succession before turning northwards to Marden. The village church is hidden down a side road to the right; Walker's Green is about a third of a mile further along the road as it takes a long curve towards Bodenham. The **Volunteer** is a 17th-century building that has

The Volunteer at Walker's Green, Marden, in 2000

been much altered and re-built in brick. James Walker was landlord in 1858, Thomas Yarnold in 1891.

Two inns in Marden were owned by Watkin's Imperial brewery around the end of the 19th century—the **Bannut Tree Head Inn** at Kitten's Gate, and the **Carpenter's Arms** at Burling. The **Bannut Tree Head** was a simple building of lath and plaster and at the end of the 19th century was let for £20 per annum to William Taylor. The beerhouse had a taproom, parlour and general shop, but only two bedrooms. Although the **Carpenter's Arms** was let for only £16 per annum, it apparently had more to offer, for it was made of brick and had three bedrooms and, in the grounds, a piggery. Neither the **Bannut Tree Head** nor the **Carpenter's Arms** are mentioned in 1858, but the **Carpenter's Arms** had William Bowen as landlord in 1891 and William Taylor ran the **Bannut Tree Head**. It seems strange that there were two 'bannut trees' within such a short distance—only some three miles apart.

THE "BANNUT TREE HEAD" INN BEERHOUSE,

Kitten Gate, Marden

(One Mile from Dinmore Railway Station).

Lath and Plaster Premises, situate on the Road to Bodenham,

Comprising Forecourt in front with pump of water, Tap Room, Parlour, General Shop, Cellar, Kitchen with oven, and Two Bed Rooms. Small Farm Yard, Stable, Barn, Cart-shed and Garden.

Also an ORCHARD and piece of ARABLE LAND, in all about 4a. 3r. 13p.

FREEHOLD.   Let to Mr. William Taylor at a Rent of **£20 per Annum**.

THE "CARPENTERS' ARMS" INN BEERHOUSE,

Marden,

A Brick and Tiled House, situate on a Bye Road off the Marden Road,

Containing Tap Room, Kitchen, Parlour, Cellar, Larder and Three Bed Rooms, Barn, Stable, Piggery, Outhouse and Garden.

Also TWO ORCHARDS and MEADOW LAND, about 4a. 0r. 21p.

FREEHOLD.   Let to Mrs. Annette Lewis at **£16 per Annum**.

Part of the Imperial Brewery sale in 1898

Marden was quite a sizeable parish with a population of some 840 in 1888. It was a hop-growing area, but also had many cider apple orchards. In addition to the four pubs in the latter part of the 19th century, Richard Taylor was listed as a cider retailer at Vauld in 1858. This must have been a successful business for in 1891 Benjamin Ridgley at the Vauld was a farmer and cider merchant, and

---

HEREFORDSHIRE.

To be SOLD by AUCTION,

BY JOHN PREECE,

At the Public-houſe known by the Name of ENGLAND'S-GATE,

In the pariſh of Bodenham, in the ſaid county,

On THURSDAY, APRIL 30, 1801,

Between the hours of Three and Five in the Afternoon,.

SUBJECT TO SUCH CONDITIONS OF SALE AS SHALL BE THEN PRODUCED,

(Unleſs diſpoſed of in the mean Time by Private Contract,)

ALL THAT FREEHOLD

Meſſuage *or* Tenement,

With a Garden, and about Four Acres of Arable Land,

Part planted with Hops, and part with Fruit Trees, (making excellent Cider.)
The above Tenement is in good repair, ſituate and lying in the pariſh of Bodenham, and now in the poſſeſſion of Joſeph Wadely, who will ſhew the Premiſes.

For further particulars apply to Mr. John Lane, Byſter's-Gate; or to the Auctioneer, Preece's Coffee-houſe, Hereford.

WALKER, PRINTER, HEREFORD.

This notice refers to the sale of a tenement at England's Gate Inn in 1801. There are several points of interest: the notice was printed by D. Walker who was Printer and Editor of the Hereford Journal *from 29 June 1791 to 31 March 1802; Preece's Coffee House was the rather dignified name for what was actually a common ale house—it was in St. John Street in Hereford, which at that time was called Milk Lane. Byster's Gate or Bye Street Gate, the north-eastern entry into the city, had its main arch demolished in 1798, but parts of the buildings remained including the City Gaol and probably the Gatehouse, occupied by John Lane*

England's Gate Inn, when it was still on the cross-roads
(Photograph : Derek Foxton Collection)

he had been joined in the trade by Alfred Pudge at Venn's Green. Alfred was also a farmer and hop-grower.

Continuing northwards, either on the road from Marden or on the more direct route from Sutton, the final destination is the junction with the A417, the main road from Leominster towards Gloucester. The road passes through part of Bodenham village and just before it arrives at the junction, **England's Gate Inn** is on the right hand side. The manor of Bodenham was purchased by Sir Thomas Coningsby in 1618; previously it had belonged to the Earl of Leicester and then to Lord Russell.

The name of the inn is often thought to reflect its position near the Welsh border, but the Coningsby Estate Records appear to provide a different solution. In 1628 there is a mention of Inland's Field and by the latter part of that century there is a mention of a Messuage called Inlands, alias England's Gate.

In the 19th century, the inn, along with most other buildings in the area, belonged to the Hampton Court Estate. A lease for the inn dated 7 July 1835 is of some interest. It is from Richard Arkwright (the son of the industrialist Sir Richard Arkwright, inventor of the Spinning Jenny, who bought the estate in 1809) to George Cox and includes the following descriptions:

House, garden, orchard and land adjoining	6a.	1r.	2p.
England's Field	1a.	3r.	20p.
England's Field	2a.	0r.	20p.
Mill Croft Meadow	1a.	0r.	37p.
Baker's Croft	1a.	3r.	27p.
Rhee meadow & Orchard	7a.	1r.	4p.
<u>Making a total of</u>	<u>20a.</u>	<u>2r.</u>	<u>30p.</u>

(For those not conversant with the intricacies of Imperial measurements,
one perch is $30^{1}/_{4}$ square yards
there are 40 perches to a rood
there are 4 roods to an acre
and, for those using metric land measurements, there are 2.471 acres to a hectare)

The lease was a standard one that was applied to all the Arkwright properties, but with some specific conditions for the inn. Thus George Cox was prohibited from sowing hemp seed or flax seed. Other conditions included 'That the said George Cox further agrees to keep a dog for the said Richard Arkwright for so long a time as he shall be required. And also will in every year ... haul to the mansion-house of the said Richard Arkwright at Hampton Court ... a wagon load of coals, free from all expenses the price of the coals excepted'. The hauling was apparently a rather vexatious issue, for it had been deleted in an earlier lease. The earlier lease (of 23 March 1827) is of interest for it describes the property as a public house. At that time it was a James Roberts who took the lease of the property.

In 1858/9 Francis Green was at the inn and in 1867 Christopher Robinson. In 1891, the inn was apparently of some consequence, for the landlord, William Purchase, was also a farmer and fly (a one-horse hackney carriage) proprietor. He had been there for some time for the *Hereford Times* of 20 March 1886 described him as landlord when they recorded that Mr. Allen Duncan, aged 38, a farmer of the Moor, Bodenham, died in a fit at the **England's Gate Inn**.

In 1904, John Hungerford Arkwright Esq. came to an agreement concerning the inn with William Childs, previously his butler at Hampton Court, but who was then taking on the tenancy. The property is described as 'All that Public House known as "England's Gate Inn" together with the gardens, stables, coach house & appurtenances thereto ...'. A condition of the lease was that 'The tenant shall at all

England's Gate Inn in the 1970s

times reside on the said premises and will daily keep open the same during such hours as are fixed by law always conducting the house and business of inn-keeper in a respectable and lawful manner'. In 1917 the licensee was Charles Francis Chilman and in 1922 John Popple was landlord.

The Royal Commission in 1932 noted that 'the house is of 17th-century date and forms an irregular T-shape with the cross-wing at the west end'. They also noted the three-bay outbuilding to the south-west which 'has curved braces between the tie beams and collars'. The 'Herefordshire Old Buildings Recording Group' described it as 'A fairly typical building of *c.*1600 with a gable entrance. It is interesting in containing evidence of a post and stud partition which must have once divided the main room into two. The wide chamfer on the beams points to a late-16th century date, the present kitchen probably having been the parlour of the original house. The present parlour wing with its small, square panels is no doubt a later 17th-century addition. The roof is of a typical Marcher collar and tie-beam type with struts and trenched through-purlins and the heavy sandstone covering was probably quarried locally. The timber-framed outbuilding has the usual square panels of the 17th century and appears to have been re-roofed

183

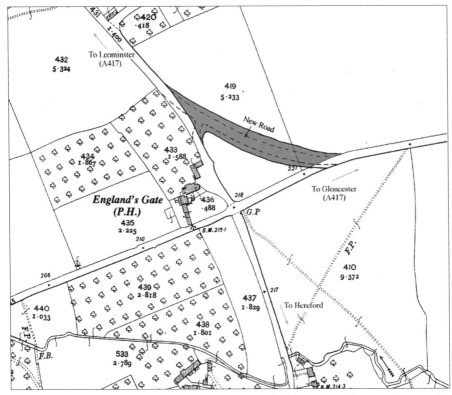

A 1904 plan of the England's Gate area with the new road superimposed

in the 19th century with the Herefordshire upper base-cruck construction typical of malt-houses and granaries'.

Now set well back from the A417, **England's Gate Inn** is in a rather quiet position, only just visible from the main road. This was not always the case and originally the inn was firmly placed on the crossroads where the traffic following the A417 road from Leominster towards Gloucester had to turn sharp left. The change took place in the 20th century and the main road now bypasses **England's Gate Inn** which is left sitting end-on to the minor road that leads through Sutton towards Hereford.

Bodenham is a large parish and in 1858 had a population of 1,113. The centre of the village is a short distance west of **England's Gate**, and is well hidden just to the south of the A417. The chief crops were then apples, hops, wheat and beans. However, the population had dropped to 879 by 1888 and this was reflected in the loss of some licensed premises. One of the more unusual was the **Royal George**

184

Inn, an inn better known as **Dyke's of the Ketch**. In the 1858 directory John Dykes was described as a cider retailer at Saffron's Cross, where the North Herefordshire Hunt had long had their stables and kennels. In 1879 Mrs. Mary Dykes was in charge of the establishment and was recorded as a beer seller. However the inn was soon to close and the *Hereford Times* for 5 October 1899 recorded that the kennels for the North Herefordshire Hunt were then located at the Ketch in Bodenham, in a converted beerhouse formerly the **Royal George Inn**. Benjamin Vale had a similar profession—beerseller—at Bowler Town about one and a half miles north of Saffron's Cross.

In addition there was a **New Inn** at Bodenham, recorded in the 1858 directory with Richard Yeoman, who was also a stonemason, as landlord. Finally there was the **Half-way House**, which is not named as such in the 1891 directory but was apparently a cider house, probably at a suitably central position on the A417. In February 1946 it was reported that the licensee was not applying for a renewal of the licence.

The alignment of a Roman road is apparent on maps, stretching northwards from the Saffron's Cross area of Bodenham and heading through the Roman settlement at Blackwardine towards Wroxeter (*Viriconium*).

Just to the west of Blackwardine is Stoke Prior and here is the **Lamb Inn**. Mrs. Hannah Volley was licensee in 1858, Mrs. Caroline Evans in 1891. The **Lamb** still survives as the village inn, but in the

The Lamb Inn at Stoke Prior in 2000

185

Wheelbarrow Castle in 2000

19th century there was a second inn in the village. This was the **Swan Inn**, where Philip Grubham was listed as victualler in 1858 and where Philip Grubham was licensee and also ran a market garden in 1891.

The situation did improve to some extent when the **Wheelbarrow Castle**, a farm on the road between Stoke Prior and Leominster, was licensed on 15 September 1982 and operated as a restaurant—a use which has since ceased.

CHAPTER TEN

Leominster—Central

That Leominster is an ancient town is beyond dispute, for it is recorded that in 658 Merewalh, King of the Magonsaete, built a monastery here for religious virgins, only for it to be destroyed in 777 by warring Britons. Since then the fortunes of the town have waxed and waned throughout the centuries as have the arguments as to the origin of the name of the town. The 'minster' part is easy as there has always been a prominent Church presence here; it is the 'Leo' element that is in dispute. For a long time it was held that the 'Leo' referred to Earl Leofric who is said to have endowed a nunnery here in the time of Edward the Confessor. It is amusing to think that, whilst Leofric was giving money to nuns in Leominster, women who were charged with keeping their clothes on, his wife, Lady Godiva, was divesting herself of hers and parading naked through the streets of Coventry in order to persuade him to spend less and reduce his tax demands upon that city! However, modern thought is that the first bit of the name merely refers to an earlier name for the area 'Leon' or 'Leen', an area of land roughly bounded by the rivers Lugg and Arrow.

The area in which Leominster finds itself is remarkably fertile and sheltered and for centuries has been noted for the quality of its agricultural products, both animal and vegetable, such virtues being extolled by many writers. For example Camden writing in the 17th century said of Leominster:

> The greatest name and fame that it hath this day, is of the wooll in the territories round about it. Leominster Ore, they call it, which, setting aside that of Apulia and Tarentum, all Europe counteth it to be the very best.

and Defoe wrote:

> This town, besides the fine woll, is noted for the best wheat, and
> consequently the finest bread: whence Lemster Bread, and Webley Ale, is
> become a proverbial saying. ... As for hops, they plant abundance indeed
> all over this county, and they are very good. And as for cyder, here it was,
> that several times for 20 miles together, we could get no beer or ale in their
> publick houses, only cyder; and that so very good, so fine, and so cheap,
> that we never found fault with the exchange; great quantities of this cyder
> are sent to London, even by land carriage tho' so very remote, which is an
> evidence for the goodness of it, beyone contradiction.

The cider, and other alcoholic beverages of the town were
obviously very good and popular for it became necessary to light the
way of the citizens making their way to and from the hostelries in the
dark months, as reported by Eric Turton from his researches into the
Borough records for 1573:

> Item. it is ordered to all and every the capital Burgesses of the Borough, and
> also to every Inn-holder and Victualler within this Borough, that they and
> every one of them shall every night that the moone doth not shine, hang out
> of there doores, windows, or other convenient place, a lanterne and candle
> burning from the feast of All Saints [1 November] until the Purification of
> Our Lady [2 February] upon payne of every Capital Burgess for offending
> to forfeit for every such offence viij s. iv d., and every other Inn-holder and
> Victualler xij d.

This was followed in 1635 by a similar order with the period stipulated
as:

> from the 21st day of October until the 2nd day of February in every year
> hang forth and keepe at their doore a sufficient lantern and candle lighted
> in it from vi of the clock at night until ix of the clock, upon payment of iiijd.
> for every tyme offending.

Eventually the borough took on the responsibility of illuminating the
populace for a trade directory comments:

> The town is clean in appearance and well-paved and lighted with gas by a
> company, established 1836, from works in Bridge Street. There are some
> wide streets and many of the houses are modern and of good design; there
> are also some fine specimens of timber-built houses, with grotesquely
> carved brackets and barge boards.

In this era, the mid-19th century, there were some 36 premises
under the general heading 'Hotels, Inns and Taverns'. Moving into the
20th century, at the Brewster Sessions in 1936, it was stated that:

Leominster Borough had 27 fully licensed houses, one beer house, two cider houses (one on and one off licence) and one wine, spirits and beer off licence. There were also six registered clubs and four shops which sold goods in addition to liquor. It was reported that 'the houses had been regularly visited and were found to be generally well conducted'. No proceedings were taken against licence-holders, but two non-residents were proceeded against for being drunk and disorderly, one of whom was convicted and the other discharged so long as he left the town.

The second half of the 20th century saw many changes, not least being the population shift from rural to urban areas and the tremendous increase in the ownership and use of the motor car resulting in travellers on the routes between the north-west and south-west, and between the midlands and mid-Wales, only knowing the little market town of Leominster as a notorious bottle-neck. The re-routing of the A49 has resulted in the traveller only being aware of Leominster as a church spire and a few rooftops seen to the west as they travel along the eastern by-pass.

The fortunes of Leominster have varied over the centuries and recently the construction of the bypass may have contributed to another decline, with some loss of casual visitors. However, in the new millennium the town is in a period of regeneration with trade increasing in such areas as antiques, specialist food shops, handicrafts, and the re-introduction of the Farmer's Market. Even though travel to Hereford and Shrewsbury is now easier, the local inhabitants find that nearly all their needs can be satisfied locally and the visitor is encouraged by free parking. Although the town is lively during the week, Sundays can remind one that Shropshire is not far away where, according to A.E. Houseman, are to be found 'the quietest places under the sun'.

Corn Square

A journey around Leominster would normally tend to be centred about the 'minster' or the Priory Church of Saints Peter and Paul as it is now known, but as our spiritual journey is of a different nature it will start at the civic hub of the town in Corn Square where may be found an imposing black and white painted public house.

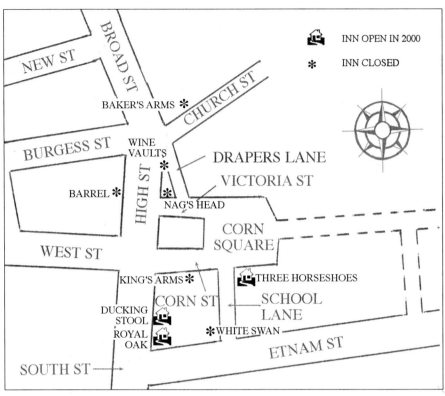

Central Leominster

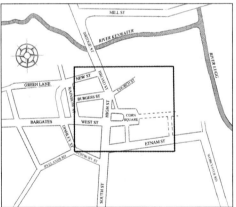

The **Three Horse Shoes**, built about 1600, has an upper story that projects on the west side and formerly also projected on the north front, but has since been underbuilt. The fronts were stucco painted in about 1780, with sham framing to look like timbers. The inn is first mentioned in a directory of 1780.

In the mid-19th century, Thomas Smith, who sometime kept the **Grape Vaults** (of which more later), recorded many aspects of life in Leominster in his apologia 'A Brand Plucked from the Burning'. Describing his apprenticeship to a draper he wrote:

I had never known up to this time what it was to be out after dark by myself, but now my early restraints quickly vanished. I was placed in the midst of

190

The Three Horseshoes in 2000

temptation without a check, without a hand to guide me, … The Tempter, ever subtle, soon placed an alluring bait in my way; a professed friend, but an enemy in disguise, offered to pay my subscription in a sweep for a large race. The winner was to receive ten of twenty pounds. I went to the draw, held in a public house called the **Three Horse Shoes**. Great numbers of young men and old men sat around the room. The cup I passed freely—the boxes were placed on the table—the names of members in one box, and the names of horses in the other. The boy took his station at the boxes –all were gazing with breathless anxiety; the turn was given, every eye was strained towards the place. My name was called, I think the first out of all the others, and now the name of a horse was called; the boy said "Cossack!". "Well done," said many voices, "that's the favourite," shouted another; compliments were heaped upon me, and success wished to the young gambler; many seemed heartily to hope the horse would win. The pay night came, lots of drink was had in, and I received the money. I was imbued now with a thirst for gambling – every sweep found my name set prominently forth. The public house was my resort, it was the place of attraction; a boy seventeen years of age to sit among men— what an honour! The money which I won must be spent. I determined to treat the young men at the shop in which I lived. I bought a few bottles of wine, I drank, and tempted them to drink. The sequel may be guessed. I grew impudent; one of the young men ordered me to my place in the shop. I refused to go—he pushed me, I struck him again; he went into the house, awaited the master's return, and told him how I had behaved. He came into the shop, told me he would not have such proceedings in his establishment, and if I would not promise to amend, I was to leave at once. I was only too glad of the opportunity, and I impudently put on my cap and wished them all good day.

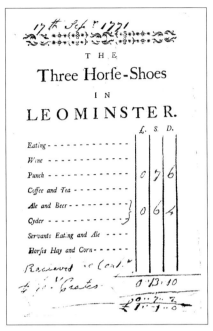

	£.	S.	D.
Eating - - - - - - - - - - - - -			
Wine - - - - - - - - - - - -			
Punch - - - - - - - - - - - - -	0	7	6
Coffee and Tea - - - - - - - - -			
Ale and Beer - - - - - - - - - - ⎫	0	6	4
Cyder - - - - - - - - - - - - ⎭			
Servants Eating and Ale - - - -			
Horses Hay and Corn - - - - - -			

A 1771 account for drink at the Three Horseshoes

From there he went first to Worcester and then to the golden pavements in London looking for more dissipation and debauchery.

In 1879 the licensee of the **Three Horseshoes** was Mrs. Susannah Bird. By 1891 Tom Mitchell had replaced her. He was also a mineral water manufacturer, a wine and spirit merchant, and an ale and porter merchant and bottler, presumably from his other property at 21 Drapers Lane. By 1937 Henry L. James was licensee.

The **Three Horse Shoes** was doubly in the news in October 1951. Mrs. Trotman, the wife of the licensee, had noticed that a Hereford man, Frederick Collins, had been tinkering with the ash trays in the pub. Early in the evening he had been asked to replace one on the mantelpiece and he had subsequently left the pub. However, he returned later in the evening and she accused him of taking other ashtrays. He appears not to have been a very clever thief, for she could see them protruding from his jacket pockets. She called her husband who in turn called the police. P.C. Eastlake arrived at the pub and first noticed 24 year-old Betty Small of Kingstone in the smoke room who was clearly the worse for drink. Mr. Trotman asked her to leave, but she refused and so he ejected her. As she tried to re-enter the pub, she hit P.C. Eastlake across the face as he attempted to bar the doorway. At her subsequent Court appearance the policeman described her as frothing at the mouth and with her arms and legs flailing. Her record showed that she had two previous offences, one for drunk and disorderliness and one for obstructing a railway officer in his duties. She was fined £1 for being drunk and disorderly and £2 for the assault. Meanwhile, Frederick Collins had admitted his thefts of ashtrays and at his court appearance 18 previous cases of theft were mentioned. In this case the magistrates felt they had no alternative but to send him to gaol for three months.

Three Horse Shoes is not an uncommon name and is thought to have been an indication that the hostelry also offered smithing services. Whilst the sign here is simply three golden horseshoes, signs in other places are more imaginative showing, for instance, a forlorn looking nag proffering a shoeless hoof.

When leaving the pub and viewing the north side of the square there are memories of Leominster's political history. From as early as 1295 the town returned two Members of Parliament, but this was reduced to one by the Representation of the People Act of 1867. In times gone by politics were far more rumbustious and dangerous to life and limb—remember the gang-ways of the House of Commons are specified as having to be two sword-lengths in width! Nowadays rival parties peacefully co-exist. Before the establishment of association offices and clubs rival parties would meet in taverns, but in 1879 Leominster did have one political association—the Leominster Working Men's Conservative Association—with their offices in Burgess Street. Now the Conservative Association has its offices and club on the north side of Corn Square.

Corn Square is an ancient enclosure where, from time immemorial, farmers and dealers in grain have been wont to congregate. In this square were, in former days, the stocks, pillory, and Barley House, a quaint-looking shed or pent-house, which was in charge of the ancient Bakers' Guild, and which gave the scantiest possible shelter from the inclemency of the weather. On the south side a Corn Market was erected in 1803 at a cost of £450. This building stood on stone pillars with a pent-house roof, but it was open at the side, and afforded no protection from the weather, so, as it was

*Corn Square in the 1920s with
the Corn Exchange*

insufficient for the increasing trade, a new Corn Exchange was built on the west side of Corn Square in 1859. This, in turn, has since been demolished.

Church Street, Draper's Lane & High Street

Not only could alcoholic liquor be bought in the public houses, Leominster also had wines & spirits, and ales & porter merchants and retailers—'off-licences' as we now know them. At the north-west corner of the Square a quaint narrow lane—Draper's Lane—leads to the western end of Church Street. Somewhere near the junction of Draper's Lane and Corn Square was the **Duke's Head**, not to be confused with the **Duke's Arms** in Etnam Street. It is mentioned intermittently in directories between 1780 and 1862, being described latterly as the **Old Duke's Head** with E. Bird as landlord.

The **Baker's Arms** was at 3 Church Street, a 17th-century building that has been re-fronted and was first mentioned in a directory in 1876 with John Weaver as landlord. In 1891 the landlord was Samuel Lewis Urwick, who was also the town's bill-poster. Mr. H. Rumsey was mine host in 1937 and the inn continued to trade until 1968 when the licence was not renewed. Amongst its customers is numbered Stanley Holland, Leominster's prodigal son and son of the landlord of the **White Horse** in West Street, who, according to Norman Reeves, reputedly owed his fall from grace, in part at least, to over-indulging and over-spending here (but more of him later).

Also in Church Street (and not to be confused with the pub of the same name in Etnam Street) was the **Bell Inn**, of which Eric Turton notes:

A deed dated 3 November 1774 mentions 'and also of and all that other Messuage or tenement and Dwelling house situate and being in Leominster aforesaid in a place or Street there called the Church Street with the Stable Court or yard thereunto adjoining and belonging, now in the occupation of the said Hugh Jones and heretofore called the **Turk's Head** but now known by the sign of the **Bell**, having a house and a backside now in the occupation of John Woolley on the East, a Messuage and backside now in the possession of Jonathan Meredith on the North, the said Messuage in the occupation of Zacheus Wyke on the West and the said Church street on the South parts'.

Returning to the corner of Church Street, it is worth momentarily stepping beyond the intended compass of this chapter and turning right to observe the name of the pub a few yards down on the right and note that this was where Thomas Smith had been landlord—the

3 Church Street, once the Baker's Arms

Grape Vaults. No! 'Do not pass. Do not go [in]'—be patient and wait until chapter twelve to enjoy the delights of this hostelry—rather turn upon your heel and return to the corner. Here is a building on an acute corner with Draper's Lane to the left and High Street to the right. Called the Hen Pen, this building has caused much confusion in researching the pubs of Leominster. The confusion is in the use of the word 'Vaults', for variously 1 High Street has been described as the **Vaults** or the **Wine Vaults** and so has 2 Draper's Lane, and, almost certainly the **Grapes** has been referred to simply as the **Vaults**. 'Vaults' also occurs in other parts of the town, but it is in this little corner that most of the confusion lies. Much of the trouble may be laid at the door of Edward Valentine Gunnell who had a wine importing business with offices at 6 Church Street and 'retail vaults' at 1 High Street and at 2 Draper's Lane. Maybe it was two separate premises 'back to back', or maybe a single unit with doors to both thoroughfares thus necessitating separate licences as occurs elsewhere, notably a pub that was reputed to straddle the border with Wales where the Welsh licence required the bar that was in Wales to be closed on Sundays whereas the bar in England could remain open. The licence for the **Vaults** was not renewed in 1966.

During the early years of the 20th century strenuous efforts were made to ensure that young children were not at risk from drink. One of

The Hen Pen, once the Wine Vaults with Draper's Lane on the left and High Street on the right [above]

Draper's Lane with the side wall of the Hen Pen and the entrance to No. 2 on the right [left]

196

the regulations, that certainly continued into the Second World War and beyond, was that it was illegal for licensees to sell drink to children under the age of 14 in bottles that were not sealed. The child could go to the 'Jug and Bottle' of the public house with father's quart bottle and have it filled from the tap. The landlord was then required to cork or replace the screw top of the bottle and seal it in place with a strip of sticky paper. This was never very successful, for the glue on the paper was usually over moistened by wiping it in the excess beer on the counter and then applying it to the stopper. Any youngster worth his salt would run round the corner and peel off the still wet seal, have a swig, and replace the paper before the glue dried thus convincing the father that the pub gave short measure! That it was common practice to send one of your children to collect the evening's beer did not prevent the rather over-zealous P.C. Worthing from summonsing Mr. G.J. Abell, the manager of the Alton Court Brewery at Leominster early in 1916, for the *Hereford Times* records:

P.C. Worthing stated that on February 3rd at 8.45 pm he saw a little boy enter the **Wine Vaults** in High Street. He took a half pint bottle from inside his coat and placed in on the counter. It was filled by Miss Jones, the manageress, who handed it back to the boy and was paid for it. The boy then came out into the street and when witness stopped him, Miss Jones came out also and asked what was the matter. Witness said to her 'Didn't you know it was wrong to supply this boy?' and she replied 'No, sergeant, not if he is 14, and I thought he was because he was at work, neither did I know it was wrong for him to be in the bar'. The boy had a half-pint bottle of stout with the cork not sealed. Florence Jones said she had managed the **Vaults** since September last and had been connected with the house for two years before that. She had never heard any complaint about the management. Mr. Wadsworth (for the defence) said that the girl had every reason to believe, and did believe, that the child was 14 years of age. He was successful in getting the case dismissed, on the basis of Miss Jones' unblemished record.

Nevertheless, P.C. Worthing had obviously taken the case very seriously indeed, for at the same court, Mrs. Alice Mitchell of 7 Bridge Street, the mother of the child, was summoned for sending her child into licensed premises. The case was withdrawn once the prosecution against Mr. Abell had failed.

Continuing along High Street, the first turn to the left, Victoria Street, leads back into Corn Square. Opposite this turn, trade directories from 1835 to 1859 indicate that there was a public house named the

Cross. Also in High Street at No. 12 was the **Barrel Inn**, first mentioned in a directory of 1876 with Charles Phillips as licensee and in 1891 when John Butland was landlord. It continued well into the 20th century, with Charles Runford landlord in 1937, but the licence was finally abandoned in February 1939. The three-storied building is probably of 17th-century date. It has been much altered and re-fronted, but there is evidence to suggest that the upper stories were once jettied out. It may be that the **Barrel** was another name for the **Cross**. Norman Reeves' list of 'Leominster's Public Houses' (*circa* 1970) includes the **Nag's Head,** which was situated along Victoria Street. In operation in the 19th century, it is also described as being in Back Lane.

Corn Street

Corn Street joins High Street to the south-west corner of Corn Square

The surviving arch of the King's Head in Etnam Street

and on the south side at Nos. 10 and 12 was the **King's Arms**, not to be confused with the **King's Head**, just round the corner in South Street. The 1934 Royal Commission describes it as a three-storey house and shops, formerly the **Kings Arms Inn**, which extended through to Etnam Street. The front block is described as being of the late 18th century, but the rear portion was of 17th-century date with exposed timber-framing in the south wall. On the west side of the yard at the back there was an early 18th-century addition of two stories with exposed framing. The lower part of the west wall was of rubble. At that time the upper storey formed a large hall.

The outbuildings in Etnam Street were of 17th-century date.

The south wall had been re-faced in brick, but timber-framing was exposed at the back. The inn was mentioned in directories between 1780 and 1862. The site of the **King's Arms** is now mainly occupied by Woolworths. The rear coach entry was at 3 Etnam St. where the old archway survives in the new houses next to the **Royal Oak** car park.

In its time this was a reasonably important town inn, for the Trustees for the Leominster Turnpike Trust held their meeting there on 20 December 1770. In 1793, following Edward Ford's move to the **Unicorn**, the inn was put up to let and in October John Thompson took it on. In 1858 George Bradford was recorded as being the licensee. The Plymouth Brethren held their services in the large rooms of this inn from 1839, before moving to the **Royal Oak**, where they stayed until 1963 when they rented Waterloo House.

School Lane

From Corn Square, Etnam Street is approached by School Lane which runs parallel to South Street. Just as School Lane is about to enter Etnam Street the sign of the **White Swan** is apparent high up on a building to the right where it owes its allegiance to the Stroud Brewery and Cotswold Beers. This pub is described in directories as being at 24 School Lane, but the 'front' appears to have been very much in Etnam Street—certainly its present frontage as a fish and chips shop is! This hostelry was first mentioned in 1792; in 1858 Richard Woolfall was licensee; in 1879, Charles Reynolds, who

The White Swan sign.
The town museum is in the background

199

This plaque, now in Leominster Museum reads:

Reynolds
THE WHITE SWAN
CELEBRATED
FOR THE SALE OF
GENUINE
HOME BREWED
OLD & MILD
ALES
WINES & SPIRITS

Charles Reynolds was at the White Swan during the last quarter of the 19th century

The Etnam street frontage of the White Swan—a fish and chip shop in 2000

was still there in 1891 when he was also described as a brewer. The premises was still licenced in the late 1930s when W. Joseph Brooks was the landlord.

Also in School Lane was the **Plough**, mentioned in directories from 1792 to 1835, and the **Coach and Horses**, mentioned in 1830.

South Street

South Street, as its name implies, runs due south from the virtual centre of Leominster where West Street meets Corn Street. The eastern side of South Street from Corn Street to Etnam Street fits more logically within this chapter whilst the western side is in chapter 12 and the southern part is included in chapter 11.

The **Queen's Head** at 11 South Street is not mentioned in any of the earlier directories, the first entry being in 1903. The Royal Commission report of 1934 describes it and its next door neighbour as:

> probably built early in the 16th century but were extensively altered in the 17th century and heightened late in the 18th or early in the 19th century. Inside the building the front room of both houses has original moulded ceiling beams and evidence of a former projecting upper storey; the beams form a series of square panels, and in no 13 the moulded joists are also exposed.

Describing an inn as the Queen's Head has been the cause of some considerable problems in times past. Elizabeth I was the subject of many early signs, some not very flattering. Such was the problem that signs that offended her were knocked down and burnt and the problem grew so great in 1563 that a royal proclamation was issued banning any future signs unless they followed an approved example. Now, many queens can be found on inn signs from Anne Boleyn, with block and axe in the background, to the queen of clubs.

The Ducking Stool, once the Queen's Arms

It may be that the problem over which queen to honour in Leominster was the reason for the change of name in 1997. It has now become the **Ducking Stool**. The recent fad of pub owners to change an old established inn name to one perceived

*The ducking stool and its accompanying plaque
in Leominster parish church*

to be more attractive frequently leads to names that do not seem to have any rhyme, reason or even connection with the building's history or situation, for example the **Jolly Frog** at Leintwardine and the **Pig in a Poke** at Wellington. However, the new name for the **Queen's Head** does have a strong connection with Leominster.

Like all towns, Leominster had a variety of methods used to punish scolds, cheats, drunks and other social malefactors, all of which involved public humiliation, discomfort, and exposure to verbal and physical abuse. The stocks, whipping post and pillory no longer exist but the town's ducking stool does. A ducking stool is somewhat like the see-saw, or teeter-totter as it is known in North America, that is to be found in children's playgrounds but with wheels under the pivot and a simple chair or stool affixed to one end of the plank.

This contraption was wheeled around the streets of the town so that the victim, well secured to the end, could be be jeered at until, at the end of the journey, the stool-end together with its unfortunate occupant was dipped into a suitable pond or river, the degree of wetting or near-drowning no doubt being left to the whim of the magistrates, those executing the sentence, or the mood of the observing crowd. Leominster's ducking stool is one of the finest preserved in the country and is displayed in the Priory Church near the re-named pub.

The painted sign outside the **Ducking Stool** depicts a struggling, reasonably well dressed but somewhat buccolic man tied to the end of a ducking stool, and it is true that such a punishment was imposed on minor offenders regardless of social standing or sex, and that

Jenny Pipes in the ducking stool

drunkenness often earned a ducking. It was also the punishment for those who gave short measure or adulterated food. Nevertheless, it is generally perceived that the ducking stool was mainly used as a popular treatment for the common scold after the mediaeval scolds-bridle, a device which clamped a piece of metal over a victim's tongue to render them incapable of speech, fell into disuse. The last recorded uses of Leominster's ducking stool both involved women. In 1809

The Ducking Stool sign

Jenny Pipes was ducked in the water near Kenwater Bridge, by order of the magistrates. She was noted for the violence of her language towards the magistrates after receiving her watery punishment, which obviously had had little effect on her behaviour.

In 1817 Sarah Leeke was the last person to be condemned to suffer this humiliation in Leominster (and England for that matter) even though she did not receive a proper ducking at the end of the parade as a drought had resulted in there being insufficient water in any of the town's three rivers. Even though it is almost two centuries since a woman was punished in this manner, it is perhaps thought to be a little politically incorrect to portray violence of any form against a woman even on an historically inspired pub sign.

The town is proud of its history and as part of its Millennium celebrations the citizens considered a proposal to commission a decorative clock featuring a working model of the device, the suggestion being that it should show a female effigy being ducked on the hour in a water butt in the town square. However, the scheme does not appear to have been accepted.

The **Royal Oak Hotel** (known as the **Unicorn** in the 18th and early 19th centuries) is on the corner of South Street and Etnam Street. It has a considerable history as a hostelry and advertizes that it has provided 'fine hospitality since 1723' and is mentioned in directories from 1780. However, in 1722 an election was held to return two MPs for the borough and after the poll the Returning Officer (Bailiff) wished to use the **Unicorn** as a place to make the count and return as the Town Hall was then closed. However, one of the candidates, Sir Archer Croft, objected and said that he

---

THIRD HALF-YEARLY ORDINARY GENERAL MEETING.

NOTICE is hereby given, that the Third Half-yearly Ordinary General MEETING of the SHAREHOLDERS of this COMPANY will be held at the ROYAL OAK HOTEL, in the borough of Leominster, on TUESDAY, the 7th day of AUGUST next, at 1 o'clock in the forenoon precisely, for the purposes of the general business of the Company. And notice is hereby further given, that the said Meeting will be made special, to make such order as may be necessary for the borrowing and securing the re-payment of a sum of money not exceeding in amount the sum authorized to be borrowed by the said Company. And notice is also given, that the books kept for the registration of transfer of shares will be closed from TUESDAY, the 24th day of JULY, to TUESDAY, the 7th day of AUGUST next, both inclusive.

By order,
JOHN CHEESE, Secretary.
Leominster, 17th July, 1855.   [6272

The Leominster to Kington railway was opened on 20 August 1857 and closed on 7 February 1955

OXFORD, WORCESTER, AND WOLVERHAMPTON RAILWAY.

THE Public are respectfully informed that COACHES, in connection with the above Line, leave the following places daily :—

Hereford, Green Dragon	3	0 a.m.
Ledbury, Feathers Hotel	9	45 a.m.
Presteign, Radnorshire Arms ...	6	20 a.m.
Leominster, Oak Hotel	8	25 a.m.
Bromyard, Bridge Inn	10	0 a.m.
Ludlow, Fathers Hotel	8	0 a.m.
Tenbury, Swan Hotel	9	10 a.m.
Arrive at Worcester	12	5 p.m.
Arrive at Euston-square, London	5	15 p.m.

Fares from Worcester to London.

21s. First Class ; 15s. second class ; 9s. 3d. third class.

The above Coaches leave Worcester daily at 3.30 p.m., on arrival of London Train from Euston-square at 10 a.m., Paddington at 11 a.m.

By Order,

W. T. ADCOCK.

General Managers Office, Worcester,
June 1, 1855. [6131

The last of the coach services—the Shrewsbury to Newport railway was fully open by January 1854, but the line from Leominster to Worcester was not completed until 1897

would run the Bailiff through with his sword if he did not make the return immediately such action resulting in rioting and blood-shed, fortunately the hapless Bailiff ran across the roof-tops and escaped with his life. In the *Hereford Times* for 10 July 1790 it is recorded that Thomas Martin succeeded James Eley as 'Office Keeper' at the **Sign of the Unicorn.** In May 1793 the *Hereford Journal* noted that Edward Ford had left the **King's Arms** and entered the **Unicorn Inn,** where there was a billiard table and a bowling green. In 1898 the *Leominster News* commented that 'James Noden (a general contractor working in the 1850s) enlarged the

Royal Oak Hotel for the late Mr Bradford … and carried out other large contracts'. This was the same contractor that constructed a passage for Mr. Bird of the **Duke's Arms** (chapter 11).

On 9 October 1746 the Council Minute Book records 'By cash expended at the **Oak** etc, it being a public thanksgiving for the victory at Culloden £4 0s. 1d.' This was the Jacobite rebellion—Culloden took place on 16 April when the Jacobites under Prince Charles were finally crushed by the Duke of Cumberland. This was the last battle to be fought in Britain.

Mrs. Leather noted that, as late as 1879,

> in memory of the escape of the merry monarch, it was formerly usual in Herefordshire to carry out the customary wearing of oak leaves or oak apples on Royal Oak day [29 May], to a much greater extent than is the case at present. Every person, young or old, male or female, wore a sprig of oak about the dress or person, and in the event of anyone being discovered not conforming to the custom, he or she was considered as having an aversion to royalty, and received rough treatment at the hands of the people. The lads of the rural districts used to be (and in some parts of the county still are) very busy, for weeks before Royal Oak Day came round, collecting eggs of small birds; blackbirds and thrushes particularly, and with these they pelted mercilessly any person they chanced to see who had neglected to obtain the conventional oak leaf.
>
> Small branches of oak were fastened by the rustic waggoners to the head-gear of their horses in almost every part of Herefordshire, and in many places, early in the morning, ropes were stretched across the village streets, on which were hung garlands composed of all the flowers in bloom at the time, besides large boughs of oak and a multitude of gay-coloured ribbons. The country children were wont to rise early on the morning of this day and proceed to the woods to gather twigs of oak with the gall adhering, which they would place in their hats, carrying in their hands leaves and branches of trees, when they would call on a number of well-disposed inhabitants of the neighbourhood, and solicit small contributions towards keeping up their juvenile festivities. In some parts this custon was termed 'Shig Shagging', the name taking its rise from some doggerel, repeated in the event of a non-successful application for alms, of which the following is one version:
>
> 'Shig-shag, penny-a-rag,
> Bang his head with Cromwell's bag,
> All up in a bundle!'
>
> From: *Antiquatis, Herefordshire Gatherer,* 1879, and quoted by
> Ella Mary Leather in her *Folklore of Herefordshire,* 1912.

Mrs. Leather comments that it is now believed that Oak-Apple Day is one of the primitive agricultural festivals, which, as its real significance was forgotten, attached itself to the anniversary of an historical event.

Leominster Turnpike Trust.

NOTICE is hereby given, that the GENERAL ANNUAL MEETING of the Trustees or Commissioners of the Leominster Turnpike Trust, will be held at the ROYAL OAK INN, in the borough of Leominster, in the county of Hereford, on WEDNESDAY, the 5th day of FEBRUARY, next, at 12 o'clock at noon, for the purpose of auditing their accounts, and reporting the state of the Roads.

And Notice is hereby further given, that at the said meeting, new Trustees will be appointed in the places of those who are dead, or who decline to act.

THOMAS SALE,

Clerk to the Trustees.

Leominster, 6th January, 1862.

The Turnpike Trusts usually met in the finest inn in the area to discuss their business

The Royal Oak in 1999

ROYAL OAK HOTEL, LEOMINSTER.

THE ANNUAL TRADESMEN and FARMERS' DINNER will take place on TUESDAY, JANUARY 21s
1862.   PRESIDENT :—Mr. JOHN MANWARING.
VICE-PRESIDENT :—Mr. THOMAS BEAVEN.
DINNER TO BE ON THE TABLE AT THREE O'CLOCK.
TICKETS 3s. 6d. EACH.

The Leominster Union Friendly Society held its meetings at the **Royal Oak and Unicorn Inn**; it was founded on 22 November, 1804, and the Articles were revised and printed in October 1827 when there were 127 members. These Articles are extremely full and elaborate with a lot of detail. Initially there was an admission fee which varied from one and a half guineas in 1804 to five guineas in 1816. However, this must have been rather unsuccessful, for in 1818 it was reduced to one guinea and after that members could be admitted without an initial payment but could not claim benefit for six years.

From 1818 a committee of 13 members was appointed annually to whom disputes, the execution of rules, supervision of the monies, etc., were referred. General meetings were held at the Royal Oak on the first Wednesday monthly for the first year (1827-8), afterwards quarterly. The payments were so

1890 advertisement

208

arranged as to provide an annuity of £20 at the age of 60 (or an annuity for the widow if the member died).

The first Wednesday in October was the usual feast day when the members walked in procession to church—the clergyman receiving the not inconsiderable sum of one guinea for the sermon. The rules allowed for the expulsion of any member who enlisted in the armed forces, but if the member was unfortunate enough to be balloted to serve in the militia, the Society paid him five pounds to provide a substitute.

Other organizations also used the **Royal Oak**: the Tories used it as their meeting place; whereas the

Royal Oak advertisements—1950s [above]; *1960s* [below]

Whigs met at the 'Lion' which almost certainly was the **Red Lion** in Broad Street rather than the **White Lion** in Etnam Street. The Plymouth Brethren also held their services in the **Royal Oak**. The inn continues to provide venues for groups wishing to meet, and also for the showing of films.

CHAPTER ELEVEN

Leominster—East and South

Etnam Street

Etnam Street is to the south of Corn Square and runs eastwards from South Street to a corner near the railway station where it joins Worcester Road. Amost all the inns were on the north side and, from the west, start with the **Royal Oak**, on the corner with South Street. On the next corner, with School Lane, is the **White Swan**. Both are dealt with in the previous chapter.

The Bell, Etnam Street, in 2000
[see over]

To the east of School Lane, the first inn was the **Iron Boat Inn**, which was at 25-29, and was probably just a beer-house. It is mentioned in the Royal Commission report of 1934 as a house and shop, 'which was formerly the **Old Iron Boat Inn**'. It was described as being of 17th-century date with two stories and attics and was refronted in brick in the 18th century. The timber-framing was exposed in the west gable and at the back. It has since been demolished. What was the iron boat, and was it used on the Kenway and the Lugg? Could it have been associated with the navigation of the river Lugg? The Lugg was made navigable from Leominster to its junction with the Wye at Mordiford

211

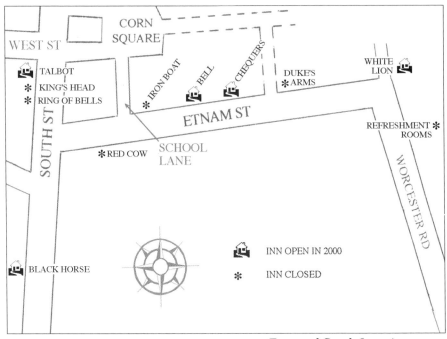

East and South Leominster

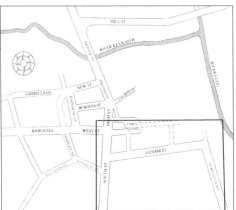

following the various Rivers Wye and Lugg Navigation Acts of 1661/2, 1695/6, 1727 and 1809.

The **Bell** at 39 Etnam Street, still provides a service to both travellers and locals. It is first mentioned in a directory in 1792. In 1879 the licence was held by Mrs. Charlotte Ovens and by Miss Eliza Lucas in the 1890s. In 1937 John J. Ree was the landlord. Writing in 1926, Monson-Fitzjohn calculated that there were then 483 houses called the Bell in England alone, not counting the blue variety. He goes on to say that it is a sign of long standing, for the Norman 'curfew' bell was once heard in every village. He even suggests that a bell was rung by the lord of the manor to inform his dependents on his estate that his great ovens were hot, ready for them to bring their bread to be baked. Bells are still common on inn signs in England, perhaps lending proof to Handel's comment that Britain was the 'ringing island'.

212

In the late 19th century the Chequers was very much 'Biddle's House' (upper)
There had been some changes to the façade by 1930 (middle), and more again by 1999 (lower)

Further along the street at No. 61 is the **Chequers Inn**. In 1934 a report by the inspector for the Royal Commission for Historic Monuments described the building as being of two stories with attics, built in the late 16th or early 17th century with a projecting timber-framed gable on the south front including a moulded bressummer and moulded and enriched barge-boards. The back wing was described as a 17th-century addition with exposed framing.

Inside the building the inspector noted the original moulded ceiling beams and a panelled cupboard door with cock's-head hinges. The staircase was seen to retain an original newel with an ornamental terminal, and in the back wing there were two 17th-century doors each with moulded battens.

213

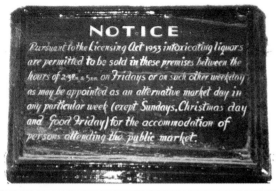

The 'Market Sign' at the Chequers, which indicated that the inn was allowed to sell 'intoxicating liquors' between 2.30 p.m. and 5 p.m. on Friday market day 'for the convenience of persons attending the public market'

The view down Etnam Street from an early 20th-century postcard. The building next to the twin gables of the Chequers has since disappeared. Further down the street is the sign for the Duke's Arms

In 1858 the landlord was James Biddle; he was still there in 1879 when the entry in the Post Office Directory described him as also being a retail brewer. As such he would not have had to look far for his raw materials and equipment for there were two coopers and two maltsters in Leominster itself, and a number of hop–growers a short distance away in Ivington.

The **Chequers** was very much a family concern, for some years later there was still a Biddle holding the licence—this was John Job Biddle. At least one more generation followed, for in 1937 Harold Job Biddle had

Gingers, once the Duke's Head, in 1999

taken on the mantle of running the inn and the brewery. Writing in the 1970s, Norman Reeves reported that cider had been made at the **Chequers** 'until fairly recently', and in the same era local and national newspapers reported that the **Chequers** had 'the fastest barmaid in the west!'.

The fading 'market sign' above the doorway at the Chequers reflects the time when public houses were compelled to close during the afternoon from 2.30 p.m. to 6 p.m. unless they had a special market day licence.

The **Duke's Arms** was at 75 Etnam Street on the corner with Duke's Lane from well before 1879. Recently it had a name change to **Ginger's**, and its future as an inn now appears to be somewhat uncertain. The building is 17th century, but the front was altered in the late 18th century. An article in the *Leominster News* in 1898 recalled:

> In the period of which I am telling [late 1850s] I do not remember any contract (for building) in the town being let to strangers except the Corn Exchange, which was built by Hardwick, of Birmingham 1857-59. Edward Bird, who then owned and occupied the **Duke's Arms** (where Mr J. Smith's shop is) would not part with a portion of his premises required for the work unless a cellar was made under the Corn Exchange which he could use as a brew-house. The cellar was accordingly made, and also a passage connecting it with the **Duke's Arms** cellar, but Bird died very soon after, killed, so he said, by the closeness of the atmosphere he had to do his brewing in, and the cellar was not afterwards used … James Noden constructed this cellar and the excavations at the Corn Exchange.

Edward Bird had already escaped death once in 1858 when a newly-made arch in his cellar fell down. In 1879 William Jenkins was listed as the landlord, but there is some confusion between directories as No. 75 was also listed as the **Wine Vaults** (an 1876 directory gives this name to No. 79). These entries are probably due to errors by the compilers as 'Vaults' do not appear in Etnam Street with any regularity.

The White Lion in the early 1930s. There has been little change to this, the eastern elevation that faces the railway

When William Jenkins was at the **Duke's Arms**, Charles Doherty had a coffee house next door. Was this to cater for those who did not approve of alcoholic liquor, or was it for the benefit of those who had over indulged in the **Duke's Arms**? By 1891 Mrs. Annie Sargant was the landlady, but she did not stay long, for the *Hereford Times* for February 1892 records bankruptcy proceedings against Henry Thomas Jones of the **Duke's Arms**.

At the western end of Etnam Street is the **White Lion** an inn that was apparently known as the **Horse and Jockey** at some time. A report by the Royal Commission on Historical Monuments in 1934 says:

> on the bend in the road this inn was built in the early 16th century but has a modern gable on the east side and modern additions on the west. It may have once projected further to the north. The timber-framing is generally exposed and the upper storey projects on the east side and south end on curved brackets and small shafts with moulded capitals; the bressummers are moulded; the south gable also projects on two curved brackets. At this end the first floor has been partly underbuilt and the bressummer is covered by a fascia-board. Inside the building, the middle part formed a single room with moulded ceiling beams forming four bays from north to south and three from east to west. The south part, also formerly one room, has similar but rather more elaborately moulded beams. The rooms above also have moulded ceiling beams.

The White Lion under repair in 1999

The White Lion from the railway bridge in 2000

The king of beasts is very well represented in English pub names, usually with a red or white prefix, but occasionally with other colours. Most stem from heraldry, many families wishing to associate themselves with the lion's reputation for courage and strength.

The **White Lion** is first mentioned in an 1835 directory and in 1858 James Noakes was landlord. 1879 saw Mrs. Eliza Smith as landlady—

she had moved from the **Star** and was still there in 1891. In 1937 the licensee was Cyril Allen.

Just around the corner in Worcester Road, Leominster railway station in its heyday included a **Refreshment Room**, and like all such establishments it had a licence to sell intoxicating drinks and thus cater for thirsty travellers. Sadly the licence for this bar was not renewed in 1954, indeed, the station is now no longer manned by railway staff.

On the south side of Etnam Street at No. 10 is Watson's Garage. This is the site of the **Red Cow Inn** which had ceased to by the end of the 19th century and by 1898 was described as the 'Mission Room'. The Royal Commission in the 1930s were somewhat uncertain about the building, for they described the property as continuing back into Miles Court and including a range of four tenements 'that was perhaps originally an inn and outbuildings'. The cellars of the inn were discovered a few years ago when the garage was digging some holes for posts.

A reference to a **Horse and Groom**, probably in Etnam Street was made in 1780, but does not occur subsequently and nothing else is known about it.

South Street

South Street is the continuation of High Street from its junction with West Street. The public houses on the eastern side between Corn Street and Etnam Street—the **Ducking Stool** and the **Royal Oak**—have been covered in the last chapter. This chapter includes all the other inns in the street, including the **Talbot** which is on the corner of South Street and West Street.

Close to the West Street junction at No.4 was the **King's Head**. In the *Hereford Journal* for 22 August 1832 there is a sale advertisement:

All that old-fashioned and well accustomed Inn and Public House called the King's Head, situate in South Street, in the occupation of William Rivers Nash, containing two front parlours, good kitchen, back kitchen or brewhouse on the ground floor; a dining room and three bedrooms on the first floor; and three bedrooms on the second floor, together with good cellar and pump, yard and excellent stabling, the whole being in good and substantial repair. Leasehold for three lives under the Corporation of Leominster at low rents, renewable on payment of Fines certain.

In the 1920s it was described as being at the 'Iron Cross'. Watkins suggests that the Iron Cross was probably a stone structure with a finial of an iron cross and mentions that there is a corporation record of repair works to the public pumps at the Iron Cross and the **Golden Cross**—an inn in West Street. In February 1728 the Minute Book of the Corporation records 'That the Chamberlain do erect a Guard House over the Iron Cross'. The first mention of the **King's Head** is in a directory of 1830; in 1879 the landlady was Mrs. Ann Sargeant and in 1890 it was held by Mrs. Olivia Edwards. It was not mentioned in the 1937 directory and may have become the **Talbot Vaults**.

Separated from the **King's Head** by only one building, was the **Ring of Bells** at 8 South Street. It was recorded in 1780 and in 1858 J. Drew was landlord, Henry Baker in 1890 and John Oliver in 1891. The inn continued through the First World War, but the licence was

8 South Street was once the Ring of Bells. A small sign above the
now-blocked archway still reads 'Bell Court'.
The building covered in scaffolding was the King's Head

Advertisement for the Talbot in 1876

not renewed in 1932 and the building is now occupied by an estate agent. The yards that were originally at the rear of both the **King's Head** and the **Ring of Bells** have now been incorporated into the rear car park for the **Talbot**.

The Talbot in the 1930s

The **Talbot** has entrances in both South Street and West Street, but as this chapter is following the east side of South Street it is logical to include it here, although the main façade is in West Street where it is numbered 5-9. However, early directories also mention the South Street approach, perhaps for the common man, for the **Talbot Tap** mentioned in a 1900 directory and the **Talbot Vaults** recorded in 1903, are probably the same entity and is likely to have been the 'back-bar'. In common with many hotels, the **Talbot** would probably have had a 'public bar' as well as facilities for

The Talbot in the 1930s.
The Lounge Bar (upper) : *The first floor* (lower)

residents. Such bars catered for the servants and others associated with the hotel's guests and frequently had a separate entrance 'at the side' or 'at the back' where locals were also welcome. However, there should be a note of caution or confusion, as the case may be, for the 1937 Kelly's Directory lists the **Talbot Vaults**, totally separate from the **Talbot** with Edward B. Owen as licensee, at 4 South Street, the same number as the earlier **King's Head**. It would appear that the

The Talbot corner of South Street and West Street in 1999

Talbot Hotel bought out the **King's Head**, which was next door just across the entry to the yard, and converted it into the **Talbot Vaults.**

The main part of the **Talbot** is three stories high and of 17th-century date. The front block to West Street was largely rebuilt and heightened in the 18th century. The back wing has some exposed timber-framing. No 9 is a separate building which, in the early 1930s,

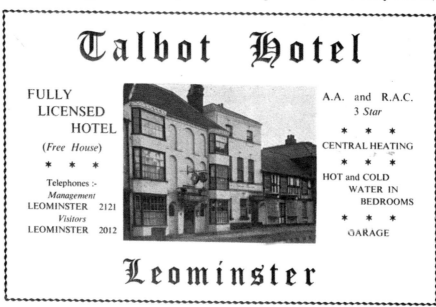

A 1950s advertisement for the Talbot

was a house and shop, also of 17th-century date but with much alteration in the 18th century. Inside the building there were two original door-lintels with a pointed head cut on the soffit.

A Friendly Society was based at the **Talbot Inn** from the mid-18th century, but it apparently had some problems. On the title page of what are described as 'the revised and amended Rules of the Friendly Society held at the **Talbot Inn**', which had been adopted in 1822, it is asserted that 'The Loyal and Friendly

Changing the menu at the Talbot in 1999

Society ... commenced August 23, 1753'. The rules are preceded by a paragraph calling the attention of the members to an evil which had been of frequent occurrence in earlier days. This related to the breaking up of a society and the division of the funds, so that members had been 'disappointed of receiving that relief, to which their payments have justly entitled them'. It was therefore unanimously agreed that the reformed society should not be broken up under any pretence. All the previous rules were cancelled and the new ones came into force on 6 February, 1823, when the stock of the old company was declared to be the property of the new one. There was no restriction on membership apart from it being limited to residents within five miles of Leominster. Meetings took place on the first Thursday of the month, members paying one shilling and three pence monthly towards the fund. The sum of ten shillings and six pence was allowed to the minister for a sermon on 'old Christmas Day'—the half-yearly meeting—and every member had to attend unless ill or forfeit one shilling. After the sermon the members dined with the stewards at a cost of one shilling and six pence. New stewards took office half-yearly, and they appointed a president from those attending the monthly meetings.

The stewards were to cause two little cups to be brought with the first carriage of ale, and members presuming to drink from others were fined two pence. The inn-keeper was to keep a good fire for meetings from Michaelmas day to May, and at other times if desired. Benefits were payable to those in need after three years' membership and amounted to seven shillings weekly during illness for six months providing that the stock amounted to £100 or more. There was a strict rule against gambling or undertaking any kind of trade during the period that pay was drawn. After six months the allowance was reduced to 3s. 6d. or other sum agreed by the members, and this would be paid for life if the disease was incurable. The society also paid death benefits and up to £6 was allowed for a funeral dependent on the length of membership. By the 1840s the Friendly Society had apparently moved to the **Red Lion Inn**.

Early in December 1794 there was a notice in the *Hereford Journal* that the **Talbot** was for sale; three weeks later the paper informed its readers that William Davis was taking it on. In 1858 E. Luscot was the licensee and in 1879 it was Francis Lucas. It stayed in the family for some time, for in 1891 Mrs. Elizabeth Lucas was the landlady. The directory may have been slightly out of date, for the *Hereford Times* of 18 October 1890 records the sale of the **Talbot** for £1,525. The directory for 1937 still has the inn at just 5 and 7 West Street and lists the licensee as John M. Thomas. By that time the hotel had a telephone—the number being Leominster 12.

Stanley Holland, Leominster's prodigal son, whose father kept the **White Horse** also in West Street, was a frequent drinker in the **Baker's Arms** and also in the **Talbot**. Norman Reeves reports that the landlady of the **Talbot** entrusted him with her financial transactions and that he emigrated to the USA in 1895 to avoid prosecution for financial irregularities—it is not known whether the landlady got her money back!

Although the talbot is a white sporting dog with black or blue spots that was used for hunting, the use of the name in Leominster

224

probably relates to the Talbot family—the Earls of Shrewsbury. They bred the dog in the 15th century and included it in their coat of arms. The dog had a marvellous sense of smell and was an ancestor of the modern fox hound.

The Black Lion, earlier the Bowling Green, in 1999

Further down South Street beyond Westbury Street was the **Bowling Green** at No.74. This inn was first mentioned in an 1830 directory. In 1858 T. Lewis was landlord and Charles Thomas was there between 1876 and 1891. It has now been the **Black Horse** for many years. This later name is a common one throughout the country and its use seems to be a reflection of its potential as a visual image— which is the case in Leominster. A black horse is now associated with Lloyds Bank, and the same sign, being used for an inn, perhaps gives the inn's customer a reassuring impression.

Other inns recorded as being in South Street have been the **Brewery Tap**, doubtless a beer house and only mentioned in the 1879 directory when A. Baker was landlord and had a side business in dealing in fish and poultry. An 1880s map shows a small building marked as a brewery, just to the west of South Street—this is likely to be the Britannia Brewery of Charles Blundell & Co. listed in the Post Office Directory of 1879. The inn could well have been associated with the brewery. To confuse the reader, an 1890 directory stated that the **Brewery Tap** was at 30 Bridge Street with John Mills in charge! Neither Mills nor the **Brewery Tap** are mentioned in the Kelly's Directory for 1891.

Square and compasses

The **Mason's Arms** has been mentioned in directories of 1835 and 1840 but not since. There is a building in South Street with an incised symbol of 'square and compasses' in South Street, but this is more likely to have been a Masonic Hall rather than a pub.

In an 1898 article the *Leominster News* commented on cider houses in Leominster:

Several cider shops, now quite extinct, did a good business. It would shock some people now-a-days who are not total abstainers if they could see Mr Martin's of the Townsend, South Street, as it used to be on a Sunday afternoon and evening. Martin had a large yard with poplars round which he placed ladders and benches for his customers to sit on and enjoy their cider. At that time drink was sold anywhere all day on Sunday and, indeed, people generally didn't keep Sunday at all well in the old days.

This was probably the establishment known as the **Poplars**, shown intermittently in directories between 1780 and 1840.

CHAPTER TWELVE

Leominster—North and West

Broad Street & Burgess Street

Broad Street is a continuation of High Street going north-north-west from its junction with Burgess Street and Church Street. Prior to 1807 when the pig and sheep market was moved to New Street it was presumably a noisome place, although persons having business at the markets would have had more opportunities for alcoholic refreshment than are now available in the street.

In Burgess Street, which connects the main thoroughfare with Rainbow Street, the **Sun Inn** is recorded between 1830 and 1840. In 1840 it was renamed the **New Inn** and continued to trade as a public house until 1927. In 1858 Mattey was the name of the landlord, John Wilson was there in 1879, Robert Stephens in 1890 and Mrs. Eliza Stephens in 1891. An article in the *Leominster News* in 1898 reported: 'I remember the premises of Mr McNish's brewery being built in 1832 by Mr Page (grandfather of Alderman Page) and William Davies, of the **Sun Tavern** (now the **New Inn**). The dwelling house at the brewery was built in, or very near, 1852, and was considered what it undoubtedly is, a very good specimen of building'. The building occupied the site between Grafton House and the old Congregational Church, which is now the entrance to the central car park.

Back at 4 Broad Street, the **Grapes** or **Grape Vaults** or **Grapes Wines and Spirits Vaults**, as it has been variously recorded, may not have been named as such at the time of the market's move but it was there in 1853 when Thomas Smith was landlord and Mr. G. Onions, a lay-preacher, arrived in Leominster to evangelize the navvies building the Hereford to Shrewsbury railway. According to Norman Reeves he suffered much indignity and ridicule at the hands of Thomas Smith, but

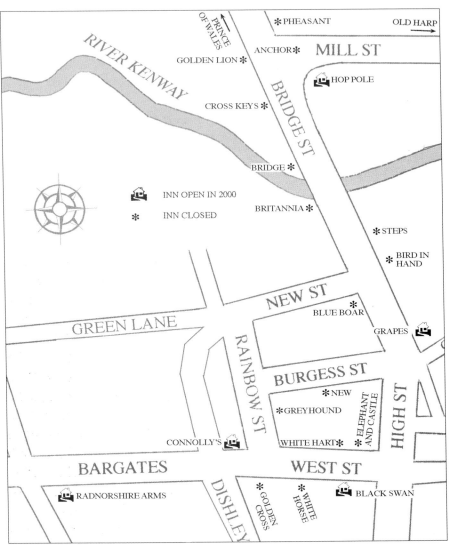

North and West Leominster

eventually converted Smith who became his assistant at the Railwaymen's Mission. In 1856 Smith wrote an autobiography *A Brand Plucked from the Burning: or My Life*, which was reprinted by Leominster Museum in

THE GRAPE VAULTS

1997. As a boy he lived with his maternal grandfather, William Cartwright, who kept the **Vaults** for many years. Thomas recorded that 'he was extremely moderate; in fact, he made a rule which he scrupulously observed, never, under any circumstances, to drink with anyone. He would not keep open beyond eleven o'clock at night for the best customer he had, and he always refused to serve a man who appeared the least intoxicated'. Perhaps this high moral upbringing was partly the cause of Thomas leaving for an early life of debauchery, locally in the **Three Horse Shoes** and then further afield. Eventually he returned to Leominster and was married in 1850. The married couple spent three weeks seeing the sights of London and then returned to Leominster with £1 in gold and some odd coppers. 'That was all we had to begin business. My grandmother left us

The Grape Vaults in 1999

about £10 of stock, and with a small quantity of spirits of each sort, we began. Fortune, often fickle, smiled upon us'. This only lasted for a while, for Thomas got round to thinking that he was in the house too much and 'I regularly went out to other public houses, and soon became a complete drunkard'. Eventually Thomas began to see the light and became 'decided for Christ'. He wrote 'I was soon counted mad. The cold shoulder of my friends I now had to endure, despised and forsaken by old companions ... my business began to fall off, my smoke-room, which before had been full, was now empty, owing to the fact that I could not mix with my companions as hitherto. Satan tempted me strongly, with the threat that business would fall off, which it did very much for about three months. But at last it took a turn, and my trade increased, especially in the out-door branch'. By 1855 he had become secretary and treasurer of a fund to build a new Place of Worship for the Leominster Town and Country Mission Society—this was on the site of a malt-house in Etnam Street and is now the Leominster Folk Museum. By this time he was enduring 'the misery of keeping a wine vault', which he described as a thorn in his side. Before the end of the year he had sold the tavern to John Langford, a wines and spirits merchant, which may explain the long version of the pub's name. He then set himself up in the drapery business, only to give this up later to become a full-time missionary.

In Thomas Smith's time the customer's behaviour was very different from that which is now seen in the Grapes for he wrote: 'I have known women come in after fighting, bathe their head in brandy and then drink it up full of blood and hair. I have seen a poor prostitute, and a man drunk by her; and when the poor wretch could take no more, get a tundish and put the small end in her mouth, put neat gin in the other, and thus force it down her throat'.

Moving forward a century things were presumably much quieter for one licensee had time to tend to his bees kept at the side of the pub. It was closed for many years and propped up on its northern side, but eventually re-opened. At the start of the 21st century the hostelry remains a small pub, opening directly onto the street, but providing homely comforts; especially in the colder weather when an old-fashioned coal fire is lit for the benefit of the customers.

Other pubs in Broad Street have not survived. The **Bird in Hand** at No. 44 was first noted in 1780. Mrs. Ann Colcomb was in charge in

1879 and William Jones in 1890, but the licence was relinquished in 1927.

The **Blue Boar Inn** was at 21 Broad Street, on the corner with New Street. It was first mentioned in directories in 1830 and by 1858 Paul Gower was landlord, William Deakin was there in 1879 and Thomas William Worthing in 1891. The pub kept going well into the 20th century with G. Sayers there in 1937. The Blue Boar is a heraldic reference to the Earl of Oxford, a leading supporter of the Lancastrian cause in 1485. It eventually closed its doors in 1971 when the licence was not renewed and is now the New Golden Dragon providing take-away meals.

The Blue Boar still serves food!

Little is known of a pub called the **Britannia**, which reputedly was at 45 High Street and had an Assembly Room at the rear. 45 Broad Street is on the southern side of the bridge over the Kenwater and includes a long stretch of buildings to the rear. It is the last house in Broad Street and seems likely to have been the **Britannia**.

Was this fine-looking building next to the Kenwater once the Britannia?

Townsend in his *History of Leominster* noted in 1863 that: 'the **Unicorn Inn** at Leominster, is now a shop in the Broad Street, in the occupation of Mr Josiah Newman. The other chief inn at this time, was the **Crown**, which stood in Broad Street, nearly opposite to the **Unicorn**, and was approached by six steps, and had a narrow entrance of wainscot'. There must be some confusion here, for it has already been established that the **Unicorn** was an earlier name for the **Royal Oak** (see p.204). Thus the **Unicorn** is entered in directories between 1780 and 1792 and the first entry for the **Royal Oak** is in 1830. In the directories for 1835 and 1840 the entries were collectively for the **Royal Oak and Unicorn.** It would appear that there was an early inn in Broad Street that was called the **Unicorn**, and that this was converted to a shop in the latter part of the 18th century. At the beginning of the 19th century the name was then taken up for a short time as an addition to the old-established **Oak** in South Street.

The **Crown** is mentioned at the start of the 17th century when the Borough Accounts for 1609 includes an item: 'paid for 6 Dynners at the **Crowne** by Mr Bailiff's appointment and others of the Company xvij s. vj d.'—quite an expensive meal for the time at 17s. 6d! During the Civil War King Charles was in north Herefordshire and the *Iter Carolinum*, a diary written by one of the King's attendants, contains this entry:

1640.   Item—paid for wine and beare by Mr Edgar
         and his company at the Crowne   xvjd.

and some years later, in celebration of the enthronement of Charles II, the entries show a considerable party spirit:

1661.   At the Crowne on the Coronation day   £2.12s.
         Hogshead of Bere   £1.10s.
         Widow Wanklin (The Landlady of the chief Inn) £5. 0s.
         More to Do   £1. 0s.

The **Crown** has long been closed—it is mentioned in directories until the middle of the 19th century, but not thereafter. Presumably this was the **Crown Inn** from which coaches used to go three times a week to the King's Head in Kington.

The 'crown' name was somewhat over-used in a 'poem' that was probably composed in the tap-room of a Crown Inn somewhere, and was obviously meant to encourage further patronage. It begins:

Come my lads, and crown your wishes,
With glee come crown your greatest joys,
Come to the Crown and drink like fishes,
Spend each a crown my jovial boys.

In the early 1800s the **Red Lion** in Broad Street was the main coaching station for Leominster with a regular service of stage coaches and wagons to many towns including a thrice weekly service to London via Worcester. The **Red Lion** was also used as a meeting place by the Whigs—the Tories meeting in the **Royal Oak**. In the 1840s it was also the home of the Leominster Loyal and Friendly Society after the society moved its headquarters from the **Talbot**. The **Red Lion** was first mentioned in a directory in 1780, and in 1858 Mary Davies was landlady, but shortly after this the premises were used as a manufactury of iron goods by Alexanders & Loverage and then became known as the 'Lion Works'. The name of the company changed to that of Alexander and Duncan—manufacturers and suppliers of agricultural equipment—whose name-plate is still evident on a number of farm buildings in the area. Not so long ago the work's site was redeveloped, but the frontage still remains surmounted by a red painted lion and now

The Lion Yard still has an imposing front in Broad Street

233

provides ball-room facilities restored in character for weddings, birthday parties and the like.

Another place used by many organizations in the past was the **Waterloo Hotel and Coaching Inn** in Broad Street, which was recorded as such as early as 1835. The place where this famous battle was fought in 1815 is a small town some 12 miles south of Brussels, in Belgium, where an allied army of several nations under the Duke of Wellington defeated Napoleon's French army. Napoleon abdicated some four bays after the battle. This was considered at the time a victory on land to equal Nelson's achievement at Trafalgar ten years earlier. Such victories were considered great opportunities to name or rename inns.

An article in the *Leominster News* in 1898 reports: 'I remember the first stucco front being done in Leominster. It is still to be seen at what was then the **Waterloo Hotel**, or, as it is now called, the **Waterloo**. The stucco was put there in 1838 by Joseph Poulton, and the style becoming fashionable he afterwards did a great number of the stuccoed fronts now to be seen in the town. His sons did a good deal of this work and he also employed Saunders and Ludlow, well-known in the trade'.

Norman Reeves reported that the inaugural meeting of the 'Mechanic's Institution' took place there in 1841 and was addressed by the Revd. Dr. Merewether, Dean of Hereford. He welcomed women to the Institution and advised its officers to avoid controversy by excluding such subjects as politics and religion.

Waterloo House, which adjoined the hotel, was used by the Plymouth Brethren for their meetings when the rooms that they had previously used in the **King's Arms** and **Royal Oak** became inadequate for their needs. Following the building of the railway the **Waterloo Hotel** closed, presumably due to the resultant reduction in the need for coaches and carters, and the premises were put up for auction in 1872. The hotel and the house were bought by the Brethren with the old ballroom being used for services and the house used as a conference centre. In the early 1900s missionaries world-wide met here for their 'Leominster Conferences' and services were held in the Waterloo Rooms until 1933 when the Brethren moved to Brook House.

Bridge Street & Mill Street

Bridge Street is a continuation of Broad Street, the name change occuring at the line of the river Kenwater in an area of Leominster also know as 'Middle Marsh', and in some records as 'Middle Mark'. At the junction where Mill Street branches off to the right, the road sign indicates that it is the Old Ludlow Road that continues straight ahead. However, to confuse locals and visitors alike, this road is still Bridge Street for several hundred yards!

On the west side of the street the first pub was the **Bridge** Inn at No. 3. It has been mentioned in directories from 1850: in 1858 it was in the care of George Mattey and in 1879 Mrs. Eliza Mattey had taken over. By 1890 Tom Mitchell was landlord and was supplementing his income by being a shopkeeper as well as an inn-keeper, but 20 years later, in 1910, the premises ceased to be licenced. The attractive black-and-white building still survives overlooking the river.

The Bridge Inn was in this half-timbered building overlooking the Kenwater

At No. 31 was the **Cross Keys**, also referred to as the **Old Cross Keys**, a 17th-century building with exposed framing to the upper storey of the easterly frontage in which are two original and slightly projecting windows with moulded frames, heads and sills. The first mention of the Cross Keys was in 1830 and by 1858 John Edwards was licensee. William Albert James was the

The Cross Keys was in this once-jettied building

landlord in 1879 and Mrs. Elizabeth Wood took over in 1891 from Isaac Harris. By 1937 Mrs. Edith Elizabeth Phillips was licensee. The inn continued until well after the Second World War, but finally the licence was not renewed in 1970 and it now called Preservation House.

Norman Reeves records that opposite this inn in 1854, a Mr. H. Trimble opened a 'Commercial School' with an announcement that advertized Mr. Trimble's own rudimentary education:

> Terms moderate; as Mr. Trimble having a very large family, who also prove useful as minor Teachers etc. under his superintendance. Mr. T has the most unexceptional testimonials. C of E is his Religion, but every party to enjoy his own Fig Tree. No tampering with Pupils as regards Religion.

The name of this inn may have been inspired by the fact that Leominster's Patron Saint is St. Peter. The keys to heaven are said to be held by St. Peter and his emblem is 'crossed keys'. The Borough Arms have St. Peter and a Pilgrim as supporters but, strangely, he is depicted holding a single key—no doubt as a result of 'artistic licence' by the heraldic artist.

The **Golden Lion** at 69 Bridge Street, opposite the junction with Mill Street, is a Grade II listed building said to be of the early 19th century, but the name 'Golden Lion' is first found in a directory of

1780. In 1858 Mrs. E. Wormington was landlady and was still there in 1879, but by 1890 she had been replaced by John Ingram. J. Allen was the licensee in 1937. In latter years this building has been used as an antiques warehouse but at the start of the millennium it appears to be unused.

Once the Golden Lion in Bridge Street

P.C. Worthing, who had attempted to prosecute the management of the **Wine Vaults** for serving a child under 14, made a similar charge against George Allen, the then licensee of the **Golden Lion**. The *Hereford Times* for 12 February 1916 recorded the following case at Leominster Borough Police Court:

P.C. Worthing stated that on Sunday January 30th he saw a little girl enter the Golden Lion Inn with a bottle. She was supplied and came out into the street again carrying a quart of cider. He asked the defendant if he supplied the child with drink and he replied "Yes, a quart of cider". Witness said "Why didn't you seal it then?" Defendant replied "I don't know, I couldn't put my hand on one just then". Witness then asked "How old do you think the child is?" Defendant replied "About 10 or 11, I think". Cross-examined, the officer said the house was well conducted and there had been no complaints against the defendant before ...Mr Wadsworth, for the defence said that the child was evidently a 'nippy young thing' and took off the bottle before Mr Allen had been paid, and while he was upstairs getting a label to act as a seal. When he came down he was surprised to find the bottle gone and the money on the bar. The defendant had been four years at Leominster and 14 years in the Licensed Trade. The case was dismissed because there was no evidence of the child's age and 'because the licensee had not completed the sale and they did not believe that he would willingly break the law, as he kept his house very well indeed'.

Like the **Cross Keys** this inn may well have taken its name from Leominster's Arms for the coat-of-arms is charged with a golden lion holding a lamb.

Where Bridge Street continues northwards beyond the Mill Street junction it leaves the part of the town known as Middle Marsh and enters the area known as Nether Marsh, sometimes referred to as Lower Marsh. This is the part of the town where much of the tanning took place to supply the flourishing leather workers of Leominster. Several hundred yards along Bridge Street was the **Prince of Wales** of which little is known except that it was recorded in 1876 as being at 121 Bridge Street with James Coleman as landlord, and that Edward Saviour was licensee in 1891. Closure followed the failure to renew the licence in 1932. Fleeting references to inns, or more likely beerhouses, called the **Mughouse** and the **Angel** have also been found in this area.

Returning to the junction of Bridge Street and Mill Street, the **Pheasant** was on the north-eastern corner and in 1879 Walter Shinn held the licence. In 1890 Mrs. Jane Edwards was the landlady, Walter Shinn presumably having retired, for the *Hereford Times* of 25 June 1892 recorded the death 'from excitement' of Walter Shinn, 71, formerly of the **Pheasant Inn**. The pub's licence was not renewed in 1910.

Someway along the north side of Mill Street was the **Harp Inn**, also referred to as the **Old Harp**. Of the building, now called the Poplands, the Royal Commission report of 1934 says:

It was built early in the 16th century on a rectangular plan. Extended to the north in the early 17th century and the west front re-faced in the 18th century when a central wing was added on the east. The gabled south end has close-set timber-framing except to the ground floor which is of modern brick. At the first floor level is an original moulded bressummer terminating at a pair of elaborately carved and scrolled brackets, perhaps of later date. The gable projects on an original moulded base-beam with a band of carving above consisting of intersecting arches with cusps and foliated spandrels. The side posts of the upper storey have attached shafts with curved brackets supporting the gable. The barge boards are carved with running leaf-ornament, and have a Jacobean apex post. The east face has close set framing up to the added wing. The north end has later timber-framing in square panels. Inside the building are some original ceiling beams.

The inn was mentioned sporadically in directories from 1792 until 1859 when it became a private residence of some standing—at one time being occupied by one of the sheriff's trumpeters amongst other notables. It was then called 'The Poplands'. The name Poplands probably comes from the 'Popeland Turnpike' which was hereabouts in the 17th century.

On the southern corner of Mill Street was the **Anchor Inn** at 46 Bridge Street. This was a 17th-century building of three stories that had been heightened and much altered, but in 1930 some original framing was still visible at the back. It was first mentioned in a directory in 1830, William Pugh was landlord in 1858 and John

The Poplands, formerly the Old Harp Inn

Christy was there between 1879 and 1891. Edwin H. Preece was there in 1937 and the inn survived the war. However, the licence was not renewed in February 1964 probably as a result of a road widening scheme to improve the junction of Bridge Street with Mill Street. Unfortunately, as with many road improvement schemes, this involved the demolition of the building.

Returning down the east side of Bridge Street, the **Hop Pole** is now the nearest pub to the corner. It is a 17th-century building that has been re-fronted and much altered. It was first mentioned in a directory in 1830 and a report of this time says:

> I remember seeing a great fight between (Tommy) Dug and Jones, of the **Hop Pole,** under the big elm tree just over Ridgemoor Bridge. After the fight had gone on for an hour some respectable people who disapproved of that sort of thing went up to Dr. Taylor, then almost the only justice living in Leominster, and got him to come down to put a stop to it. I was a boy at that time, but I remember well how when the old doctor came on the scene all the people cried out 'Oh, please to let them fight, sir!' So the incarnation of English justice, who was called to curse and to stop the fighters, stayed half-an-hour to bless them, and was then conducted home by some of the gentlement present, after which the fight continued another hour-and-a-half. I remember Jones's face was already a fearful sight when the doctor arrived, but he pluckily kept on and wore Tommy Dug out.

The Hop Pole on the corner of Bridge Street and Mill Street

In 1858 John Jones was landlord, in 1879 it was Joseph Durham who also offered his skills as a carpenter, in 1890 William Coles was in charge. At one time the hop vines used to be trained up hop poles, but now they grow up strings attached to a wire frame. In the 19th century there were many hop yards around Leominster. However, it has been suggested that this was one of the oldest inn signs to be found not only in England, but on the Continent. The original sign usually took the form of a long pole with a wreath of hop leaves hung from the extreme tip by four strings so that the wreath was at right angles to the pole. The general description followed the Roman 'bush' sign, but hops were only introduced to this country in the early 15th century.

This building could well be the Steps

There has been some form of retail outlet for alcoholic liquor at No. 30 Bridge Street. A William Pounds has been recorded as a 'beer retailer' operating from this address, it has been described as the **Steps** and also as the **Brewery Tap**. References are scanty and confusing but there is a building in this vacinity which does have steps and does have the remains of a sign frame, but there is no sign left to tell tales!

At 22 Bridge Street was the **Crown & Sceptre**. It was first mentioned in a directory in 1830, Charles Rowlands was landlord in 1879 and Mrs. Elizabeth Phillips in 1890. It was present in the early 1920s when it was described as being at Middle Mark. The licence was not renewed in 1925.

West Street, Rainbow Street and Bargates
Leaving Corn Square from the south side and going westwards along Corn Street, the street opposite is the aptly named West Street

240

(South Street being to the left going south, and High Street to the right going north).

The **Talbot Hotel** is at Nos. 5-9 and has been included in the previous chapter due to its frontage in South Street. In West Street it started off as Nos. 5 & 7, but eventually 'collected' No. 9.

The even numbers in West Street are on the northern side and at No. 6 was the **Elephant and Castle**. The first record is in a directory of 1830; in 1858 landlord was James Cheshire, in 1879 is was Thomas Prichard who was also described as a maltster, and in 1891 the landlord was Harry Best. An article in the *Leominster News* in 1898 reported: 'The **Elephant and Castle** 50 years ago did about the best business of any public in the town. It was kept by a man named Garrett who committed suicide'. The name has its origin in the arms of the cutlers' company, which, since 1622, have included an elephant with a howdah on its back, the latter looking very much like a miniature castle. The

6 West Street, once the Elephant and Castle

Elephant and Castle ceased to be a public house in 1915 during the Great War and by 1937 was a café run by Henry Foster. It is now the Central Bakery.

Two doors further up at No. 10 West Street was the **White Hart**, a 17th-century building with a modern front, but with an original gable with exposed framing at the back. It is first mentioned in a directory of 1780. William Mapp was licensee in 1858 and was apparently still there in 1879. It certainly seems to have been a family concern for Mrs. Jane Mapp held the licence in 1891. It ceased to hold a licence in 1933 and is now a shop—Skelton's Sound and Vision. The origins of this common sign probably date back to Richard II's time, for it was his heraldic symbol. Tavern keepers of the time would have shown their allegiance to the king by displaying the sign above their door. Modern

10 West Street, Onve the White Hart

usage is more generic; Dickens gives a fine description of the White Hart in Southwark where Sam Weller first met Mr. Pickwick.

A short way beyond the **White Hart**, the turning for Rainbow Street bears off to the north, parallel to High Street. This contained the **Greyhound Inn**, mentioned in direct-ories from 1840 and where John Price was landlord in 1858. Richard Price was licensee in 1879 and William Price in 1890—seemingly another father-to-son establishment. William Price was also listed as a farmer. By 1937, the chain had been broken and Ernest R. Guy was the landlord. The greyhound was formerly used in the chase, but it is now mainly associated with greyhound racing. At one time an 'All-seeing Eye' was painted on the front of the building, for the Oddfellows met regularly in a room at the back of the inn. Oddfellows' Hall was first used by the 'British School for Boys' in 1857 and Reeves records that in 1859 the fees were 2d., 3d., or 4d. per week depending upon the subjects studied. The Hall

The Greyhound in 1999

The 'Bottle and Jug' in the leaded lights at Connolly's reflects earlier drinking habits when this was the Bull's Head!

was also used by the Railwaymen's Mission, also known as the Town and Country Mission, whilst their Mission Hall was being built in Etnam Street—an enterprise then organized and funded by Thomas Smith the recently converted landlord of the **Grape Vaults** in Broad Street. The premises are now used by a firm specializing in adventure sports such as ballooning and canoeing and include bunk rooms and dormitories at the rear for hen and stag parties.

The last house in West Street, next to its junction with the inner relief road, is the **Bull's Head**, which is first mentioned in a directory in 1792. From the 1850s to the end of the century the house was in the

Connolly's—until recently the Bull's Head

243

hands of the Pritchard family—once again it appears to have been a family concern. In 1937 Ernest J. Burford was licensee. The inn name may well have heraldic implications—a bull's head was introduced into the arms of that rather beefy monarch, Henry VIII, after he had defied the papal bull of 1538. The building is still a public house, but now goes under the more exotic title of **Connolly's**—an Irish pub.

On the opposite side of the street, the **Talbot** takes up the whole of the corner block including numbers 5-9 West Street. There is then a gap for a short distance before arriving at the **Black Swan** at No. 33. The **Black Swan Inn & Posting House** is a Grade II listed 18th-century building which is mentioned in every directory from 1780. In 1858 W. Ensoll was landlord, Mrs. Ann Luscott was there in 1879, and Elijah Molyneux in 1891. According to Reeves, he was still there in 1908 when, together with Mr. R.B. Sandiland, a chemist, and Mr. C.H. Lewis, a milliner, they became the first three customers to use electricity in Leominster. It was supplied from a dynamo driven by an

The Black Swan in West Street

oil engine situated in Edward Bellow's yard in Burgess Street and was provided to the three properties by wires taken over the intervening buildings. Andrew Thompson was the landlord in 1937.

On a sadder note, in March 1946, the funeral of the late licensee of the **Black Swan**, Mr. Charles Gregory, took place at Blackpool where he had formerly been the chairman of the New South Promenade Private Hotels Association. In the mid-1980s, a landlady at the inn obtained her flying licence and on the same day collided with a microlight aircraft and was killed. The **Black Swan** has survived all its difficulties and still operates as a traditional public house.

Three doors further up at No. 39 was the **White Horse** which was first mentioned in an 1835 directory. In an 1858 directory W. Prosser is given as landlord; 1879 saw Richard Clayton there, and Thomas Holland in 1890. The inn ceased to trade in 1921 and in 2000 is empty and for sale. Norman Reeves describes how in 1895 Stanley Holland aged 28 and the son of the then landlord, was Surveyor to Leominster Corporation and was found to be embezzling, probably necessitated by his frequent over-spending in the **Talbot** and in the **Baker's Arms**. He was given the choice of being prosecuted or emigrating, so he opted for America where he put his considerable mathematical ability to more acceptable uses and became a successful bridge engineer making a fortune that amounted to some half a million pounds upon his death. Whilst in the U.S.A. he supported many Leominster charities,

including buying playing fields for the schoolchildren, and for this he was made the first Freeman of the Town. When he died in Chicago in 1936, his body was brought back to England and buried in the Priory Church in accordance with his wishes—his funeral being conducted by the Bishop of Hereford and attended by thousands of townfolk.

A little further up the street was the **Golden Cross**, a 17th-century building with a modern front, which had exposed timber-framing and an original gable visible on the east side in the 1930s. It was first recorded as an inn in 1830 and in 1858, 1879

39 West Street, once the White Horse

245

49 West Street was at one time the Golden Cross

and 1890 John Seaborn was listed as landlord—either a long-lived landlord or a family reluctant to change forenames. There is a corporation record of the repair of a public pump at the Golden Cross, which Alfred Watkins suggests was near the public house although he acknowledged in 1917 that the site, close to where Dishley Street meets the Bargates, is not now called by that name. In 1937 Miss C.J. Edwards was the landlady; the licence was finally abandoned in 1958.

Two other public houses described as being in West Street, but without a secure provenance, are a second **King's Head**, mentioned in 1840, and where, in 1858, Mrs. A. Sergeant was landlady; and the **Millwright Arms**, noted in directories from 1830 to 1851.

The sign for the Radnòrshire Arms

The Radnorshire Arms in Bargates

From the junction with Dishley Street, now the inner relief road, West Street becomes Bargates and a short distance along there on the south side of the street is the **Radnorshire Arms**, which was originally the **Fox Tavern**. The **Fox** is mentioned in directories from 1840 to 1850; the **Radnorshire Arms** in directories from 1851 onwards. This also involved a street name change for the **Fox Tavern** was on the corner of Fox Lance; the **Radnorshire Arms** is now on the corner of Westfield Walk. In 1858 Samuel Prosser was landlord and a directory of 1879 also described him as a farmer and haulier. By 1891 John Gill had become landlord and in 1937 William Henry Brown was licensee.

A little way south of Bargates is a small side road which is simply called Sandpits and it is here that the **Castle Inn** was active in the second quarter of the 19th century. Also known as the **Sandpits**, it was described in 'An Old Leominster Man's Recollections' in the *Leominster News* in 1898:

There was a Sandpits wake held every Sunday afternoon in the summer time at the **Sandpits Inn**, kept by a man named Evans, and also Saunderson's wake, a great resort in the cherry and apple season, held at **Baron's Cross**. In the summertime, on a Sunday afternoon and evening, all the way from Mr

Preece, the lawyer's (corner of Westbury and South Street), to the **Sandpits** there used to be stalls for the sale of cakes and eatables for the people who went to see the cock-fighting, boxing, etc, going on at the Sandpits wake. At the Sandpits wake cock-fighting was the great sport. One of the chief cock-fighters 70 years ago was 'Black 'un' Jones, sawyer in the Bargates, who kept a noted breed of black cocks, hence his nickname. Robinson and John Rodd were noted cock-fighters as also was Saunderson of **Baron's Cross**, but he fought his cocks at the **Sandpits**. Fighting in all its branches, whether between men, cocks or dogs was much more the go in those days.

There was another **Lion**, described as being in Middle Marsh, and mentioned in directories between 1840 and 1851. Here, one Thomas Smith, after a visit to Kinsland fair:

repaired to a public house called the Lion; here the first scene that presented itself was a number of human beings fighting like devils. I went into the house—it was not long before I was assailed; I did not know what to do; I was afraid that I should be killed. Free Trade was at this time a question that agitated the public mind. I got on top of a settle, and advocated the part of freedom of competition; this saved me from fighting. At about three in the morning I arrived home to my distressed and miserable wife.

Other Leominster pubs with no provenance include the **Boot** (late 18th century), the **Bull** (near the **Waterloo,** in 1830), the **Globe** (mid-19th century), the **Leopard** (late 18th to early 19th centuries), **Nelson's Head**, **Pack Horse** (late 18th century), **Six Bells** (home of the Leominster Benefit and Friendly Society in 1845), and finally, the **Last Inn** (late 18th century).

CHAPTER THIRTEEN

West from Leominster
THE ARROW VALLEY

Leominster town has always had a strategic position, situated as it is close to the border with Wales. Through the middle of the town (until the recent by-pass was built) ran the A49, the medieval replacement for the Roman road that once joined Caerleon to Chester. From Bromyard in the east of the county came the A44, the old coaching route from the south midlands into central Wales. Earlier, Leominster had been the final point on the navigation of the river Lugg, from its junction with the Wye at Mordiford, south-east of Hereford.

Just to the south-east of Leominster, the Lugg is joined by a major tributary, the river Arrow. Both rivers provided valley routes into Wales—the A44 subsequently followed the less tortuous Arrow valley through Eardisland and Pembridge to Kington and thence the Vale of Radnor, whilst the Lugg valley takes a course just to the north of Kingsland, then bears sharply north through the Aymestrey Gap, only to curve back westwards to leave Herefordshire heading for Presteigne.

The river Arrow takes a course to the south of Leominster, but the A44 went straight through the middle of the town climbing up Bargates and into Baron's Cross Road. Here is Baron's Cross where the A44 originally continued straight ahead towards Eardisland. The signposts have been changed and the A44 now accompanies the A4112 bearing off to the south-west through Monkland, to turn northwards past Burton Court and thus by-pass Eardisland. Baron's Cross was historically an important junction and well deserved its

The Baron's Cross about 1900

two public houses—the **Brickmaker's Arms** and the **Baron's Cross Inn**. Now the junction is surrounded by housing estates and the Baron's Cross road junction is partially masked by a nearby roundabout that provides access to a new supermarket.

Who was the baron commemorated by the name? Leominster gave the title of baron (Lempster) to the Fermors, Earls of Pomfret, but the title became extinct on the death of the 5th Earl in June 1867. Could one of the Fermors be the baron celebrated here, or is the name much earlier?

Directly on the junction is the **Baron's Cross Inn**. It is of some considerable age, being mentioned in a directory for 1851. In 1858 William Powell was the landlord and in 1891 Edward Stanton.

The other pub, a little closer to Leominster, has closed, or at least changed its way of life. This was the **Brickmaker's Arms**, not mentioned

Baron's Cross Inn in 1999

250

The Bird Cage, now a restaurant, but at one time the Brickmaker's Arms

in an 1891 directory, but present in the 1903 register of public houses, where it is described as a beer-house with a pencilled note confirming that it had changed its name to the **Bird Cage**. It was built and owned by a Mr. Tunks, a farmer from Ebnal Farm who also had a brick works at Baron's Cross. The Tunks were Mormons, probably converted when Brigham Young (who was later to succeed Joseph Smith, the founder of the Latter Day Saints) visited Herefordshire in 1840, and it was at their farm that Mormons from throughout the area met. About 1860 Mr. Tunks decided to emigrate to Salt Lake City, but only his two eldest sons accompanied him as the rest of the children had gone into hiding. These children and their mother Mrs. Tunks were left in the charge of Isaac Tunks, his brother, as was the **Brickmaker's Arms**. Unfortunately, Isaac preferred to live a riotous life and Mrs. Tunks and the remains of her family ended up living in poverty in London. The **Bird Cage** was granted a full licence in 1960, although at that time there was concern about the state of its toilets! Of course they have been improved and the building is now a licensed restaurant, although still called the **Bird Cage.**

About a mile and a half along the A44/A4112, heading west, is Monkland, a small village on the banks of the Arrow where it is joined by a small tributary, the Moor Brook. It was at Monkland that the Rev. Sir Henry Williams Baker was vicar, one of the chief compilers of 'Hymns Ancient and Modern'. Monkland has had several inns, but only one survives to the present day.

Norman Reeves noted in his 1980 book *The Leon Valley* that the earliest inn in Monkland for which he had found a record was the

The Seven Stars at Monkland some time before 1928 (upper)
The same building in 2000 with a raised roof and lack of thatch (lower)

Seven Stars, where the court leet met in 1758. This was the manorial court which was held annually and regulated the life of the village. The last court leet in the area was held at the **New Inn** in 1854; manorial courts were finally abolished by the Real Property Act of 1922. Reeves goes on to comment 'The building still exists, being one of the oldest in the village; it is the cruck house known today as Church Cottage, just a little west of the bridge, near the church'. The **Seven Stars** is on the Old Road through the village some 150 yards from the church and has since had a name change to Manor Cottage. The present occupants understand that it was closed as an inn in 1785. It has lost the thatched roof that was noted during the Royal Commission survey and apparent on a pre-1928 photograph, but still has its medieval cruck.

The **New Inn** at Monkland had William Barnett as landlord in 1858 and Edmund Seymour in 1879, who was also a blacksmith and agricultural implement maker. By 1891 the licensee was David Ferguson. Although still operating at the beginning of the 20th century, the licence was not renewed in 1913, for by that time it had become a private house. The Inspector for the Royal Commission on Ancient Monuments, visiting some time before 1934, confirmed that it was by then a house that had been largely rebuilt in the 18th century although the back wing could be earlier. The building that was the **New Inn** is a quarter of a mile west of the church on the south side of the main road

and is now called 'The Beeches'. According to Reeves, it had very spacious rooms in the 18th-century block which faces the road. In the older, once timber-framed, rear part of the house there was a great fireplace with inglenooks and an end-wall chimney.

The **Red Lion** was of a similar vintage, for it had Hannah Phillips as mine host in 1858, James Powell in 1879, and Alfred Brown in 1891. The

The New Inn at Monkland, now a private house called 'The Beeches'

The Red Lion at Monkland at the beginning of the 20th century (upper)
The rebuilt Red Lion, now the Monkland Arms (lower)

two pubs were clearly in competition and the **Red Lion** eventually won the battle. In the earlier years of the 19th century it had a name change and was called the **Travellers Arms**. An early 20th-century postcard shows a half-timbered building set back from the road with an attractive garden in front of it. Apart from the slightly wider section of road, there was no need to make provision for parking when this photograph was taken. Unfortunately this half-timbered building was burnt down in 1910, to be replaced by a new building now called the **Monkland Arms.**

A short distance to the south-east of Monkland, and only accessed by minor roads, but still close to the river Arrow, is Ivington. There does not seem to have been a pub here, but the records indicate that there was a Cider House in 1903 and probably later, but the licence was not renewed in 1943.

Upstream from Monkland is the well-named Arrow Green and then Eardisland, a substantial village now on a B class road since the A44 was diverted along the A4112. Previously the main A44 crossed the river and the adjacent mill race in the centre of the village, and it is here that the **Cross Inn** continues to thrive. It was the **Cross Inn** in 1858 when J. Macklin was the landlord—was he the same person as the George Macklin who was recorded as being there in 1879? The landlady in 1891 excelled herself; not only did she have an appropriate name—Miss Elizabeth Cross—but she somehow managed to get an exceptional mention in the Kelly's Directory entry for Eardisland where the compiler noted that there was 'Good accommodation for visitors. Excellent fishing in the Arrow'. It almost seems as though the inn was named after its illustrious landlady!

In 1902 the new licensee, Benjamin Goodenough, kept up the publicity record for he provided 'good accommodation for anglers with one and a half miles of private trout and greyling stream'. In the latter part of the 19th century the landlord also brewed his own beer, but Goodenough changed this and supplied Arnold Perrett's Gold Medal Ales and Stouts. These excellent drinks were made at the City Brewery in Hereford, now lost underneath the Maylord Orchards

A 1931 advertisement for the Cross Hotel, Eardisland

255

*The Cross Inn with an AA box in the garden
and the war memorial close by*

development. In the 1920s the inn was used by the local football teams both for changing and, inevitably, for refreshments.

Of course, the **Cross Inn** was not named after the late 19th century landlady; the sign shows an ornate cross. There are hundreds of different shapes of cross used in heraldry and the sign painter may just have chosen an ornate appealing sign. Artistic licence can often completely obscure the origins of a name. However, the inn now has a proper cross adjoining it, for it was here that the war memorial was erected.

Also in the grounds of the inn is one of the early relics of motoring— a well kept AA box no. 321 from Legions Cross!

Also surviving in Eardisland is the **White Swan Inn**, which in the 1858 directory was entered as the establishment of James Bassett, an industrious landlord who was also a carpenter. By 1879 he was followed by George Bassett, possibly his son, who was also a farmer. Perhaps this was not a very successful inn, for later in the 19th century the landlord also worked as a plasterer. However, in the 1890s Walter Stinton was landlord and did not have any other stated profession. By 1902 William Thomas Yates had become licensee, in

256

The White Swan at Eardisland when Mrs. C.M.N. Bishop was landlady in the late 1930s and 1940s (Photograph : Derek Foxton Collection)

1913 it was Charles Prothero, and by 1934 Reginald Miles. Arthur Bishop and his wife followed by 1937. The inn is on the south side of the village road a short distance south of the bridge over the river Arrow. It has the appearance of a late 18th- or early 19th-century building, but almost hidden to the rear is the timber framework of a 17th-century building. On that section there is obvious evidence that the roof was raised when the front building was added.

Lyme Lane leads northwards from the village towards Lyme Farm. Along here was the **Bull**, now a private dwelling called 'Crabtree'. It is not mentioned in the directories for 1858 and 1891 and was probably a beer house.

The White Swan at Eardisland in 2000

Whilst Eardisland is disappointingly short of inns, Pembridge, the next village along the river Arrow, reverses the trend, for from time to time it has had up to eight inns. Pembridge is an attractive place that seems to survive quite well with the main A44 running the whole length of the village. Indeed, one of its main functions during the coaching era was as a half-way point between Leominster and Kington. At a first glance there appears to have been little change in this village of half-timbered houses, but this impression is somewhat erroneous, for early trade directories give some indication of the variety of occupations that were practised here. A late 19th-century Kelly's Directory records that in 1881 the population of Pembridge parish was 1,318. This included the hamlets of Broxwood and Marston. There was a National School in the village and two schools at Broxwood (one established church and the other catholic) with average total attendance of 175. There were two post offices, one at Pembridge and the other at Broxwood. In the parish, apart from the three named inns—the **New Inn**, the **Greyhound** and the **Queen's Head**—there were also four beer retailers and one cooper to provide the barrels. Trading was well represented with four general shops, three butchers and three boot and shoe makers. There was a baker, who doubtless depended on the two millers (water mills), a tailor, and a dressmaker. Two blacksmiths and three wheelwrights ensured that vehicles were kept in good condition, whilst other villagers made a living as masons (two), a carpenter, a chimney sweep and a sexton (who was also a cowkeeper). The station, which was the central point on the Leominster and Kington Branch of the Great Western Railway, was half-a-mile north of the village. Here was the coal merchant and an office of the Old Radnor Lime, Roadstone and General Trading Company Limited. The Pembridge Village Post Office also dealt with Money Orders and was a Telegraph Office.

At the turn of the century trains ran on a regular basis from Leominster to Kington with connections to New Radnor. Also from Kington or from Titley Junction trains ran to Eardisley and Presteigne. With five or six trains each day, and even a Sunday service, the station must have been a centre of activity. The railway finally closed in 1955, although a special train ran from Leominster beyond Kington as far as Dolyhir on 27 July 1957 to celebrate the centenary of the line's opening.

Leominster, Kington, Eardisley, Presteign, New Radnor

LEOMINSTER	a m	a m	a m		p m	p m		p m	p m	Sun p m
LEOMINSTER dep	5 30	...	9 55	...	1 0	4 5	...	5 50	8 40	5 50 6 40
Kingsland	5 41	...	10 5	...	1 11	4 16	...	5 59	8 50	5 41 6 50
Pembridge	5 51	...	10 13	...	1 20	4 24	...	6 7	8 58	5 51 6 58
Titley	6 5	...	10 24	...	1 31	4 37	...	6 19	9 10	6 5 7 10
KINGTON arr	6 10	...	10 28	...	1 36	4 42	...	6 23	9 15	6 10 7 15

Kington	...	9 10	11 15	...	3 25	...	6 25	...	...	
Titley	...	9 15	11 22	...	3 31	...	6 30	...	...	
Lyon's Hall	...	9 20	11 27	...	3 39	...	6 35	...	...	
Almeley	...	9 30	11 37	...	3 51	...	6 45	...	...	
EARDISLEY ar	...	9 35	11 42	...	3 57	...	6 50	...	...	

Kington dep	6 50	...	10 32	1 20	...	5 5	...	6 30	...	...
Titley	6 56	...	10 37	1 32	...	5 10	...	6 37	...	...
PRESTEIGN ar	7 10	...	10 50	1 46	...	5 25	...	6 50	...	...

Kington dep	...	...	10 31	...	1 45	5 5	...	9*30	...	...
Stanner	...	...	10 40	...	1 54	5 14	...	9 39	...	...
Dolyhir	...	...	10 45	...	1 59	5 19	...	9 44	...	...
NEW RADNOR	...	...	10 50	...	2 5	5 25	...	9 50	...	...

NEW RADN'R d	a m	a m	a m	p m	p m	p m	p m	p m	p m	Sun p m
NEW RADN'R d	...	...	10 55	...	2 15	...	5 50	10*0		
Dolyhir	...	...	11 1	...	2 22	...	5 56	10 6		
Stanner	...	...	11 6	...	2 27	...	6 1	10 11		
Kington arr	...	...	11 13	...	2 35	...	6 8	10 18		

PRESTEIGN dep	7 20	...	11 0	...	2 20	...	5 45	7 10		
Titley	7 35	...	11 25	...	2 48	...	6 0	7 24		
Kington arr	7 40	...	11 30	...	2 53	...	6 5	7 28		

EARDISLEY dep	...	9 55	...	12 0	...	4 30	...	7 10		
Almeley	...	10 0	...	12 10	...	4 35	...	7 15		
Lyon's Hall	...	10 11	...	12 28	...	4 46	...	7 26		
Titley	...	10 16	...	12 37	...	4 51	...	7 31		
Kington arr	...	10 20	...	12 42	...	4 55	...	7 35		

KINGTON dep										a m p m
KINGTON dep	7 50	...	11 15	...	2 40	...	6 12	7 40	8 0 7 45
Titley	7 55	...	11 20	...	2 45	...	6 18	7 45	8 5 7 50
Pembridge	8 5	...	11 31	...	2 55	...	6 28	7 55	8 15 8 0
Kingsland	8 14	...	11 40	...	3 4	...	6 38	8 5	8 24 8 10
LEOMINSTER	8 25	...	11 50	...	3 15	...	6 45	8 15	8 35 8 20

1899 train timetable

The loss of this great variety of local trades and trading means that there are now only two inns left in Pembridge—the **New Inn**, perversely one of the oldest inns in the county, and the **Red Lion**. The **New Inn** is a well-known building on the north side of the square that also contains the Market Hall. James Wathen, who sketched it in 1804, described it as **Cooke's Public House**. The main structure of the **New**

Cooke's Public House in 1804 as painted by James Wathen

*The New Inn, Pembridge, at the turn of the century
when John Chandler was licensee*

Inn is of early 17th-century date and Wathen shows it as having a full range of attic rooms with small dormers, probably providing quarters for the servants. Wathen also shows a two-storey porch on the front of the building which has also disappeared.

The main block has cross-wings at each end whilst the four-gabled wing at the rear is a rather later addition. It has a western wing of 17th-century date that was apparently detached, but was eventually joined to the main building by a stable block. A second wing, similarly placed to the rear, is also of 17th-century date. The timber-framing is exposed throughout the various buildings. The upper storey projects at the southern ends of the two cross wings of the main building, with moulded pendants hanging from the corners. The western doorway has a moulded frame and a door with strap-hinges. Within the building many of the ceiling beams are exposed, some being moulded. The staircase has an original newel with a moulded terminal and moulded handrails.

The rear view of the New Inn as seen from the A44

In front of the **New Inn** stands the early 16th-century market-hall. It would originally have included a first-floor room, but this had been removed even before Wathen visited. One of the eight pillars that support the roof sits on the socket stone of a 14th-century cross, a squarish stone considered by Alfred Watkins to be a mark stone for a local ley line. The Pembridge stocks were kept at the upper end of the Market Hall and in 1924 the aged Mr. Gough could well remember a drunken man 'decorating the stocks'.

The *Hereford Times* for 7 July 1855 records the sad death of Anne, the wife of William Neighbour of the **New Inn** at the relatively young age of 38. However, William continued to run the inn and is shown as landlord in 1858, but by 1879 there had been a change and George Garwardine was the licensee. The inn was the Meeting Place of the Loyal Westonbury Lodge No. 3303 in 1856.

A turn-of-the-century photograph shows a building much as it is today, but the sign records John Chandler as being 'licensed to sell British and Foreign Spirits, Ale, Cider, and Tobacco'. In 1891 he was a farmer as well as being landlord. In 1955, the proud proprietors of the **New Inn**, Mr. and Mrs. Eric Bettington, produced a postcard with their name and telephone number firmly imprinted on the front.

The Greyhound in the late 1920s

Another well-known inn in Pembridge was the **Greyhound**, closed some years ago and now taking on a new lease of life as the Visitor Centre and Tea Rooms. According to the Royal Commission the main part of the building was erected early in the 16th century and the cross wing was added

The Greyhound is now a café and the Tourist Information Centre

at the east end later in that century. The upper storey projects along the whole of the south front, the original block having shafted posts with moulded capitals and curved brackets carved with roses and foliage. The later wing had plain curved brackets. The upper storey also projects at the back of the original block on curved brackets springing from simple shafted posts. The whole building has close-set timber-framing. Inside the building the original block has moulded ceiling beams. An auction sale was held on the premises on 26 June 1858 when Elizabeth Parry was licensee. In 1891 the landlord was Arthur Richard Saunders.

The 'Greyhound' was a famous mail coach that ran between London and Birmingham, but here in Pembridgee the name is more likely to refer to the use of greyhounds in hunting. On a similar vein, there was, until recently, a **Greyhound Dog** in Hereford.

The **Queen's Head** was the meeting place for the 'Amicable or Friendly Society', first mentioned in 1796. In 1858 William Holder was landlord, and in 1891 it was George Rowlands, who also acted as the village saddler. He may well have been related to Mrs. Mary Rowlands, identified in a directory as one of the four beer retailers in the parish.

Other inns in Pembridge that were, from time to time, open to the public included the **Duke of Marlborough's Head**, mentioned in deeds between 1756 and 1806, but not included in the 1858 directory; the **Oak**, a beerhouse mentioned in an 1858 directory with Thomas

Old Oak House in 2000

Hawkins as landlord; and the **Red Lion** in the same directory also as a beerhouse with James Rowlands in charge. These may well be the unnamed beerhouses of the 1891 Kelly's Directory. The **Oak** is probably the building

The Red Lion in 2000 with the detached bell tower of
Pembridge church behind

now called the Old Oak House, on the eastern edge of the village; the **Red Lion** still survives, on the main street just to the east of the **New Inn**.

It would also seem that Ye Olde Steppes, now the village shop and post office, was also an inn or beer house, for in February 1916, at the

Ye Olde Steppes, now the village shop
and post office

Kington Licensing Sessions, the licence of the **Steps**, Pembridge, was transferred from Mr. Chester to Mr. C.A. Heynes.

At Bearwood (or Barewood), a hamlet just over a mile south-west of Pembridge, was the **Builders Arms**. This is not mentioned in the trades directories consulted, but the compiler of the 1891

264

directory seems to have been somewhat confused, for there is an entry for Thomas Powles of Bearwood, a beer retailer, under Pembridge, and a similar entry under Eardisland.

The building is shown as a beer house on the earlier 20th century Ordnance Survey maps, but at some time changed its name, for in January 1951 the licence of the **Bearwood Inn** was transferred from Mr. C. Slater to Mr. W. White. The building still survives, almost central to Bearwood hamlet. It is now called simply 'The Old Inn'.

The Old Inn (Once the Bearwood Inn)

Between Gorsty Common and Broxwood, on a minor road almost two miles south-west of Pembridge, was the **Yew Tree Inn**. It is not

The sign for the Yew tree still survives, hidden amongst the vegetation

mentioned in 1858 or in 1891, but sale details exist for 1919. However, an 1891 directory mentions a beer retailer at Gorsty Common. This was Charles Powles, presumably a relative of Thomas at Bearwood. The building is described in the 1934 Royal Commission Inventory as being on the west side of the road and of 17th-century date with a roof that had at one time been heightened.

From Pembridge the Arrow continues to wind westwards through the small village of Staunton-on-Arrow, which never seems to have had an inn, and then curves south-west-

Once the Yew Tree Inn at Gorsty Common

wards to pass to the south of Titley. At Horseway Head, a hamlet on the hill between Staunton-on-Arrow and Lower Mowley, the farm at the top of the hill was at one time a cider house catering for carters to refresh themselves and their horses.

An 1891 directory comments about Titley that 'The surrounding scenery is beautiful, and on a neighbouring hill are traces of an extensive encampment. Offa's Dyke passes through the parish'. In addition to such glory, the village achieved its measure of fame during the railway period, for Titley Station, on a side road leading towards Lyonshall, was the junction where the two lines running to Eardisley and Presteigne left the main Leominster to Kington line. The population of the parish in 1881 was 389.

The one inn in Titley is on a sharp bend on the main road from Kington to Presteigne. It may well have suffered several changes of name, for there is an inn of long standing in this village. In 1802 the **Balance Inn** was the home of the 'Amicable and Friendly Loyal Society'. It was still the **Balance Inn** in 1833 when there was a sale there, but by the 1850s the only inn recorded was the **Stag's Head Inn**, where William George was both landlord and shopkeeper. In the 1863 Kelly's Directory, it is described once again as the **Balance Inn** and in 1879 although no inn was mentioned, a David Rowland was a farmer at Balance Farm. Again in 1891 there was no inn mentioned, but Edward Thomas, a farmer, is recorded as living at Stag House. The **Stagg Inn**, as it is now known, was recently closed for a while, but now has a new lease of life and a more promising future, offering food of quality.

The present day inn sign on a post in the grounds of the **Stagg** shows the coat of arms of the Greenly family—a green shield with three stags and a chevron. When devising arms it is common for

The Stagg Inn, early in 2000

heralds to make play on the names and attributes of the family and in this case the shield colour is green. The manor of Titley was leased from the Warden and Fellows of St. Mary's College, Winchester in 1679 by John Greenly and then bought from them in 1865 by Charles William Greenly, the family living at Titley Court. The Greenly family also owned a farm at Lower Mowley and a deer park at Staunton-on-Arrow, the stags in the arms no doubt being a reference to this. In 1833 Eliza Greenly, a well known diarist and energetic reformer, gave the **Stagg** its brick frontage and built a grocery and butcher's shop next to it. She renamed the inn the **Stag's Head** after her family crest.

Inn-keepers often chose a sign for their premises that declared their allegiance to their landlord or indicated their previous service with a notable family. Servants' livery often displayed emblems derived from their master's arms or crests, or badges of the family, embroidered upon the uniform or engraved upon its buttons. Such emblems frequently feature as inn-signs, such as the Swan, which is a badge of the Bohun family. The Greenly crest would also have been

The Greenly crest (above)
The Stagg inn sign (right)

displayed on Greenly property in the area on such things as carriage doors and gate posts as well as the servants' livery, cutlery, linen etc within the house.

A leaflet available at the inn includes a story from its chequered history. Apparently the inn was closed for many years when the rail workers from Titley junction got too drunk on Sundays for the Greenlys of the day—allegedly they called Mr. Greenly 'turkey legs' when he wore red stockings to church. The **Stagg** reopened in the '60s when David Forbes of Titley Court purchased the second pint, as he did in 1998 when the inn was re-opened with the present landlords after a short period of closure. It is uncertain when the second 'g' in **Stagg** was first used. Often the use of idiosyncratic spelling such as this was a leftover from when spelling was anything but standardised. The preservation of spellings such as 'The Swann' and 'The Starr' into modern times shows that the inn concerned was of considerable age. However, in the case at Titley, the idiosyncratic spelling would seem to be modern!

CHAPTER FOURTEEN

West from Leominster
THE LUGG VALLEY

The river Lugg flows to the north of Leominster, having passed through Aymestrey, Mortimer's Cross and Kingssland to the north-west. The minor road, the B4360, takes a similar course from Leominster towards Kingsland. Here houses, many of which are traditional black-and-white, stretch from the junction with the main road—the A4110—for a considerable distance south-eastwards along the village road. The church, with its rather odd Volka Chapel opening off the porch, and the earthworks of what appears to have been a substantial castle, are to the south of the village road; the Lugg flows to the north.

The Post Office Directory for 1879 divides Kingsland into two main parts—'West Town', with Alfred Brown at the **Three Horseshoes** (now the **Monument**), and George Stephens as shop-keeper and beer retailer at an unnamed beerhouse (possibly the **Bell**); and 'Longford', with John Allen at the **Corners**, William Reece at the **Red Lion**, and George Burden as a butcher and beer retailer (presumably at the **Angel**). The junction between West Town and Longford would appear to be the village cross roads where a minor road runs northwards crossing the Lugg on its way towards Yarpole.

Approaching from the south-east, The **Red Lion Inn** was close to the sharp-angled bend at the eastern extremity of Kingsland village road. This was the home of a Friendly Society, apparently with no specific name, first mentioned in 1838. In an 1858 directory, John Crump is described as being a blacksmith and agricultural implement maker at the **Red Lion Inn**. Another section makes it evident that

The Red Lion at Kingsand in retirement

Elizabeth Crump was the licensee, whilst her husband, John, is described as assistant overseer. In 1891 James Preece was the landlord. Writing in 1980, Norman Reeves noted that it 'fairly recently became a private house'. The building now shows little sign of ever having been an inn. It is quite small in a typical Herefordshire style with a central doorway and external chimney stacks on each gable. It has recently been extended.

In the centre of the village, on the north side of the road almost opposite the turn to the church, is the **Angel Inn.** Reeves describes it as Kingsland's most ancient inn and comments that 'it is the Kingsland inn *par excellence*, because it is named after the church's patron, St. Michael, and it is very near the church'. He suggests that the building next door—Angel House—was probably the original hostelry. The **Angel Inn** is a 17th-century building of L-shaped plan with the wings extending towards the east and north. Angel House, immediately west of the inn, was built at least a century earlier on a T-shaped plan with the cross wing at the southern end against the road. Although the front has been refaced in brick, the upper storey projects at both ends. The building was extended to the north in the 17th century. In 1891 Mrs. Elizabeth Burden had the double job of landlady and shopkeeper.

For many years the price of beer was fixed by law, and at the Flower Show on 26 August 1920, Divisional Inspector Wynn of the

The Angel at Kingsland in 2000

Ministry of Food went into the drinks marquee. He saw that the notices indicating the fixed prices of bottled beer were not up, and was charged 9d. instead of the maximum 8^{1}/2d.. for a bottle of beer. Anne Reynolds of the **Angel Inn,** who was running the marquee, was subsequently prosecuted. In her defence she said she was sorry, but did not know that it was an offence not to display the sign at a flower show. The court decided to give her the benefit of the doubt as to displaying the notice, but for the fact of overcharging, she was fined £1 with 2 guineas costs. Writing in 1980, Norman Reeves noted that the inn was open again after a period with no licence.

Continuing westwards along the village street, it is not long before the traveller finds the **Corners Inn**, also on the north side of the road, and appropriately at the crossroads in the centre of the village. The *Hereford Journal* of 5 February 1794 advertised a sale by auction 'at the dwelling-house of Mr. James Blashfield, called the **Corner Inn**, in the Borough of Pembridge'. In 1858 William Phillips was the landlord; in 1879 John Allen, and in 1891 it was Henry George Harrison. The front of the building has been faced in brick, but the side elevation exhibits two periods of 17th-century timber-framing.

In 1946 there was some tension between a crowd of local youths and the licensee of the **Corners Inn**, Mr. F. Pursey. He refused to sell

271

The Corners Inn at Kingsland in 2000

Dennis Evans and Geoffrey Amos any cigarettes, so, as part of a gang of five, they threw down several gates on land that he owned. They said they only did it 'for a lark', but the magistrates felt that the activity was dangerous and 'must be stamped out'. They were each fined £4 plus costs. The contretemps does not seem to have put Mr. Pursey off running his pub, for he was granted a full licence (to enable him to sell spirits as well as beer and cider) in February 1951. His application was supported by a petition indicating that the nearest inn with a full licence was 2 1/2 miles away. He had to pay £375 for what was called 'the monopoly value'. By that time he had held the licence for 42 years, and apparently as part of the deal he submitted plans for some structural alterations to the building.

The **Bell Inn** was on the opposing corner to the **Corners,** opposite the 'Croase House', the fourth corner being taken up by 'the Old Workhouse', a building of late 16th-century date that is now several cottages. In 1886 the inn was known as the **Blue Bell**, but was not mentioned by name in the various 19th-century directories consulted and was doubtless a simple beer house. Its position suggests that it was probably the last building in West Town (from the west) and was most likely to

Once the Bell Inn, this building is across the junction from the Corners.
The two elevations are totally different, the one side having had a Georgian brick face added

be the home of George Stephens, shopkeeper and beer-retailer, in 1879. An 1891 directory would seem to confirm this for it includes Stephens and Broad, who are described as grocers, drapers and beer retailers. It was certainly in the register of inns for 1903, but the licence was apparently not renewed in 1922. It was certainly operating in 1899, for in the *Hereford Times* of 19 October there is the report of an inquest into the death of Richard Jones, aged 54, of Kingsland. Apparently he drank plenty at the Goose Fair and at the **Bell Inn**. He then slept in the stables and apparently died of exposure. In 1980 the bell of the sign was still just visible painted on the south-east wall.

South of Kingsland, on the minor road leading from Cobnash to Lawton, Norman Reeves notes that there had been a **Dog Inn**, the name surviving in the road which is known as Dog Lane.

The **Crown Inn**, well over half-a-mile south of Kingsland, on the A4110, at Shirl Heath, was recorded in 1858 with William Davies as landlord. This was probably the cider house run by Charles Bassett in 1879, but there is no mention in the 1891 directories, so it had presumably closed.

The **Monument Inn** is at the north-western end of the village on the junction with the A4110. Reeves suggests that in 1801 it was known as **Mortimer's Cross**, but in the second half of the 19th century it was certainly called the **Three Horseshoes**, with Alfred Brown as licensee in 1879, and Mrs. Ann Price as landlady in 1891. Perhaps there was some confusion with the inn of the same name a mile northwards? The **Monument** was still described as the **Three Horseshoes** by the Inspectors for the Royal Commission during their visit in the early 1930s. They noted that it was of 17th-century date, but had little else to say. The name change, which must have been shortly afterwards, reflects the Monument to the Battle of Mortimer's Cross that stands outside the inn.

The Monument Inn and Brasserie in 1999

It reads:

> This pedestal is erected to perpetuate the Memory of an obstinate, bloody and decisive battle fought near this Spot in the civil Wars between the ambitious Houses of York and Lancaster, on the 2nd. Day of February 1461, between the *Forces of Edward Mortimer*, Earl of March, (afterwards *Edward* the *Fourth*) on the Side of York and those of *Henry* the *Sixth*, on the Side of Lancaster.
>
> The Kings Troops were commanded by *Jasper* Earl of Pembroke, *Edward* commanded his own in Person and was victorious. The Slaughter was great on both Sides Four Thousand being left dead on the Field and many Welsh Persons on the first distinction were taken Prisoners amongst whom was *Owen Tudor* (Great-Grandfather to *Henry* the *Eighth* and a Descendent of the illustrious *Cadwallader*) who was afterwards beheaded at Hereford.
>
> This was the decisive Battle which fixed *Edward* the *Fourth* on the Throne of England who was proclaimed *King* in London on the Fifth of March following.

The Monument has a bench mark inscribed at the bottom left (297.6 ft.)
Growing to the sides of the monument are red roses and white roses.

The monument records the battle as occurring on 2 February 1461, but an earlier monument, erected by public subscription in 1799 recorded it as 2 February 1460. This change was noted by Woolhope Club members when they visited in June 1890. It was explained that the 'New Style' of calendar was introduced into England in the year 1751, before which time the legal year did not commence until the 25th March. Consequently by the Old Style the year would be called 1460 until that date (25 March) arrived. The earlier monument now has a place of honour in the Mortimer's Cross Water Mill, much closer to the actual battle site.

The battle took place about a mile to the north of the **Monument Inn** where the so called Battle Field Oak or Gospel Oak was described as being about the centre of the Lancastrian position. Sadly it is no more, although it was inspected by the Woolhope Club members who agreed that it had probably been present in 1461 and could well have given shelter to Owen Tudor the night before the battle. It was of such antiquity that it formed the boundary mark between the four parishes of Kingsland, Luston, Aymestrey and Shobdon.

Going from the **Monument** in a north-westerly direction, the road runs parallel to the Lugg until it takes up the line of the Roman road just south of the Mortimer's Cross cross-roads. Here the main road is crossed by a minor road (B4362) that takes a meandering course from Ludlow to Presteigne. The battle was fought in the fields to the south-east of this junction; the **Mortimer's Cross Inn** is on the opposite corner.

This is an inn with a long reputation for hospitality. It was on 21 September 1852 that 'The Woolhope Club members met at breakfast at 9 a.m. at the **Mortimer's Cross Inn**, those who had come from Hereford having greatly enjoyed the ride of fifteen miles through the charming scenery of that district'. The geologists amongst the party visited several quarries that are now just names—the north-field quarry, containing an excellent example of Downton sandstone; the Croft quarry, where Upper Ludlow rock was worked, and from there to the quarries near Lucton. They also visited a quarry at Aymestrey, where there was a fine escarpment of rock, perhaps 100 feet high, quite even and wall-like. The rock was described as being so jointed that as it was worked it preserved the evenness of the surface. The company then returned to **Mortimer's Cross Inn**, where, according to their records, 'they carried out the spirit of the poetic resolution:—

"I am resolved:
The mind shall banquet, though the body starve"

in a manner much more satisfactory than a literal fulfilment could possibly have been. The mind having "banqueted," the body was treated with equal justice. After partaking of an excellent dinner, on the cloth being removed, the Chairman gave the usual loyal toasts'.

Signs from the Mortimer's Cross Inn reflect different aspects of the battle between the Lancastrians and the Yorkists.
Left: *An allegorical pastiche where the central figure is the White Lion of March, representing Edward, holding the banner. The suns represent the parhelion—a rare meteorological condition where three suns are seen—which occurred on the day of the battle. The red and white roses are at the base; the red rose being pierced with a sword. The sign is surmounted by a castle, the crest of the Mortimers. The sign is very much Yorkist—but then, they were the winners!*
Right: *The monument to the battle is in the background with two figures representing the two armies, one with a red rose and the other with a white one*

Turnpike Trust Meetings at Mortimer's Cross Inn

The *Hereford Times* for 31 October 1857 noted that the Trustees of the Blue Mantle Hall Turnpike Trust met in the house of Mrs. Anne Bradford, **Mortimer's Cross Inn**, Aymestrey, to consult about moving the then toll gates at Kingsland to a place between the Brook End Bridge and the Harbour House. Ann Bradford was still the licensee in 1858; by 1879 it was David Knight, and by 1891 Charles Roberts was the landlord. The inn has suffered a series

278

The Mortimer's Cross Inn in 1999

of ups and downs in recent years and although it was spruced up in 1999, this does not appear to have been very successful.

Both road and river continue in a northerly direction for another mile or so to Aymestrey where the river bears off in a north-westerly then westerly direction. Here, just next to the bridge, is the **Riverside Inn**. For many years it was known as the **Crown Inn**, where, in 1858, William Butler was landlord, in 1879, Charles Preece, and in 1891, Charles Hope provided 'stabling and accommodation for travellers'. Even at such a remote inn, there was occasionally trouble and the *Hereford Times* for 11 July 1891 records that 'At the Wigmore Petty Sessions in July 1891 John, George, Richard, and John Jnr. Cook, were charged with being disorderly and refusing to leave the **Crown Inn**, Aymestrey when requested to by the landlord, Charles Hope'.

Substantial improvements were made to the building in the late 1960s by Jim Crump, and in the 1980s there was a regular summer

AYMESTRY, HEREFORDSHIRE.

VALUABLE

NAVY OAK TIMBER

FOR SALE BY AUCTION,

At the CROWN INN, in the village of Aymestry,

BY MESSRS. RUSSELL AND SON,

On THURSDAY, the 23rd day of JANUARY, 1862, at Three o'clock precisely, (subject to such conditions as shall then be produced,) in the following lots, viz. :—

LOT 1.—80 Oak Timber Trees, standing in Merchant's Grove, near the village of Aymestry, numbered with white paint from 1 to 80 inclusive.

Lot 2.—80 Oak Timber Trees, adjoining Lot 1, and numbered from 81 to 160 inclusive.

Lot 3.—5 Ash Timber Trees, numbered from 1 to 5 inclusive, and 1 Wych Elm, all marked with white paint, and standing on Lots 1 and 2.

Lot 4.—52 Oak Timber Trees, standing in Raisnor Grove, in Aymestry, numbered from 1 to 52 inclusive.

Lot 5.—54 Oak Timber Trees, adjoining lot 4, and numbered from 53 to 106 inclusive.

Lot 6.—11 Ash Timber Trees, numbered from 1 to 11 inclusive ; 9 Wych Elm Timber Trees, numbered from 1 to 9 inclusive ; and 1 Lime Tree ; all marked with white paint, and standing in Lots 4 and 5.

Lot 7.—70 Oak Timber Trees, standing in the Garden House Wood, in Aymestry, numbered from 1 to 70 inclusive.

Lot 8.—70 Oak Timber Trees, adjoining Lot 7, and numbered from 71 to 140 inclusive.

Lot 9—70 Oak Timber Trees, adjoining Lot 8, and numbered with white paint from 140 to 210 inclusive.

Lot 10.—69 Oak Timber Trees, adjoining Lot 9, and numbered with white paint from 210 to 279 inclusive.

Lot 11.—16 Ash Timber Trees, numbered from 1 to 16 inclusive ; and 5 Wych Elm Trees, numbered from 1 to 5 inclusive ; all marked with white paint, and standing in the Garden House Wood aforesaid.

Lot 12.—17 Birch Trees, numbered from 1 to 17 inclusive ; 8 Maple Trees, numbered from 1 to 8 inclusive ; and 5 Beech Trees, numbered from 1 to 5 inclusive ; all marked with white paint, and standing in the Garden House Wood aforesaid.

Lot 13.—9 Sycamore Timber Trees, numbered from 1 to 9 inclusive, and 2 Walnut Timber Trees, all marked with white paint ,and standing upon the Farm occupied by Mr. Thomas Mason, at Yatton, in the said Parish of Aymestry.

Several of the above trees are of large dimensions, and all of them are of easy access to the Turnpike Road at Aymestry, within four miles of the Kingsland Station, on the Leominster and Kington Railway.

For a view of the several lots apply to Mr. JOHN FREEMAN, of Aymestry, near Leominster, and to the Auctioneers.

The coming of the railway made transportation of timber relatively easy.
Sales took place at local inns, here at the Crown at Aymestrey in 1862.
Previous to the arrival of the railway, timber for the navy
would have been floated down the river Lugg

The Riverside Inn in 2000—at one time the Crown

festival at which George Melly would perform. The **Riverside Inn** has changed its image along with its name and now has an emphasis on food, being a popular restaurant and inn. It is an attractive black and white building with grounds going down to the river Lugg.

Returning to Mortimer's Cross, the road to the west takes a more direct route in the direction of Wales than the river, and after some two miles arrives at Shobdon. Here is the **Bateman Arms**, a fine 18th-century three-storey listed building of fairly striking and unusual appearance with dormers lighting the attic rooms in the roof space. In 1858 E. Smith was landlord, but by 1891, Fred Biddle was mine host for what was then the **Bateman Arms Commercial Inn & Posting House.**

A recent article in the *Sunday Telegraph* (21 May 1999) under the heading 'Taste of the Dragon' gives an insight into the problems of modern day cooking:

> Jane Sharp, who cooks for the **Bateman Arms**, in the Herefordshire village of Shobdon, used as a sideline to supply 'Red Dragon Pies' to an organic food shop in nearby Leominster. A trading standards officer called to ask what her pies were made from. When she explained that they contained aduki beans, which

the Chinese say 'give you the strength of dragon', the official solemnly replied: 'If there are no dragons in the pies, you cannot call them dragon pies'. When Jane jestingly suggested 'I suppose I cannot call them pies either, because they have a potato topping', the official agreed. 'What about my cottage pies?' Jane asked. 'Should they have bits of cottage in them?' 'No,' he replied. 'Cottage pies and shepherd's pies are exempted from the Trade Descriptions Act'.

Shobdon, of course, is known locally for its airfield. Constructed in the summer of 1940, this was originally called Pembridge Landing Ground. During the Second World War it was initially the base for No. 8 Anti-Aircraft Cooperation Unit. They moved to Madley in 1941 and new runways were installed at Shobdon by May 1942 for No. 5 Glider Training School. During the period up to 1945, the School was responsible for 96,925 separate glider launches! No doubt the **Bateman Arms** hosted many a party throughout the war. Shobdon Airfield now

The Bateman Arms at Shobdon in 2000

has a civilian role—sufficiently successful for the **Airport Bar** to have provided drink for thirsty aviators for over 20 years.

Having circled to the north of Shobdon Hill Wood, the Lugg and the Presteigne road again converge in the vicinity of the small villages of Coombe and Byton. On the main road south of Byton and east of Coombe at Coombe Moor was the **Bell Inn** with Thomas Davies as landlord in 1858, Mrs. Martha Evans in 1879, and James Taylor in 1891. It was then called a public house, but on later Ordnance Survey maps it is indicated as a simple beer house. The combined total of inhabitants of both parishes in 1881 was less than 250. The inn has been closed for many years.

The old Bell Inn at Coombe Moor in 2000: there is still
a small bell above the door

Finally, one-and-a-half miles north of Byton, and on the Limebrook, a tributary of the Lugg, is the **Royal George** at Lingen, a small village lost in the midst of rolling hills. In 1858 Lingen had two beer retailers—Joseph Burgoyne (who was also a shopkeeper) and John Davies (who had an additional trade as a hurdle maker). By 1891 Thomas Preece was the landlord and also doubled as a grocer. The inn was named after the Royal George, a ship that was built at Woolwich in 1756 and sank in Portsmouth harbour in 1782 with the loss of 800

The Royal George inn sign

lives. It is said that the captain survived and set up the pub, which was, of course, built of ships' timbers! There is a poem by William Cowper on the loss of the Royal George.

The Inn incorporates the village shop and post office and has an original Automobile Association sign on the wall. At one time the Royal George had its own brewery.

The Royal George, Lingen, in 2000
(above)

The AA sign reads London 152¹/₄ miles
(right)

284

CHAPTER FIFTEEN

North and North-east of Leominster

The northern part of Herefordshire and parts of South Shropshire are associated with the course of the river Teme as it flows eastwards from Knighton to enter the county just to the west of Brampton Bryan. Through Leintwardine, where it is joined by the river Clun, and Downton it stays within the county, but then takes an excursion into Shropshire to visit Bromfield, where it picks up the river Onny, and then south-eastwards to encircle Ludlow. From there it heads rapidly southwards to re-enter Herefordshire near Brimfield and then follows the course of the A456 eastwards to Little Hereford finally to leave the county at Tenbury Wells.

The first route in this chapter takes the line of the Roman road from where it was left at Aymestrey in chapter 10, and follows it through Wigmore to the Roman station at Leintwardine (a main route which has always had a good helping of wayside inns). Diversions to east and west identify those village inns that have long since closed. The latter part of the chapter covers routes north from Leominster.

The road northwards from Aymestrey squeezes through a gap in the hills and then skirts the edge of what was a moor, keeping the hills just on the west. The high ground coming down from Radnorshire between the rivers Lugg and Teme converges and descends towards the east until it forms a spur or ridge, bounded to the south by a steep narrow valley and to the north by the moor after which Wigmore gets part of its name. (The other half comes from the old English *wicga* meaning 'beetle, or something that wriggles'). The remains of the castle sit astride this ridge and are bounded on the west by a deep, apparently man-made ravine which traverses the ridge and cuts off the eastern portion from the higher, broader ground to the west. The ridge, as it continues to the south-east, includes the church, about 400 yards from the main part of the castle, before dropping down to the present main road. The line of the Roman road, which originally joined Caerleon to Chester, crosses Wigmore Moor about half-a-mile east of the present road on its way to *Bravonium* some 3 miles to the north.

The first castle at Wigmore was built by William FitzOsbern, just after the Norman Conquest, and was held by Ralph de Mortimer. The Mortimer family continued to hold the castle, gradually gaining in importance through several hundred years, having much influence on several kings and queens. Eventually Richard, Duke of York, became the heir to the vast Mortimer estates and, following his death, the inheritance passed to his son Edward. It was this Edward who gathered together a small army from the Wigmore area and, although outnumbered, defeated Owen Tudor at the Battle of Mortimer's Cross, almost within sight of the ancestral home, and subsequently claimed the throne as Edward IV. Wigmore castle, as Crown property, probably had little or no use after this time, Ludlow being the preferred residence. The castle was, however, apparently repaired by Bishop Lee, President of the Council of the Marches (1534-43), who found it 'utterly decayed in lodging', and again by Sir Henry Sidney (1559-86) who used it as a prison. After that it was allowed to decay until English Heritage took a hand and consolidated the crumbling stonework whilst carefully preserving the sensitive ecological environment. In the words of the then chairman, 'we've spent a million, and have nothing to show for it'!

In the 19th century Wigmore continued to have some local importance as a Petty Sessional Division of the County, but like most villages with a relatively small population (417 in 1888) its importance gradually decreased. It was more fortunate with its secondary school, which continues to provide education for the whole area, and with its pubs, for it has only lost one since the 19th century. This was the **Castle Inn**, on the western side of the main street, now replaced by the Castle Garage. In 1774 the **Castle Inn** was the home of a Friendly Society called the 'Amicable Society'. By 1858 the name had been changed to the rather cumbersome **The Castle Inn Hundred House** with John Phippen as landlord. He was also postmaster for Wigmore. It must have been the end of the postal route for Adforton and

The Olde Oak Inn at Wigmore in 2000

Leintwardine to the north, although in Herefordshire, had their postal services provided from over the border in Shropshire. Letters only arrived at 12.30 and were dispatched to Leominster at 2 p.m. The landlord in 1891 was Thomas Edwards. There was apparently a fire at the inn and as a result the licence was not renewed in February 1929.

The two inns to survive are the **Olde Oak Inn**, facing the main road in the centre of the village, and the **Compasses**, a short distance down Ford Street, the road leading towards Ludlow. The **Olde Oak Inn** is a timber-framed building on the edge of what was probably the market place. It was a originally a beer and cider house and is probably the establishment run by Mrs. Elizabeth Burgoyne, described simply as a 'beer retailer' in the 1891 directory. It continued in this simple role until 1961 when it was granted a full licence. It was altered in the 1970s from two small rooms to a single bar with a restaurant to the rear. There is now no trace of the oak after which it was presumably named.

The **Compasses Inn** was run by Joshua Gillam in 1891. He was a busy man for he was also the village baker. It was extended in the 1930s and has a well-established trade. A single compass would probably refer to the instrument that appears in the arms of the masons, but

*The Compasses in the early years of the 20th century. Archie Hughes was
the landlord—he is probably the rather portly, waistcoated
gentleman standing proudly outside the door*
(Photograph : Derek Foxton Collection)

multiple compasses such as at Wigmore are found in the arms of the
joiners (two) and the carpenters (three). More modern signs tend to
interpret it as the compass rose that is associated with ships, but at
some inns with this name there is a tradition that the original name was
the House of Compassion—originally hospices for travellers and especially pilgrims.

Just over a mile along the road towards Ludlow is Leinthall
Starkes and here was the **Fox Inn**. This was a well-established hostelry
with John Jones as landlord in 1858. The 1891 directory showed a
measure of favouritism with the entry '**Fox Inn**: beds and accommodation for travellers' with William Rickards as landlord. The **Fox**
closed many years ago.

However, the main road from Wigmore continues to the north
and somewhere along it must have been the hostelry mentioned by
Thomas Blount in his 1675 manuscript *History of Herefordshire*.
Having described Wigmore church he continued northwards to the
Grange at Adforton, which he rightly recognised as the remaining part
of Wigmore abbey founded in 1179 by Hugh Mortimer for Augustinian
Canons. By that time the abbey church had been reduced to simple

The Compasses in 2000

walls with no memorials left to the great Mortimer family. He goes on 'Among the outbuildings contiguous to the highway leading from Leintwardine to Wigmore Town, there is an Ale house, which they say was heretofore the Abby Prison for Malefactors'. Blount puts his prison firmly on the main road from Wigmore to Leintwardine, but also describes it as being amongst the outbuildings. It may well be that at that time the main road ran past the Grange to rejoin the Roman road at Paytoe, a short distance to the east, and thence to Leintwardine. If

Wigmore Abbey—buildings on the roadside in the 1920s

this assumption is correct then the Ale House could be the 14th century building that still adjoins the road. It was apparently adapted at some post-reformation time into an outer gate-house by cutting an opening through the middle of it. One part or the other could easily have been described as having been a prison. Perhaps the Ale House continued, in a small way, the ancient tradition that monasteries provided a 'guest house' for travellers.

This continued in the village, for during the 19th century there were at least two beer houses at Adforton. In 1858, in this small road-side hamlet, there was John Pritchard, who was a blacksmith and shop-keeper in addition to selling beer and cider, and Richard Titley, who apparently made a living simply selling beer and cider.

Whichever road is taken from Adforton, all lead to Leintwardine, not quite half-way between Kenchester (*Magnis*) and Wroxeter (*Virconium*). The village now occupies much of the area that was taken up by the Roman fort, a roughly 10 acre rectangular site formerly enclosed by earth banks and centred on High Street. The fort was built on rising ground north of a ford across the river Teme. Between the fort and the river was a small annexe that contained a reasonably elaborate bath house. The fort stayed in use until late in the 4th century. The several 'Leint—' prefixes in this area are derived from the 'river Lent', an otherwise lost name for a local river. Thus Leintwardine is 'the enclosure on the river Lent', an appropriate name for what would have

The Lion Hotel at Leintwardine at the beginning of the 20th century
(Photo : Derek Foxton Collection)

290

The Lion at Leintwardine

still been seen as an enclosed area long after the Romans had left.

Leintwardine really is a small town if the number of inns is taken into consideration, for it has had more than either Weobley or Wigmore, both failed boroughs associated with large and important border castles.

Close to the bridge and facing the attractively named Rosemary Lane is the **Lion Hotel**. The name was coloured in the 18th century when the Friendly Society simply known as the 'Amicable Society' met at the **Red Lion Inn** between 1775 and 1795, but by 1839, the otherwise unnamed Friendly Society met at the uncoloured **Lion**. In the 1850s it had a secondary role for it was then the **Lion Hotel & Posting House**, with John Robert as both licensee and sub-postmaster (letters arrived from Shrewsbury and Ludlow at 8 a.m. and were dispatched on their return journey at 6 p.m.).

Having travelled from Hereford in a brake supplied by Messrs. Bosley (of the Green Dragon), on 26 July 1853, the **Lion Inn** was the first port of call for the Woolhope Club outing. They reached the Lion at 9 a.m. where they had an 'excellent breakfast'. Leaving at 11 a.m. they first visited the limestone quarries on the Ludlow road, a mile from Leintwardine, and then went 'through the beautiful demesne and woods of Downton, to Burrington and Leinthall. Thence they directed their course to Wigmore'. The walk had taken some six hours and they ended up at about 5 p.m. at the **Hundred House Inn** 'where they refreshed their exhausted frames with an excellently served dinner'. This was the inn otherwise known as the **Castle** in Wigmore.

By 1867 the **Lion** had once again become coloured, for it was listed as the **Red Lion** with John Pearce as licensee, but by 1876 it had once again reverted to being a plain **Lion** with John Whitehead as mine host. By 1891 Charles Samuel Hall was the proprietor of what was described as a 'family and commercial hotel & posting house; cyclists and tourists well catered for by arrangement'. Besides running the hostelry and the posting house, Hall had a third string to his bow as a farmer.

In the 1950s it was run by the Goldbourns and then the Espleys who carried out many alterations, creating the present lounge bar and changing the emphasis from a hotel to an inn and restaurant. 'The Top Bar' was (and still is) a popular local bar whose barmaid, Rose Watkins, served there for years. Once frequented by fishermen and otter hunters, the small office on the left of the entrance used to be the bar. The inn is rather low-lying and has always been prone to flooding from the river Teme.

In the 1970s the locals often called it 'the **'Otel**', as it offered a few bedrooms, a dining room, and a lounge. The public bar was entered from the side where those in overalls, muddy boots etc were expected to drink. It is rumoured that the Earl of Plymouth in muddy walking boots was sent there on one occasion! Nowadays it tends to be a pub that is more dependent on passing trade, due to its attractive location by the bridge and river.

1980s advertisement

The **Sun Inn** is a short distance along Rosemary Lane from the Lion. It is a survivor, a gem, a small untouched front room pub. The local village leaflet notes it as 'parlour bar, no spirits, no food. Only three inns in Herefordshire are included in the CAMRA guide to good pub interiors—this is one; the others are the **Olde Tavern** in Kington and the **Hop Pole** at Risbury. The **Sun** is easy to miss—just a simple board with the name and an entry that looks like every other front door. The **Sun** was not mentioned by name in the 1851 and 1867 Directories, but was included in the 1876 directory with William Jones as landlord. This is presumably the William Jones of 1867 who combined the trades of beer retailer and tailor.

The Sun, hidden down Rosemary Lane, Leintwardine

As befits a beer house, it was not included in the 1891 directory by name; it was probably run by one of the two beer retailers mentioned at that time, either James Saviger or James Lippett. In the 1903 register of licensed premises the Sun was classified as selling Beer & Cider only. In 1936 the licence was transferred to Mrs. E. Edwards, the widow of Charles Edwards, the former licensee. This must be one of the few pubs left without a spirits licence. In the 1970s it was run by Charles Lane and his spinster sister. It had no bar and was just their sitting room with drinks being brought from the back. If the

Lanes did not consider you to be a 'native' then you were not always considered welcome. Charles died some time ago. It is still run by octogenarian Floss Lane, mainly for her locals, she took over some 15 years ago following upon the heads of her parents and grandparents. Indeed, the inn was listed under the Lane family as early as 1938.

Whilst outsiders have sometimes been discouraged from visiting the inn, at other times they are made welcome even if they are then perplexed at the local information with which they are provided. One of the favourites is to raise the subject of the renowned local delicacy, Squirrel Pie. Details are gone into its preparation and taste, but when the question is asked 'How do you catch the squirrels?', to which the reply is given 'By the tail of course!', one could wonder what other parts of, in this case, the human body are being pulled.

One visitor, not the butt of any humour himself, did exact a certain revenge on behalf of outsiders. Being the chief horologist at the National Maritime Museum, he promptly noticed that the old clock in the bar had stopped. On being told that it hadn't worked for a while, he asked if he could have some needles or skewers and some cooking oil as he could probably fix it. This was initially met with disbelief, which passed through stages of uncertainty to an eventual willingness to let him have a go. He duly fiddled away and soon the mechanism was working, and the clock put back in its place. As the bar filled up there happened to be a slight pause in the conversation and the clock could be heard ticking away. 'Here, damn it,' one of the locals was heard to say, 'she's got the clock fixed. Now she'll know when to call time!'

The **Swan Inn**, in the appropriately named Watling Street, the main village street that runs parallel to the main road—High Street— was run by John Wollaston in the 1850s and '60s, although latterly he also worked as a farmer. It was the home of the Swan Friendly Benefit Society, which is first recorded in 1811. By 1876 Mrs. Elizabeth Wollaston had taken the reins and she was still there in 1891. On the west side of Watling Street, the building, of late 16th or early 17th century date, is built of rubble and extensively altered.

During much of the 20th century it was run by the Edwards family, and in the 1970s it was the most popular pub in the village, with a strong local trade. When Clive Edwards died (he was also the bell-tower captain) his wife tried to run the inn for a short while, but

*The old Swan Inn at Leintwardine with, inset, the faded sign
that is still above the window*

her mind began to fail and she just closed it, leaving glasses on the tables and bottles on the shelves. She still lives there, and the faded notice above the window still records that C.L. Edwards was licensed to sell 'Ales, Wines & Spirits, Cider & Tobacco,' and one of the doors still has a brass door-knocker in the shape of a swan.

The **Rose & Crown** is not mentioned in the 1891 directory, but was recorded as a Beer & Cider House in 1903. It obtained a full licence in time to celebrate Christmas in 1961, but the trade did not increase and it closed in 1968. The **Coopers Arms** was in the High Street, and again is not mentioned in the 1891 directory, being a simple Beer & Cider house. Although on the main through street in the village, it was not a successful pub and the license was surrendered in February 1957. However, there were two beer retailers in Leintwardine in 1858—Miss Elizabeth Bird (who also ran a shop)

Mixed names! Is it the Jolly Frog, or the more traditional Cottagers Comfort? Or simply the Poker!

and Samuel Evans. It would seem likely that they were responsible for these two houses.

Less than half-a-mile north-east of Leintwardine is the small village of Kinton. There was certainly a drinking establishment here throughout most of the 19th century, for in 1858 John Evans was a beer retailer there, to be replaced with Richard Higginson by 1867 and in turn by John Tipton in 1891. He had a secondary trade as a tailor. Was this the establishment known by the evocative name **The Kinton Thatch**—an unlicensed house that provided accommodation for travellers?

Kinton is on a side road, but the main road towards Ludlow, the A4113, passes first through The Todding where there is a hostelry with a confusing set of names that has not been resolved at the present day! This is the **Cottagers Comfort**, or is it the **Jolly Frog**, or is it still known to the locals as the **Poker**? Built in the late 18th century, this enigmatic house was sometimes known as the **Todding**, but then, and for a long time afterwards it was always referred to as the **Poker**. This was because the beer served there was usually so cold when brought up from the deep cellar that a hot poker had to be plunged into it to warm it up. Indeed. some locals do say that the inn sign used to show a blazing fire with a large poker in front of it. This wayside inn was originally one of the Downton Estate pubs. The estate was sold up in 1917, when the pub, together with 7 acres, fetched £750. This was yet another beer and cider house that served passing and local trade for many years. It finally obtained its full licence on 8 March 1960.

Leintwardine 266

BAR SNACKS, LUNCHEONS and EVENINING MEALS

Good food and a friendly atmosphere amidst beautiful scenery.

AA Approved

In 1951 concern was expressed at the general state of the **Cottagers Comfort**, and the brewing company was asked by the magistrates to take action in the near future. They were of the opinion that it needed a 'sharp reminder'.

By 1976 it had been in the same family for a number of years, but had become run down and was only used by a few locals. It closed some time after 1984 when the last of the family decided that they could no longer cope. However, it has been reopened and the names continue to confuse the visitor with the **Cottagers Comfort** on one elevation and a rather more doubtful **Jolly Frog** on the other. As it is situated on a steep hillside, it is doubtful that any self-respecting frog would wish to live here, and one that did would certainly not be jolly!

The small villages around Leintwardine all seem to have been well equipped with Beer Houses, probably due to the influence of the Downton Estate, which seems to have owned most of them. Some 4 miles north-east of Leintwardine there was the **Downton Inn**, described as being at Gravel in the small settlement of Brakes. In 1858 John Monnington was landlord. Brakes had a population of only 143 in 1851—hardly enough to support an inn! However, it survived for a little while and became the **Downton Castle Inn** in 1867 with Joseph Edmonds as mine host. He was evidently unsuccessful for there is no mention of the inn in 1876 or any subsequent directory.

Walford is in the opposite direction, about a mile to the south-west of Leintwardine on the road to Knighton. In 1858, Samuel Howells was the energetic grocer, miller and beer retailer, and in 1867 William James mixed the trades of beer retailer and wheelwright, both at inns with long-forgotten names.

Another mile along the road is Brampton Bryan with the remains of its famous castle in the grounds of Brampton Bryan House. During the Civil War practically the whole village was raised to the ground, but it was rebuilt and has many pleasant looking buildings around the village green. One of these was the **Oxford Arms Commercial Inn**, with Charles Hancox as proprietor in 1891. He provided 'comfortable accommodation, home comforts, horse & trap for hire'. Half-a-century earlier in 1858 Mary Ireland had been the licensee, but the inn had been in existence much earlier for it was the home of a Friendly Society which was apparently founded in 1817. The inn may well have been named after Robert Harley, the 1st Earl of Oxford. He entered pariament as a Whig in 1689 and was elected Speaker in 1701 and by 1704 was Secretary of State. Shortly afterwards he joined the Tories and became chief minister to Queen Anne in 1711. In 1714 he was dismissed for alleged treasonable acts and was sent to the Tower. He was acquitted two years later by the Peers, after which he left London and spent his retirement at Brampton Bryan, dying in 1724. The last memories of the Earl have gone for the inn has now been closed for many years. Brampton Bryan is the last village in Herefordshire as the A4113 heads towards Knighton, but it is not as remote as it seems, for it is less than one-and-a-half miles to Bucknell, just over the border in Shropshire, where there is an inn and a station on the Central Wales Line.

There are two roads going more or less directly north from Leominster and for most of the way through the county they are separated by the Hereford to Shrewsbury railway line. The westernmost one, the B4361, goes through Luston, bypasses Yarpole and Orleton and leaves the county at Richard's Castle. The main A49, a little way to the east, winds through the small village of Ashton and then bypasses Brimfield, leaving the county just before the cross-roads at Woofferton. From Stockton Cross, some two miles along the A49 from Leominster a third road, a north-easterly continuation of the A4112, passes through Kimbolton on its way to Tenbury Wells, where it meets the A456 from Woofferton.

Luston, the first village along the western road, was in the ecclesiastical parish of Eye. There were two townships in 1858—Luston and Eye on the one part and Ashton and Moreton on the other. Richard Collins was innkeeper of the **Balance Inn** in 1858. It became part of the Hereford Imperial Brewery empire and was part of the 1898 sale. At that time William Wynn was paying £22 per annum rent. The public

---

THE "BALANCE INN" PUBLIC HOUSE,

Luston,

About Three Miles from Leomister, and near Berrington and Eye Station on the Great Western Railway.

A Brick and Slated House,

Containing Private Parlour, Bar, Tap Room, Kitchen, Back Kitchen and Pantry, good Cellar in Basement, Four Bed Rooms, Cider Cellar with Loft over, Stable, Piggery, Kitchen Garden, Pump and well of water, Stone and tiled Store House, and Stable fronting Road.

Let to Mr. William Wynn at a Rent of **£22 per Annum.**

And TWO ORCHARDS, together about 2a., 0r., 7p.,

Let to the same Tenant at **£23 per Annum.**

FREEHOLD.

Details of the Balance Inn included in the 1898 sale
of the Imperial Brewery

The Balance Inn at Luston in 2000

rooms included a bar and tap room and the landlord may have made his own cider, for there was a cider cellar with a loft over. The change in ownership resulted in a change in tenant and Mrs. Mary Ann Turner was there in 1891.

Licensees were often in trouble due to the price fixing regulations, and Bessie Gibbons of the **Balance Inn** was no exception. She was charged under the Spirits Prices and Distribution Order of 1920 for selling one-fifth of a gill of whisky above the maximum price. Inspector Wynn was charged 6d. instead of 5$\frac{1}{2}$d., which he calculated at giving the licensee an excess profit of 13s. 4d. per gallon. Luston village has grown since the 1920s and the **Balance Inn** continues to provide for both residents and passing trade.

Yarpole is at the junction of several side roads about half-a-mile west of the main road. Here is the **Bell Inn,** an attractive black and white free house with a sign that states that it was established in 1550. It included a cider mill which now forms part of the restaurant. The barn and house are joined by a 1970s building and there are modern extensions on the side and to the rear. The original pub had front and rear bars, but they are now opened up into one. Even though the **Bell** has had a long history as a hostelry, it was always a beer and cider

house, not obtaining a full licence until 1960. It is not mentioned by name in the 1891 directory, but was doubtless the house of Thomas Bengree, described as a beer retailer.

A little further along the main road is the **Maidenhead Inn**, at the junction of the road that leads off to the east to Orleton Village. Orleton was roughly half way between Leominster and Ludlow, and this must have accounted in part for the relatively large number of

The Bell at Yarpole in 2000 after 450 years of service

The Maidenhead at Orleton in 2000

inns in the 19th century. Apart from the **Maidenhead**, there was the **Boot** in the centre of the village, and both these survive, but other inns existed at the Folly, a short distance to the north, where the B4362 heads eastwards towards Woofferton.

The **Maidenhead** is an attractive roadside hostelry that appears in all the directories. It was the home of the Friendly Brothers Society which was first recorded in 1800. In 1851 Thomas Norgrove was the victualler there, whilst in 1858 it was George Durnall. By 1867 William Shenton had taken over to be replaced by 1876 by John Pearce who was also a farmer. The Record Office hold details of a draft mortgage relating to the **Maidenhead** dated 18 November 1878. The mortgage for £450 was to William Rowlands Berkeley of Leominster, gentleman, and from William Daggs, the Leominster manager of the Herefordshire Banking Company. It relates to 'All that messuage with the outbuildings yard garden orchard situated in the parish of Orleton in the County of Hereford called **The Maidenhead Inn**, bounded on the east by the Turnpike Road leading from Ludlow to Leominster, on the west by land now or formerly of James Haynes, on the North by the highway leading from the said Turnpike Road to Orleton Common

The Boot at Orleton in 1903

and on the South by land of Richard Keysall Yapp ... which said premises were formerly copyhold held of the Manor of Orleton in the County of Hereford but were enfranchised by an Indenture dated 23 May 1878.' Even in the 19th century extensions to opening times had to be applied for, but they were apparently usually given. Even so, the extension granted to Sarah Preece of the **Maidenhead** for a ball during the whole night of 15 January 1885, must have been exceptional! Sarah Preece did not stay long and by 1891 Arthur Well was the landlord.

The **Boot Inn** (or **Boots Inn** in 1934 according to the Royal Commission on Historic Buildings) is a half-timbered building of 17th-century date and was built on an L-shaped plan with the wings extending towards the south-west

303

The Boot Inn, Orleton, in 2000

and south-east. It has been suggested that it was originally three shops—a butchers, a cobblers and a funeral parlour. This may partly explain the variety of trades that past licensees were involved in. Thus in 1851, John Price was also a mason, whilst in 1876 Charles Lawrence was a butcher. He was followed by George Lawrence, presumably his son and also a butcher. In 1903 it was the meeting place for the Ancient Order of Foresters. The inn name may have some relevance, for late in the 19th century Alfred Drew and William Jones were both boot makers, living and working near the **Boot**. Alternatively, beer and cider was sometimes served in a leather 'jack' or 'boot'.

The **Boot** was a simple beer house and in 1951 an objection was raised to the renewal of the landlord's beer licence. Apparently two plain clothes police officers, one male and one female, visited the pub and had asked for a whisky and a gin and orange. On being told there was no orange, they still asked for the gin. Once these had been served, the female officer went to summon her uniformed senior colleague who had waited outside. As soon as he appeared the landlord emptied the two glasses onto the floor of the pub. When questioned, he said he did not feel like talking as his health had not been good lately, so the police officers searched the premises finding a quantity of spirits.

At the subsequent court hearing, one of the magistrates, Mrs. Williams, asked 'Is it right that a police officer should go in and break the law in asking for a drink?' adding that she presumed the offence was to actually drink it. The response she received was that 'It raises a fine point as to whether the constable could be charged with aiding and abetting' but that this charge was not being pressed!

The landlord, it appeared, had been running the **Boot** for some 10 months, having previously been a businessman in Walsall, who had decided on a change in direction fearing that his previous business may have been about to be nationalised. He said he had run the inn as a beer house, but had always kept a few bottles of spirits for customers who had wanted it. He was fined £25 plus costs, and had his spirits confiscated. However, it did not prevent his licence being renewed.

A recent visitor to the inn tells of rumours of a ghost. This apparently concerns a painting of the pub in the back room in which a figure (Joe Vale) has been painted out after arguing with the landlord. His ghostly figure is said to return from time to time to take his revenge on the landlord.

The various inns at the Folly are a mite confusing. The main one was the **Plough Inn**. Between 1851 and 1876, George Matthews is included in the various directories variously as 'victualler',

The Folly, Orleton

305

'innkeeper', and 'cider retailer'. By 1891 the long reign of the Matthews family was over and the landlord was probably John Phillips who, in 1876, was a farmer and beer retailer at Comberton, only a short distance from the Folly. This beer and cider house continued to ply its trade into the 20th century, but the licence was not renewed in 1907 and it has since been a private house.

Clare Wesbury informs me that her ancestor, one Richard Powell, lived at the **Bull's Head Inn** at The Folly where he died in 1818. It was still apparently in use as an inn about 1840 with James and Elizabeth Powell as landlord and landlady. However, there is no further mention and it is suggested that there was a change of name around the middle of the 19th century, the **Bull's Head** being transformed into the **Bay Horse.** The 1851 and 1858 directories includes a Benjamin Wall as a victualler in Orleton, but he apparently died for the 1867 directory has Mrs. Sarah Wall as a beer retailer at the Folly. She must have lived there for perhaps half-a-century, for she was still listed in the directory in 1891 as a beer and cider retailer. The **Bay Horse** continued long after the **Plough** had closed and was run by Jack Bowen for some time before it finally closed in the mid-1960s. It may have had a secondary name as the **Brick House**.

The Castle Inn at Richard's Castle in 2000

The last inn on this back road to Ludlow is in Richard's Castle, an odd village that is partly in Herefordshire but principally in Shropshire. However the one pub, the **Castle Inn** is in Herefordshire. It has been an inn for many years and was once part of the Moorepark Estate. It was built around 1830 and Mary Taylor was recorded as licensee in 1858. This was once again a cider house, making its own cider in the barn at the rear. There used to be a rival pub, called the **Tan House** or the **Salway Arms**, which was across the road, but it closed about 1900. Apparently a brick wall was deliberately built so that there was no direct view from one pub to the other. The estate was sold in 1952 and the inn became part of the Wrekin Brewery chain which was eventually taken over by Wem Brewery. It finally reverted to being a free house in 1990. The inn still sports its early AA sign recording the distance from Richard's Castle to London as 138½ miles.

The A49 takes a direct route north from Leominster and provides no opportunity for a stop. Brimfield now has a bypass, and the intrepid traveller has to bear off to the east to visit the **Roe Buck Inn**. In 1858

The Roebuck at Brimfield in the early 20th century

The Roebuck at Brimfield in 2000

Elizabeth Wood was landlady; in 1891 the licensee was Richard Allen. In 1936, Mr. W. H. Elborn of the **Roebuck** at Brimfield asked at the Brewster Sessions on behalf of all the licensees in the Leominster Rural area for the start of the two hour Sunday afternoon opening period to be brought forward from 12.30 to 12 noon. This fundamental change was agreed and presumably continued until the more relaxed licensing hours of the present day. In the early 1990s the **Roebuck** included Poppies Restaurant, which had a well-known chef and was renowned for its food. Also in Brimfield, but only mentioned in the 1858 directory, was the **New Inn** with Thomas Pocock acting both as landlord and village butcher.

This is really the last pub in Herefordshire, but as it is only just over the boundary and on the junction of the A456, it is worth mentioning the **Salway Arms** on the Woofferton crossroads (as opposed to the **Salway Arms** at Richard's Castle). Richard Salway of Richard's Castle was a consistent supporter of the old republican principles during the 17th-century Civil Wars and in 1654 was the Commonwealth's ambassador to Constantinople.

A section of the road from Woofferton to Tenbury Wells and an area to the north of it is in Herefordshire and includes the parish of Little Hereford. There is no record of an inn in this remote corner of Hereford until the **Temeside Hotel** obtained a licence on 17 September 1970.

However, the other road from Leominster towards Tenbury has much more of interest. A short distance from the A49 is the parish of Kimbolton which includes the village of Stockton. Here is the **Stockton Cross Inn**, a 17th century building with an added late 17th-century staircase wing on the north and various modern additions. Inside the building the staircase has shaped slat-balusters, moulded strings and rails; there is an original doorway with a flat pointed head. The 1858 directory doesn't mention an inn in Kimbolton, but records William Phillips as an innkeeper, presumably at this hostelry. Often known simply as the **Cross**, this inn had James Priest as landlord in 1891.

The Stockton Cross in 2000

There was an explosion at the **Cross Inn** in November 1945. Harold and Annie Pugh were aware that one of their gas cylinders was empty and needed to be filled. They started to disconnect the empty cylinder but the subsequent hissing noise alerted them to the fact that they hadn't turned off the cylinder which still held some gas. As they attempted to do this there was an explosion which badly burnt them both and did some damage to the pub. Seventy-eight year old John Bigglestone, who was in the bar, recalled seeing a sheet of flame and then a badly burnt Mrs. Pugh coming into the room—indeed she was so badly burnt that she died in hospital two days later. Another pub regular went to fetch buckets of water, and the fire engine also arrived. It appears that the flame that caused the explosion came from the fire in the grate in the main bar; the gas having flowed along the floor, under the stable door by the bar and had eventually reached the fire some 15 feet away from the gas cylinders. The **Cross** recovered from this catastrophe and still serves the regulars of Stockton and Kimbolton. There was another pub in Kimbolton around the turn of the last century. This was the **Perseverance**, recorded in 1903, but the licence was not renewed in 1935.

The Duke of York at Laysters in 2000

Further along the road is the **Duke of York Inn** which is in Middleton-on-the-Hill parish although often described as being in Laysters. It was functioning over a hundred years ago when John Went was landlord. There have been many dukes of York and some inns of this name may well be named after Richard, whose claim to the throne led to the Wars of the Roses. However, most people relate the name to the song about the Grand Old Duke of York. This was Frederick Augustus, the second son of George III, who commanded the English army in Flanders in the 1790s. The song misrepresents the duke, for he was only 31 years old, had 30,000 men under his control and certainly had no hill to climb in Flanders!

Sources & References

GENERAL WORKS

The Itinerary of John Leland, ed. L. Toulmin Smith, 5 vols., 1908
    (reprint 1964)
A Tour through the Whole Island of Great Britain, (Daniel Defoe), ed.
    P.N. Furbank & W.R. Owens, 1991
The Life of Samuel Johnson, James Boswell, 1791

THE COUNTY

The History of Kington, Parry, 1845
Nooks and Corners of Herefordshire, H.T. Timmins, 1892
The Folklore of Herefordshire, E.M. Leather, 1912
An Inventory of the Historical Monuments in Herefordshire, Vol. 3,
    Royal Commission on Historical Monuments, 1934
The Inns of Herefordshire, H.P. Bulmer, *c.*1955
The Last Great Pub Crawl, J. Slane, 1976
A Drink for its Time, M.B. Quinion, 1979
The Leon Valley, N.C. Reeves, 1980
Hops and Hop Picking, R. Filmer, 1982
Domesday Book, Herefordshire, F. & C. Thorn (eds.) 1983
Herefordshire Place-Names, B. Coplestone-Crow, 1989
Ludford Bridge and Mortimer's Cross, G. Hodges, 1989
Hereford and Worcester Railways Remembered, L. Oppitz, 1990
Alfred Watkins, A Herefordshire Man, R. Shoesmith, 1990
The Archaeology of the Welsh Borders, S.C. Stanford, 1991
Herefordshire in Old Photographs, A. Samdford, 1992
The Folklore of Hereford and Worcester, R. Palmer, 1992
Hereford: History and Guide, R. Shoesmith, 1992
Bridges on the River Wye, A. Crow, 1995
Castles and Moated Sites of Herefordshire, R. Shoesmith, 1996
The 1675 Thomas Blount Manuscript, N.C. Reeves (ed.) nd.

JOURNALS AND NEWSPAPERS ETC.

Transactions of the Woolhope Naturalists' Field Club, 1851 to date
Gurney's Graphic Guide to Hereford, nd but about 1900
Hereford City and County Guides, various years
Kelly's Directories of Herefordshire, various years
Hereford & District Directory, Chamber of Commerce, 1950-51
Hereford Citizen and Bulletin
Hereford Journal
Hereford Times

INNS AND TAVERNS

Quaint Signs of Olde Inns, G.J. Monson-Fitzjohn, 1926
    (Reprint, 1994)
The Old Inns of England, A.E. Richardson, 1948
A History of the English Public House, H.A. Monckton, 1969
Stories of Inns and their Signs, E. Delderfield, 1974
Pub Names of Britain, L. Dunkling and G. Wright, 1994
The Pubs of Hereford City, R. Shoesmith, 1998

Index of Inn Names

In the following index common names are used—others are cross-referenced. Adjectival descriptions are normally used except for 'new' and 'old'. To avoid confusion the parish is shown for country inns; in Kington and Leominster the street is shown with 'K' for Kington and 'L' for Leominster. Only main entries are indexed.

Also from Logaston Press

Churches of Herefordshire & their Treasures
by John Leonard   ISBN 1 873827 91 1   £12.95

This book is an exploration of Herefordshire's churches. It is not a straight gazetteer, for the author is concerned to place the churches in context, to tell the story of their evolution over a thousand years, and to indicate those buildings which are most rewarding to visit because of their architectural, artistic or religious interest.

Introductory chapters tell of the origins of the churches, of the influence of the Welsh, Anglo-Saxons and the Normans; and then follows a description of the treasures of the churches—the Herefordshire School of Romanesque Sculpture; the fonts; roofs,; screens; stained glass; memorials and effigies which enrich the great majority of our churches.

The book then divides the county into areas in which the author indicates his personal choice of the medieval churches that he considers to be the most interesting to visit. All the medieval churches in a gazetteer of each area, often with reference back to the earlier chapters. Finally, the post-medieval churches, from the 17th to the 20th centuries, are considered across the county as a whole.

This book is richly endowed with illustrations, containing over 290 photos and plans, some of them dating from the 1800s.

Also from Logaston Press

Ludlow Castle
Its History & Buildings

Edited by Ron Shoesmith & Andy Johnson   ISBN 1 873827 51 2
£14.95

Ludlow Castle has often played a pivotal role in the history of the Welsh Marches, indeed of the whole of the United Kingdom.

Commenced about 1075 to help control the Welsh border, it became the power base of the de Lacys whose importance escalated on the demise of the fitzOsbern earls of Hereford. Captured by King Stephen during the Anarchy, it passed to the de Genevilles, staunch allies of both Edward I and II. When they died without male issue, the castle passed by marriage to the Mortimers. On the death of Edmund Mortimer in 1425, the Mortimer inheritance passed to Richard, duke of York who was married to Edmund's sister. When Edward claimed the throne as Edward IV, the castle once again became a royal possession, Ludlow and its castle flourishing under its Royal lords. In later years this continued under the Council in the Marches of Wales which lasted to 1689. It was one of the last Royalist garrisons to surrender in the Civil War, was on the point of being used as a PoW camp in the Napoleonic Wars, might have been about to be demolished to make way for a country house, and became a focus of the Picturesque. It still draws devotees.

This book draws together the history of the buildings and its owners to provide a developing picture of the castle and its role in both border and national history and to interpret the changes that occurred in the buildings themselves.

With over 125 colour and black and white illustrations.

Also from Logaston Press

Radnorshire from Civil War to Restoration
A study of the county and its environs 1640-60 in a
regional setting
by Keith Parker   ISBN 1 973827 86 5 (Pbk) £12.95
ISBN 1 873827 96 2 (Hbk) £18.95

Whilst this book is a record of the social, political, religious and military state of affairs in Radnorshire from before the Civil War to the Restoration, by its nature much reference is made to events in neighbouring counties and further afield. Many of those affecting the course of events in Radnorshire had a base elsewhere, and the military almost universally operated from outside the county.

Keith Parker has made much use of primary sources of information to confound the generally held view that Radnorshire was both a poor county at the time of the Civil War and essentially Royalist in outlook. A more confusing picture emerges of strongly held views by a few on each side, though most notably the pro-Parliamentarians, in a sea of neutrality, bewilderment and opportunism.

This is a story of Radnorshire gentry, farmers and clergymen caught up in an age of both danger and vibrant political and religious debate, when many had a rare chance to shape the future.

Keith Parker, a native of Kington and graduate of Birmingham and London Universities, lives in Presteigne where he was formerly deputy head of John Beddoes School. For many years he has lectured on local history for the Extra-mural Department of the University of Wales, Aberystwyth, and for the Workers' Educational Association. 1997 saw the publication of his popularly acclaimed *A History of Presteigne*, also published by Logaston Press.